THE BYZANTINE WARS

JOHN HALDON

T0307316

The History Press

This edition first published 2008

Reprinted 2009,2012

The History Press
The Mill, Brimscombe Port
Stroud, Gloucestershire, GL5 2QG
www.thehistorypress.co.uk

British Library Cataloguing in Publication Data.
A catalogue record for this book is available from the British Library.

ISBN 9780752445656

Typesetting and origination by
The History Press

Contents

A Note on Transliteration

Books dealing with the Byzantine world generally open with a note on the transliteration of Greek or Latin words and technical terms, for the simple reason that there are several different systems in use. I have decided to use the simplest: Greek terms will be transliterated as literally as possible, but without employing macrons on long vowels (thus no ê or ô for the letters eta and omega) or the phonetic rendering of certain letters (b will be kept as 'b' rather than 'v', for example, which is the way it would have been pronounced in most contexts). There are a few concessions towards standard Modern Greek phonetic transliterations – thus Thessaloniki, rather than Thessalonike – because these are now the common form, but not many.

Greek was the language of culture and government from the later sixth and seventh centuries, but both Greek and Latin were employed before that time. Indeed, the empire included at various times considerable areas where Latin was the main or only language – parts of Italy, parts of the northern Balkan region and central and western North Africa. To Latinize Greek names of the medieval period looks odd, just as Hellenizing earlier Latin names and terms appears unreasonable or confusing. I have, inevitably, had to compromise. Technical terms and names will, therefore, be presented usually in their Latin form for the period before the year A.D. 600, and in their Greek form thereafter. This leaves many contradictions, but is the best that can be done. Where standard English versions of technical terms, personal names or placenames exist, I have used them (thus Constantine rather than Konstantinos).

Introduction

In its thousand years of existence – from the reign of Justinian I (527-565) until that of the last emperor, Constantine XI (1445-1453) – the Byzantine (or medieval eastern Roman) empire was almost constantly at war with one or another of its neighbours. This reflected its geography and strategic situation, centred as it was on the southern Balkans and Asia Minor. It had constantly to fend off challenges to its territorial integrity from, on the one hand, the Persian and then Arab or Turkish Islamic powers to the east and, on the other, its Balkan neighbours to the north – various barbarians groups, in particular Slavs and the Turkic Avars, in the sixth and seventh centuries and then, until the thirteenth century, the Bulgars. To complicate matters, relations with the western medieval states which grew up amid the ruins of the western Roman empire from the fifth and sixth centuries on were rarely easy, and there was an ongoing political tension between the patriarchate at Constantinople and the papacy, the two major sees in the Christian world (the others being Alexandria, Antioch and Jerusalem). As the western and central European powers grew and matured – first in the form of the Carolingian empire, then the German empire and the kingdom of Hungary – so Byzantine political pre-eminence began to be challenged, until by the end of the twelfth century the empire had become a second-rate state, subject to the power politics of powerful western kingdoms and the commercial strength of Italian merchant republics such as Venice, Genoa and Pisa.

Throughout its history military matters were of prime importance to the empire, and it is therefore no surprise that a very considerable part of the annual revenue of the state was spent on soldiers or related issues. But while the army and the physical defence of its lands were of first-order importance, the empire's political situation meant that diplomacy and politics played an equally important role. Indeed, given its limited territory and population, they were absolutely crucial to its survival, for shortage of manpower alone meant that the casual expenditure of such a valuable resource was, wherever possible, to be avoided. Hence the Byzantines' reputation for clever diplomacy and, in the post-Crusader western tradition, cunning and deceitfulness – hardly deserved in reality, especially in view of the record of the western powers in their dealings with the Byzantines, but an unfortunate result of western cultural prejudice. Byzantium was a society in which the virtues of peace were extolled and war was usually condemned, certainly when taken for its own sake. Fighting was to be avoided at all costs. Yet the empire nevertheless inherited the military administrative structures and, in many ways, the militaristic ideology of the expanding pre-Christian Roman empire in its heyday. These tensions were overcome through the blending of Christian ideals with the political will to survive and the justification of war as a necessary evil, waged primarily in defence of the Roman world (as understood by the Byzantines, who described themselves as 'Romans') and the Orthodox faith. Late Roman and medieval Christian society in the eastern Mediterranean/south Balkan region thus generated a unique culture which was able to cling without reservation to a pacifistic ideal while at the same time legitimating and justifying the maintenance of an immensely efficient and, for the most part remarkably effective, military apparatus.

In the following chapters we will look at the development of this military organization and illustrate its performance through a series of examples of actual battles. The history of the armies and their successes is not simply a military matter – the ups and downs of imperial military history parallel those of the state, both in its political as well as its social and economic aspect. There were notable peaks and troughs. In the sixth century, with the resources of a still dominant empire at its disposal, the armies were able to effect a series of remarkable reconquests in many regions conquered in the previous century by

Germanic peoples such as the Goths (in Italy) and Vandals (in North Africa), as well as holding off barbarian inroads into the Balkans and defeating the other major player in the western Eurasian world, the Sassanid Persian empire. In contrast, the seventh and much of the eighth century saw the massive loss of territories following the Islamic conquests of the Middle East, Egypt and eventually North Africa, with a consequent restructuring of military organisation within the empire. By the tenth century the empire had taken up the offensive once more, and by the 1030s was once again the dominant power in the eastern Mediterranean basin, its armies well led and disciplined, to the extent that the mere rumour that an imperial army was on the way was sufficient to bring most recalcitrant former allies or neighbours to heel. Yet by the time of the Fourth Crusade in 1204 the empire had been reduced to a shadow of its former self, with armies consisting mostly of foreign mercenaries and ineffective local militias. Thereafter, although it was able to make a slight recovery in the second half of the thirteenth century, the Byzantine state was an empire in name only, its armies constantly on the defensive, reduced in numbers, largely modelled and armed along western lines and barely affordable. Given this picture, the present volume will concentrate on the period up to the middle of the twelfth century, focusing in equal measure on victories as well as defeats, and the reasons for both.

In presenting the historical framework within which the various battles and encounters took place, I have drawn on the most recent modern studies of Byzantine and medieval warfare and military organisation. But the sources for the descriptions of the battles themselves are often very partial and frequently lacking in the sort of detail needed to make sense of the tactics employed, the movements of troops before and during the battles, the numbers of men and the types of unit involved, as well as physical details of the terrain and contours of the localities at which the clash occurred. Those battles which are treated by the sources in some detail have received frequent attention, although interpretations of what actually happened vary. Thus the battles of Adrianople (378), at which the emperor Valens was defeated and killed by the Goths, Chalons (451) when the Romans defeated the Huns, the battles described by Procopius and Agathias for the reign of Justinian, as well as Manzikert in

1071 are relatively well studied. Yet there is enough information on many other encounters to justify a little more than a brief mention of the outcome, and I have attempted in this volume to extract as much information as possible about such battles.

In some cases, details can be supplied in whole or in part by visiting the sites (or attempting to locate) the sites in question. I have myself been to most of the relevant sites, where they can be identified, or to the areas in which the battles in question took place, and this has guided me in my interpretation of the written sources. In other cases, one can supply depth and colour by drawing on other accounts of similar battles at the same period and in the same area, sometimes by the same medieval writer or writers. In this respect, therefore, I must confess to using some informed guesswork and a little imagination, but always grounded in what the medieval sources tell us, in order to flesh out some of the details of some encounters. Where this is the case I have noted the fact in the section on sources and literature at the end of the book.

I

The Geography of Byzantine Warfare

Before beginning our survey of warfare and military organization, it is worth glancing briefly at the physical context in which these are to be situated, since it is obvious that neither can really be understood without some appreciation of the landscape and other related factors which affected them. Resources, communications, population size and settlement patterns are all relevant here, and just as modern strategists must take these features into account, so Roman and Byzantine generals and politicians had to pay serious attention to such matters in planning and executing any military strategy.

The Byzantine world in the sixth century was dominated by three major regions: the Balkans, sometimes stretching northward as far as the Danube; Asia Minor (Anatolia, approximately the area occupied by the modern state of Turkey); and the Middle Eastern regions of Syria, western Iraq and Jordan, with Egypt, North Africa, Italy, and the seas which linked these lands. Different climatic patterns determined patterns of agricultural and pastoral activity in each area and thus what the government at Constantinople could hope for in the way of human and material resources.

The Balkans presents a very rugged and fragmented landscape, though the broad plains of Thrace, of Thessaly and the south Danubian area are productive and relatively densely settled. The region as a whole is dominated by mountains, which cover some two thirds of its area. The Dinaric Alps run through the western Balkan region in a south-easterly direction and with the associated Pindus mountains dominate western and central Greece.

Outlying extensions of these ranges stretch into southern Greece and the Peloponnese. The Balkan chain itself extends eastwards from the Morava river for about 550km as far as the Black Sea coast, with the Rhodope range forming an arc reaching to the south through Macedonia towards the plain of Thrace. The river and coastal plains are relatively limited in extent. Distinct climatic variations thus exist, between the fairly mild conditions of the coastal regions and the continental conditions of the inland and highland regions, particularly in the northern zone. The accentuated settlement pattern reflects this in a series of fragmented geo-political units separated by ridges of highlands, fanning out along river-valleys towards the coastal areas.

Five main routes appear time and again in accounts of Byzantine war-making in the Balkans:

1. The *Via Egnatia*: Constantinople – Herakleia in Thrace – Thessaloniki – Edessa – Bitola – Achrida (*Ohrid*) – Elbasan – Dyrrachion (*Dürreš*) on the Adriatic coast.
2. Constantinople – Adrianople (*Edirne*) – along the Maritsa – Philippoupolis (*Plovdiv*) – the pass of Succi (guarded at the northern exit by the so-called 'gates of Trajan', and barred by a wall and forts) – the pass of Vakarel – Serdica (*Sofia*) – the Nisava valley – Naissos (*Niš*) – key crossroads along the routes southwards to the Aegean and Macedonia, westwards to the Adriatic, south-eastwards to Thrace and Constantinople, and northwards to the Danube) – the valley of the Morava – Viminacium (near modern *Kostolac*) – Singidunum (*Belgrade*). This was a key military route, and it was complemented by a number of spurs to East and West, giving access to the south Danube plain, the Haimos mountains and Black Sea coastal plain, as well as, in the west, the valleys of the West Morava, Ibar and Drin rivers.
3. Thessaloniki – the Axios (*Vardar*) valley and the pass of Demir Kapija (alternative easterly loop avoiding this defile and leading through another pass, known to the Byzantines as Kleidion, *the key*) – Stoboi (*Stobi*) – Skopia (*Skopje*) – Naissos (*Ni*).
4. Constantinople – Anchialos (*Pomorie*) – Mesembria (*Nesebar*) – Odessos (*Varna*) – mouth of the Danube.
5. Adrianople – across the Sredna Gora range – over the Shipka pass through the Balkan range itself – Nikopolis (*Veliko Trnovo*) – Novae (*Svistov*) on the Danube.

From the point of view of campaigning strategy, it is to be noted that all these routes pass in several places through relatively narrow and often quite high passes, easily blocked both by human agency and by natural phenomena. Such terrain was, and is, ideal for ambushing an enemy army; and combined with the weather (in which winter snows can drift to very considerable depths), made for tough campaigning conditions. Even today transit is very difficult at certain times of the year. The history of the Balkan region has been clearly marked by these features, and the pattern of communications and the degree and depth of Byzantine political control show this especially clearly, since there is no obvious geographical focal point in the south Balkan region – the main cities in the medieval period were Thessaloniki and Constantinople, both peripheral to the peninsula and its fragmented landscape. In the mountainous regions, especially the Rhodope and Pindus ranges, government power was always circumscribed by distance and remoteness, whether in the Roman, Byzantine, Ottoman or more recent periods. These were regions where paganism and heresy could survive with only limited possibilities for interference from a central government or from the Church authorities. And while they were certainly regions where popular resistance to a central political power was difficult to combat, they were also sources of hardy soldiers.

This geophysical structure also affects land use. The highland regions are dominated by forest and woodland; the lower foothills by woodland, scrub and rough pasturage. The possibilities for extensive arable exploitation are confined to the Danube plain and the plains of Thessaly and Macedonia, with the few river plains and the coastal strips associated with them offering similar but more restricted opportunities. Production here includes orchards, as well as vine and olive cultivation, apart from the staple grain production. As noted already, the settlement pattern and distribution of both larger urban centres and rural communities is determined by these aspects of the landscape. At the same time, the political, military and cultural history of the region is inflected by the relationship between this landscape and the sea. Except along its northern boundary, it is surrounded by the sea, and the extended coastline, with its gulfs and deep inlets, acts as an efficient link between neighbouring and more distant regions and as a medium for the dissemination of common cultural elements. This easy seaborne access from the west, the south or the north-east via the Black Sea had its disadvantages, however, opening the southern Balkan peninsula – Greece and the Peloponnese especially – to invasion.

Asia Minor, the site of much of the empire's military activity until the later thirteenth century, can be divided into three clearly separate zones: coastal plains, central plateau, and the mountain ranges which separate them. The climate of the plateau is typified by very hot, dry summers and extreme cold in winter. This is in stark contrast to the friendlier Mediterranean climate of the coastlands, in which the most productive agricultural activity and the highest density of settlement is to be found – making such areas of great importance to the government as sources of revenue. Except for some sheltered river valleys the plateau is dominated by a chiefly pastoral economy – sheep, cattle and horses.

The most densely settled regions of Asia Minor were the narrow coastal plains in the north and south and the much broader plains of the Aegean region, dissected by the western foothills of the central plateau which run from east to west. It was here that urban settlement was concentrated, although some inland regions, where a more than averagely favoured situation offered protection from the extremes of warm and cold weather, also supported small towns and villages. Throughout the medieval period and until very recently (with the introduction of modern fertilizers and mechanized farming) the exploitation of the land was predominantly pastoral on the plateau, while the fertile coastal regions supported the cultivation of grains, vegetables, vines and olives. Cities always depended upon their agricultural hinterlands for their economic survival, since the cost of transporting bulk goods such as grain overland were prohibitive over more than a few miles. Cities with port facilities or other access to the coast could develop as centres of long-distance as well as local trade and exchange and could afford to bring in supplies by sea in times of scarcity; these were thus not as dependent upon the size of their agrarian hinterland for their size.

The pattern of roads and network of communications in Asia Minor was subject to similar constraints to that of the Balkan region. Armies, whether large or small, faced several difficulties when crossing or campaigning in Asia Minor, in particular the long stretches of road through relatively waterless and exposed countryside and the rough mountainous terrain separating coastal regions from central plateau. But such features affected hostile forces to the same degree, and could be used with great effect against an invader. Middle Byzantine strategic planning was largely determined by these features. The Roman and Hellenistic road network was complex, and while much of it continued in use locally, there evolved a series of major military routes in the Byzantine period, along which developed also a string of fortified posts and military bases as the same routes became corridors of access to Arab raiders. As in the Balkans, this network evolved according to the requirements of the period, so that routes might fall in and out of use as time passed. Several routes are mentioned in the various accounts of Byzantine warfare and hostile invasion in the period stretching from the sixth and seventh through to the twelfth and thirteenth centuries. Those which seem to have been used most frequently were as follows:

1. Chrysoupolis (opposite Constantinople) – Nikomedeia – Nikaia – Malagina (an important imperial military base) – Dorylaion – (easterly route via Kotyaion/westerly route via Amorion) – Akroinon – Ikonion/ Synnada – Kolossai/Chonai. There were two options to turn off to the south along this last route, the first down to Kibyra and thence across the mountains to the coast at Attaleia or, farther west, at Myra. Alternatively, the road from Chonai led westwards via Laodikeia and Tralles to Ephesos on the coast.
2. Ikonion – Archelais – Tyana/Kaisareia.
3. Ikonion – Savatra – Thebasa – Kybistra/Herakleia – Loulon – Podandos – Cakit gorge (through the Anti-Taurus mountains).
4. Kaisareia – Tyana – Loulon – Podandos – 'Cilician Gates' (*Külek Bogazı*) – the Cilician plain – Tarsos/Adana.
5. Kaisareia – (i) – Ankara/ Basilika Therma – Tabion – Euchaita/ (ii) – Sebasteia – Dazimon – Amaseia
6. Sebasteia – Kamacha/ Koloneia – Satala.
7. Dorylaion – valley of the Tembris river (mod. Porsuk Su) – Trikomia – Gorbeous – Saniana – Timios Stavros – Basilika Therma

– Charsianon Kastron – Bathys Ryax – Sebasteia – (and on to Kaisareia, north to Dazimon, east to Koloneia and Satala, or south-east to Melitene).

8. Saniana – Mokissos – Ioustinianoupolis – Kaisareia.

Some of these routes were more regularly used than others, a reflection as noted of their strategic importance at particular periods. The most frequently employed were those which led south and eastwards, and from the middle of the eighth century a series of major depots or bases, with attendant livestock supplies, were established to facilitate campaigning in these regions. These were set up at Malagina, Dorylaion, Kaborkin (between Trikomia and Midaion), near Koloneia, Kaisareia and Dazimon.

Several important routes of access were used by the Arabs, and later the Turks, for access from the Cilician and north Syrian regions into Asia Minor.

1. Cilician Gates – Podandos – Loulon – Herakleia – Ikonion/ Loulon – Tyana – Kaisareia.
2. Germanikeia (Mar'as) – Koukousos – Kaisareia
3. Adata – Zapetra – Melitene – Kaisareia – Lykandos/ Kaisareia – Sebasteia/Melitene – Arsamosata (Šim at) – Khliat (on Lake Van).
4. Mopsouestia (al-Massisa) – Anazarba ('Ain Zarba) – Sision – Kaisareia.

It is important to note that many of these routes do not follow the major paved Roman roads, preferring instead lesser and often much more ancient routes which provided better opportunities for watering and pasturing animals and provisioning armies. For most roads there were parallel alternatives, some suitable for wheeled vehicles and paved, others more like tracks, often accessible only to men in single file and sure-footed beasts of burden. Local knowledge of such tracks was essential to successful campaigning in the guerrilla-type warfare conducted along the eastern frontiers. Many of these routes evolved in response to the situation which followed the loss of the eastern provinces to the Arabs in the seventh century. Another major change came in the later years of the eleventh century, when the focus of imperial strategy in Anatolia had to change as a result of the Seljuk occupation of much of the central plateau. A new frontier zone evolved, stretching along the belt of marginal lands which divided the lowlands and coastal plain from the interior and plateau. By the 1160s and 1170s fortresses such as Chonai, Choma (Soublaion), Philomelion, Kotyaion, Dorylaion, Ankyra and Kastamon now figured as the most advanced frontier posts, covering the territories recovered from the Turks, with a network of smaller outposts and fortresses guarding the most important routes from the interior into the coastal regions. But they signal the high-water mark of the efforts made by the emperors of the Komnenos dynasty. Although their efforts were used to advantage by the emperors of Nicaea during the period of the Latin empire (1204-1261) following the Fourth Crusade, the advance of the Turks was to prove irresistible.

In marked contrast to the fragmented geography of the Balkans and Anatolia, the remaining territories of the empire were less rugged, although Syria and Palestine were broken up by the hilly country around Jerusalem and Tiberias and the rough and inaccessible mountains of the Lebanon, with the steppes of the great Syrian desert in the east effectively separating the spheres of Roman and Persian power in the region. The fertile Nile valley and the rich agricultural lands of Palestine and western Syria were (and are) much wealthier than the Balkans and Asia Minor and, until their loss in the seventh century, provided the greater part of the imperial revenues. The extended coastal plains of Tunisia produced both olives and cereals, the latter in great quantities, and Rome imported most of the grain to support its population from Africa, just as Constantinople was heavily dependent upon Egypt for the same requirements.

While it originally included all these lands within its boundaries, throughout the greater part of its existence the lands of the empire were restricted to the Balkans and Asia Minor, along with the Aegean islands, Crete and Cyprus, and parts of southern Italy. Although our survey begins on the Syrian and Mesopotamian fronts, Asia Minor and Thrace were the setting for the battlefields upon which the fate of the empire was partly decided.

It was certainly the system of military roads, constructed largely in the period 100 BC – 100 AD, which made the Roman army so successful and efficient in its campaigning. The Roman road system also eased and aided non-military communications, in particular the movement of goods, people and information. For a variety of reasons, the regular maintenance of roads, which was a state burden upon towns and which was administered and regulated at the local level, seems during the later Roman period to have suffered a serious decline. An important consequence of this change and the difficulties it created for the use of wheeled vehicles was a much greater dependence on beasts of burden. Strict regulations were established during the later third and fourth centuries on the size, loads and types of wheeled vehicle employed by the state transport system. This was divided into two branches, the fast post (faster-moving pack-animals, light carts, and horses or ponies) and the slow post (ox-carts and similar heavy vehicles) and although the service was drastically reduced in medieval times, it seems that a unified transport and courier service continued to operate through the Byzantine period.

There were many types and standards of road: wide roads, narrow tracks or paths, paved and unpaved roads, roads suitable or unsuitable for wagons or wheeled vehicles are all mentioned in the sources. Roads of strategic importance were generally more regularly maintained. After the sixth century, it would appear that only certain key routes were kept up, largely by means of compulsory duties imposed on the local labouring population and any skilled craftsmen relevant to the task in hand. The road system in Anatolia, with its imperial and provincial marching camps situated at strategically important points, was in consequence less extensive but still effective from the middle of the seventh century. Similar considerations apply in the Balkans, too, although marching camps such as those in the Anatolian region are known only from the twelfth century and later. The maintenance of these stretches was a localized and irregular matter, and the limited evidence suggests that many became little more than paths suitable only for pack-animals, with paved or hard surfaces only near towns and fortresses.

Transport by water was generally much faster and certainly far cheaper than by land. Long-distance movement of bulk goods such as grain was generally prohibitively expensive – the cost of feeding draught-oxen, maintaining drovers and carters and paying local tolls, combined with the extremely slow rate of movement of ox-carts, multiplied the value of the goods being transported beyond the price of anyone who might have bought them. Although the bulk transport of goods over long distances did sometimes happen, it was really only the state, with some activity funded by wealthy private individuals, which could pay for this. The cost-effectiveness of shipping, entailing the carriage of large quantities of goods in a single vessel handled by a small crew, gave coastal settlements a great advantage with regard to their access to the wider world.

2
Justinian's Wars

Strategic Arrangements

At the beginning of Justinian's reign in 527 the armies of the East Roman empire were organized into five mobile field armies and a large number of smaller regional divisions along and behind the frontier regions of the empire. The field army units were referred to as *comitatenses* and each was commanded by a *magister militum*, or 'Master of the Soldiers'. The five divisions were those of the East (a huge region including the Armenian and Mesopotamian fronts with Persia, as well as the Egyptian desert front), Thrace, Illyricum, and two further 'praesental' corps (literally, 'in the presence' of the emperor) based in north-west Asia Minor and in Thrace to defend Constantinople. In the days when emperors had personally commanded their field troops, these had been their divisions. By Justinian's time this tradition of personal command had lapsed somewhat, although under Heraclius in the Persian war (622-629) it was revived. The troops making up the frontier divisions and permanent garrisons were known as *limitanei*, mostly composed of older legionary units and associated auxiliary units, backed up by mixed corps of auxiliary and legionary cavalry to provide local reserves.

Justinian undertook several reforms of these arrangements, introducing new commands for Masters of Soldiers in Africa and Italy after their recovery and establishing a Master of Soldiers for Armenia out of the older eastern field command. By the end of his reign there were over twenty-five regional commands behind the frontiers and deeper inland, serving both as military and police force for internal matters and stretching from Scythia in the north-west Balkans through the Middle East and Egypt to Mauretania in north-west Africa. The real differences between field troops and garrison units were not always very clear, mainly because of cross-postings from one type of army to the other and because so many field units were more or less permanently based in and around garrison cities.

Justinian established a strategically very important new field command, known as the *quaestura exercitus* (loosely translated as 'regions allocated to the army'), which was similar to that of a *magister militum*, but whose incumbent was entitled *quaestor*. His command comprised the troops based in the Danube frontier zone (the provinces of Scythia and Moesia II) but included in addition the Asia Minor coastal province of Caria along with the Aegean islands. The aim was to supply the Danube divisions by sea from an Aegean hinterland and thus relieve the oppressed local population of the frontier regions and their hinterland from the burden of supporting a large military force. In addition to the regular corps, the empire maintained a substantial numbers of allied forces: Arab clans and tribes were essential to the empire's strategic arrangements in the East, and were subsidized with food, cash, vestments, imperial titles and weaponry.

The emperors had also several guards units based in or near the imperial palace, or in the districts about Constantinople. The most important were the Schools, or *scholae palatinae*, and the *excubitores*. The former were organized in seven divisions of 500 heavy cavalry soldiers. Originally elite shock units recruited largely from German peoples, they had become by the middle of the fifth century little more than parade units. In their stead as active guards the emperor Leo I (457-474) recruited a much smaller elite unit of a mere 300 men. Although they remained active throughout the sixth century, during the seventh century they seem also to have become more of a parade unit, like the *scholae*.

Imperial naval forces were relatively limited – several small flotillas maintained along the Danube, a fleet based at Ravenna, and a squadron at Constantinople.

The empire's strategy was based on a first line of defence which consisted of a linear frontier screened by fortified posts, major fortresses and a connecting network of minor fortified positions. This was supported by a second line made up of a reserve of mobile field units scattered in garrison towns and fortresses across the provinces behind the frontier. By the end of Justinian's reign the gap between the different functions of the 'frontier' and 'field' armies had been narrowed, for the reasons noted already, and in the 560s and 570s garrison units seem to have reinforced and fought alongside field army units. In effect, the late Roman army was a relatively expensive force of very variable quality, which consumed a large proportion of the state's fiscal revenue each year, both in respect of cash payments and in terms of equipment and maintenance in kind for troops on campaign.

Tactics

Well into the fourth century Roman armies were still made up largely of infantry. Roman tactics were focused upon the heavy infantry, who formed the main battle line, with auxiliaries – slingers, archers, javelin-men – as light-armed troops. Cavalry operated as an ancillary arm, employed chiefly in the role of scouts, flank and rear guard, or to exploit weaknesses or an enemy withdrawal.

From the later fourth and especially the fifth century, there was a relative increase in the importance of cavalry, although they were not yet the dominant element and the proportional relationship between cavalry and infantry units remained at approximately 1:3 (it was of course lower in terms of absolute numbers of men, unit sizes in the cavalry being much smaller) until the later sixth century at least. Of the total number of mounted units, about 15% of those in the field armies were of the very heavy cavalry type (*cataphracti* and *clibanarii*).

During the later third and fourth centuries the Roman heavy infantry panoply (including the *lorica segmentata* and the helmet with neck-guard) had gradually been replaced by a lighter one, including mail and scale armour. This reflected a change in infantry training and tactics as the emphasis moved towards the infantryman as one of a mass, his effectiveness depending not on individual skills so much as on unit coherence, in contrast to the highly trained individual, fighting within a distinctive tactical sub-unit, who characterized the first and second centuries. Archaeologically, this shift can be tied in with the generalized adoption of the Germanic long sword or *spatha* instead of the older short stabbing sword or *gladius*. There was also an increase in the diversity of weapons used within individual units. The chief characteristic of Roman armies remained their tactical discipline and training in close-order drill and battlefield manoeuvring. Combined with the heavier personal armour issued to soldiers who stood in the front ranks of the battle line, these features gave Roman infantry a continued advantage over their barbarian enemies in the European and Balkan theatres.

The slow increase in the importance of cavalry from the 250s AD onwards reflects changes in the armament and tactics of Rome's main enemies, especially in the East – mounted shock troops had a significant impact on Roman warfare, particularly in the wake of defeats at the hands of Sassanid Persian forces at this time. Heavily armed cavalry now supplemented the standard cavalry formations, deployed to strengthen the main battle-line of the Roman army and to act as a counterweight against such units on the enemy side. But they remained a (very expensive) minority – disciplined Roman infantry formations, correctly handled, could usually hold their own, even against the Sassanid heavy cavalry.

Well-trained and disciplined infantry continued to be seen as essential. But discipline was increasingly a concern; poor pay and difficult conditions contributed to several mutinies during Justinian's reign and in those of his immediate successors. In an effort to stiffen discipline and fighting spirit, commanders are often reported to have stressed the traditional high standards of Roman discipline and efficiency. Belisarius was anxious about the steadiness of his infantry on more than one occasion, and the speeches put into the mouths of both Belisarius and the Persian leader Firuz at Dara in 530 allude to the usual weakness and lack of order in the Roman infantry. This may be a reflection as well as a cause of the fact that the emphasis does swing towards cavalry during the sixth century. Yet in many battles of the period reported by contemporaries such as Procopius (an eye-witness in many cases) and Agathias, infantry continued to play a key role: at Tadinae/Busta Gallorum (see below) in 551/2 infantry made up the centre of the main Roman line, and their order and discipline is stressed by Procopius. Similar remarks occur in connection with the battle of Mons Lactarius the following year, and for the battle on the Casilinus river Agathias describes the classical battle order of the late Roman period, with infantry forming the main battle line and the front rank more heavily armed than the troops behind them. Similar descriptions are recorded for later encounters elsewhere – in an engagement during the eastern wars in 556/7, for example, where well-armoured Roman troops advanced with linked shields to drive the enemy centre back.

But it is clear that Roman traditions and styles of mounted fighting were beginning to alter as a result of contacts with new enemies, in particular the steppe nomads of central Asia. To combat these effective mounted archers, the Romans needed troops trained in such skills, which was achieved in part by recruiting mercenaries or allies from such peoples and in part by training their own soldiers in such skills. By the time Procopius was writing about the campaigns of Belisarius, a number of units of archer-lancers had been established, and although they were probably relatively few in number, they played an important role in several of the battles described by Procopius and Agathias. Roman archery, based on the Hunnic model, seems to have been more effective than that of the Persian, or at least this is what Procopius claims, although there is no doubt that the massed Persian archery always remained a major tactical problem for Roman forces.

It was probably the nature of much of the warfare of the middle and later sixth century which stimulated the greater emphasis on cavalry, for the empire recruited substantial numbers of new cavalry units at this time. In the Italian and North African wars infantry continued to play a key role, but the guerrilla aspect which the campaigning took on was especially suited to fast-moving cavalry. As often as infantry appear as the mainstay of the Roman line, cavalry also appear increasingly in a central role as both shock- and missile-troops. On several occasions cavalry forces fought with minimal or no infantry support, while infantry units sometimes acted merely as a reserve or formed a protective square or wall for retreating cavalry. The importance of cavalry acting independently becomes especially apparent in a series of victories won by the general Priscus along the Danube in 600, and in the campaigns of the emperor Heraclius against the Persians in the years 622-626. Infantry nevertheless remained a significant element in late Roman armies of the sixth and first half of the seventh centuries. In the wars with the Persians, whose own infantry were often quite numerous, if less well-trained than Roman troops, as well as in the Balkans, infantry were in some situations essential. Only infantry units were suitable for garrison duties, manning major defensive installations as well as minor outposts and fortlets, while in the thickly wooded, broken and hilly terrain of parts of the Balkans infantry were indispensable, especially against the Slavic tribes that were infiltrating in considerable numbers across the Danube. The general tendency by the early seventh century appears to be one in which infantry are increasingly passive and defensive, serving both as a reserve once the enemy has been repulsed or turned and a safe haven for defeated or withdrawing Roman cavalry units.

Tactical Structures

Units of the middle of the sixth century varied considerably in their regimental organization. The older legions and auxiliary forces continued to exist, divided into *alae* of cavalry and *cohortes* of infantry, nominally of 500 and 1,000 men respectively; although under Constantine I new infantry units called *auxilia* often replaced these cohortes. Newer legions, numbering 1,000-1,500, had also been created during the second and third centuries, and this number seems also to have applied to the original legions by the fourth century. Apart from these were units called *vexillationes*, originally detachments from various units formed for a particular reason during the period around 150-250 AD, which had been turned into permanent units in their own right. This term, vexillation, was applied in the fourth century to most of the new cavalry units recruited at that time. Although some of these technical differences survived into the sixth century, the general term for most units was by then the word *numerus* or its Greek equivalent, *arithmos* or *tagma*, which simply meant 'unit' or 'number' (of soldiers). There were some important differences, however, notably between units recruited as 'federates' and those recruited as regular 'soldiers'. The former grew out of regiments of foreign allied soldiers settled on Roman territory, but by the sixth century represented a sort of foreign legion. Federate soldiers could be indigenous Romans or foreigners, and although originally spread out throughout the armies, by the later sixth century they seem to have been brigaded together as a special elite corps. In Justinian's reign they were regarded as slightly superior in their fighting qualities to the regulars. Each commanding officer also had his own personally recruited guards, known as *bucellarii*, paid for out of his own pocket. Some had quite substantial forces of private guards, including Belisarius whose *bucellarii* numbered over 1,000. Again, by the later sixth century it seems that such forces had been taken over and were henceforth paid for by the government, and established as a special division of elite soldiers.

The Battle of Dara

The battle outside Dara fought in 530 was one of the first victories of the young general Belisarius, one of Justinian's most able officers and the successful commander of the invasion and conquest of the Vandal kingdom in North Africa, as well as of the initial phase of the reconquest of the Ostrogothic kingdom of Italy.

Dara (also called Anastasioupolis, modern Turkish Oğuz) was a fortress built by the emperor Anastasius I in the years 505-507, to serve as a military base on the Roman-Persian frontier, where the *doux* of Mesopotamia was based c. 527-532; the *magister militum per orientem* may also have been established there from 540-573, when the city was taken by the Persians. Retaken in 591, it fell again to Persian forces in 604, was recovered at the end of the great Persian war in 628, and fell to the Arabs in 639. The fortress was situated on the road from Nisibis (mod. Nusaybin) to Mardes (mod. Mardin), some 15 miles northwest of Nisibis, and at the head of a dry watercourse which, in the winter season, flows down to the Khabur river farther south. The terrain of the region is fairly barren, consisting for the most part of an undulating plain dissected by several shallow dry watercourses and occasional ridges. The strategic importance of Dara was considerable, since it covered a major route into Roman Mesopotamia and beyond into both north Syria or north-westwards into Asia Minor.

War had broken out between the Sassanid Persian kingdom and the Roman empire during the last year of the reign of the emperor Justin I (518-527). The causes were several: the Persian king Kavad tried to impose Zoroastrianism on the small, predominantly Christian kingdom of Iberia, which was under Persian overlordship. The king of Iberia rebelled and called upon the Romans for support, before fleeing into Roman Lazica, on the Black Sea coast to the west, where Persian forces pursued him. At the same time, Kavad wished to secure the neutrality of the Romans in his efforts to have his third son, Khusru (Chosroes) confirmed as his successor, in view of the opposition at the Persian court to this plan. He proposed to the emperor Justin that Khusru should become his adoptive son, a plan approved by the emperor but rejected by his advisers, who then had the emperor write that, since Khusru was a barbarian, he could be adopted only on the same basis as the Roman emperor adopted German tribal leaders. Understandably, the Persian king and his son were deeply insulted by this, a response which reinforced their resolve to deal with the king of Iberia quickly. Justin ordered a counter-thrust into Persian-controlled Armenia under the young officers Sittas and Belisarius. Initially successful, they were soon defeated and expelled by a larger Persian force. In Mesopotamia, meanwhile, and in response to raids into Roman territory by Beduin allies of the Persians, Roman forces had pushed towards the Persian fortress of Nisibis, but were defeated and forced to withdraw.

At the beginning of August 527, however, Justin I died, and the new emperor Justinian began by proposing a peace treaty with the Persians. But the Persians temporized, leaving the Roman ambassadors to wait in vain at Dara: Justinian's plans to establish a new fortress to guard the Roman frontier close to the fortress city of Nisibis, which had been lost to the Persians during the reign of the emperor Anastasius (491-518), met with strong objections from the Persian king. Rather than negotiate, indeed, the Persians sent a sizeable army of some 30,000 men, which defeated the Roman covering force and destroyed the building works. The war was prosecuted with little success in 529, but in 530 the general Belisarius was appointed commander-in-chief of the eastern field army and sent to re-establish Roman dominance in the region.

Belisarius and his second-in-command Hermogenes had assembled a total of some 25,000 men, most of the field army of the East, and they took up position outside Dara, across the road to Nisibis, awaiting the agreement of the Persians to renew the negotiations. But the Persians despatched a force somewhat larger – perhaps as many as 40,000 men – under the Persian *Mirran*, the sole commander, named Firuz (rendered as Perozes in the Greek sources). This force arrived at Nisibis in June 530, before marching out and establishing a camp about 20 *stadia* (roughly 4.5 km) from the Roman position, at a place called Ammodios (a *stadion* was reckoned at 7 or 71/2 to the Roman mile, in turn reckoned at about 1570m. See E. Schilbach, *Byzantinische Metrologie*). In spite of the disparity in numbers, the Roman commanders decided not to withdraw into the fortress of Dara, but prepared instead a defensive position to receive the Persian attack, probably because much of the Persian force consisted of a rather unreliable conscripted peasantry only poorly armed and of little tactical offensive value. The victory which ensued re-established the Romans' bargaining power, and in spite of a heavy Roman defeat in 531, the death of Kavad in September of the same year nevertheless led to a negotiated settlement, ratified as 'the endless peace' in early 532.

Procopius of Caesarea, Belisarius's military secretary, provides an eye-witness account of the battle, and although not entirely clear in all details, enough information is given to provide a fairly detailed account of the course of the battle. The confrontation stretched over two days. The Persians broke camp just before sunrise on the first day, and as soon as they came within site the Roman forces were drawn up in pre-arranged formation. Belisarius had prepared a position partially shielded by a series of defensive ditches dug across the main road from Dara to Nisibis, consisting of a short central section recessed behind two longer flanking trenches, to which the middle sections were joined by two transverse sections, with numerous crossing places for troops to pass through. The bulk of the Roman infantry was drawn up in the centre in a single deep line, under Belisarius and Hermogenes. On the far left of the Roman line was stationed a detachment of Herul cavalry under their commander, Pharas, and to their right was a much stronger force of cavalry under the commander Bouzes. In the angle of the trench on the left of the Roman centre were positioned two units of 300 Hunnic cavalry under their commanders Sunicas and Aigan. Dispositions on the Roman right mirrored those on the left: a small force of some 600 Hun cavalry, under the officers Simmas and Ascan, and to their right, probably behind the trenches, a considerable force of cavalry under John son of Nicetas, with subordinates Cyril, Dorotheus, Marcellus and Germanus. Procopius is unfortunately not clear on where the two wings were positioned in relation to the trenches – in front or behind. From his account of the later course of the battle, it is clear that the centre division was behind its section of trench. The wings were probably similarly disposed. The trench would thus serve as a defence against the superior numbers of Persian cavalry, allowing the Romans to cross over the narrow passages left for this purpose to mount their own attack or to pursue the enemy. It would have been dangerous to place them in front of the trenches, which would then have been in their rear, since in the event of an overwhelming attack and the need to beat a hasty retreat, there would have been a high risk of the Roman troops falling foul of the very obstacle dug to hinder the Persians.

The Persian forces were drawn up in two lines, one held back some distance behind the other, with the centre commanded by the Persian general Firuz, the left under Baresmanes and the right under Pityaxes. The opening phase of the Persian attack involved a thrust by cavalry of the Persian right against the forces under Bouzes, which withdrew as the Persians advanced. But fearing an attack against their flank from the Hunnic units in the Roman centre, these soon stopped, at which point Bouzes gave the order to counter-attack. The Persians retired in some haste, losing, according to Procopius, seven men in their withdrawal. There then took place an incident not uncommon in pre-modern warfare, assuming that Procopius can be believed in this aspect of his account, as a Persian soldier rode out to challenge the Romans to individual combat. Unusually, the challenge was taken up not by an enlisted soldier but by a certain Andreas, a personal attendant in the retinue of Bouzes and a wrestler by profession. Andreas was able quickly to unhorse his opponent, and dismounting, kill him. This greatly enhanced Roman morale, of course, and a second, apparently more experienced Persian soldier rode out to repeat the challenge. Although Bouzes is reported by Procopius to have forbidden him to do so, Andreas again answered the challenge, and was again victorious, although each man unhorsed the other to begin with. The Persian forces seem to have been cast down by this misfortune, and since dusk was by now approaching, began to withdraw to their base at Ammodios.

The next day the Persians received some 10,000 reinforcements from the troops based at Nisibis and, following an exchange of letters in which the Romans asked the Persians to come to the negotiating table and the Persians accused the Romans of being untrustworthy and deceitful, the armies took up the same positions once more. At midday both sides began a heavy attack with arrows, the Persians' being far more numerous but having only limited effect since contrary winds reduced the force of their missiles. Nevertheless, both sides suffered some casualties. Belisarius, meanwhile, had at Pharas's suggestion sent his small cavalry force behind the hill on the extreme left of the Roman position, with the intention that, should the opportunity offer itself, he could break out from the flank into the rear of the Persian right flank.

Shortly after the exchange of arrows had ended, the Persians launched a general assault along the whole line, with their right wing under Pityaxes pushing forward with a strong attack on the forces under Bouzes. The Roman forces were compelled to withdraw in some confusion. But at this point both the Hunnic units to the right of Bouzes's position and the forces concealed behind the hill to his left swept in on the Persian cavalry, driving them in on one another and causing them to break and flee back towards their original positions, where they were sheltered by the Persian second line. Some three thousand Persian cavalry were killed in the Roman counter-attack. There seems to have followed a short pause during which both sides regrouped. In this pause Firuz decided to mount his main attack on his left, against the Roman right and the forces under John, and despatched a large force from his second line to this position, accompanied by his crack units, drawn from the Immortals, the Persian kings' elite troops. The final phase of the battle began with a general assault once more, but with a powerful attack on the Roman right which forced the cavalry units under John to give way and withdraw in disorder. From his position in the centre, however, Belisarius realized what was happening and quickly despatched reinforcements of infantry and cavalry to help the Hunnic units under Simmas and Ascan, adding the other Hunnic units from the Roman left under Sunicas and Aigan. The Roman counter-charge seems to have been very effective, for it sliced into the enemy line and cut it into two unequal parts. The larger part continued to advance after the retreating Roman cavalry, but the smaller section was now cut off from both the main Persian line and the advancing Persian units and found itself in desperate straits. The standard of the Persian commander, Baresmanes, fell, and at this point the main body of the advancing Persian units, now ahead of them and to their left, realized what was happening. Wheeling around to their right they began to move to attack the Romans from the rear, at which point Belisarius ordered the cavalry nearest to them to engage them. At the same time, the retreating Roman units under John rallied, faced about and counter-attacked, taking the hitherto victorious Persian left in the rear. This was the deciding moment in the battle. Baresmanes himself was killed in the mêlée, and the Immortals began to break up and withdraw. Some five thousand of the Persian troops in this sector of the battle fell, and as the Persian units here broke, so the whole Persian line began to break up, eventually falling into headlong rout. Procopius remarks on the great slaughter which followed as the Roman line moved forward to pursue their now broken foe, but Belisarius and Hermogenes called the troops back after a few miles, fearing the enemy might rally and turn defeat into victory if the Romans permitted their forces to fall into too much disorder.

As Procopius remarks, the battle of Dara marked an important moment in the long drawn-out warfare on the eastern front, for it was the first time a Roman force – and a numerically inferior one at that – had been able to defeat the Persians in battle for some years. Both Roman and Persian morale were affected. From the tactical perspective, it is perhaps significant that it was largely the Roman and Persian cavalry that were engaged. The Roman infantry were held back in the centre in a well-defended position behind the central ditch, while the Persian infantry, who probably composed most of their second line, appear to have played little or no part in the battle until the final rout.

The Reconquest of Italy

The Ostrogothic kingdom had evolved out of the confused situation in the last 30 years of the fifth century after the disappearance of the western empire. In 476 the general Odoacer, probably of Hunnic origin, was commander of the Germanic troops who had rebelled against the last Roman emperor in the west, Romulus Augustulus. Although proclaimed king by his soldiers, he seems never to have made this claim himself, and tried to obtain formal recognition of his position as representative in Italy of the Roman emperors from the emperor Zeno in Constantinople. In spite of bestowing the title of *patricius* upon Odoacer, Zeno eventually instigated the Ostrogothic king Theoderic to invade Italy (chiefly to free the Romans from the Ostrogothic presence in the Balkans), and in 489 Odoacer was defeated and besieged in Ravenna. After apparently agreeing to share Italy between them, Theoderic had Odoacer murdered and in 493 established the Ostrogothic kingdom of Italy. In 497 his rule was formally recognized by the emperor Anastasius I. The new regime achieved a degree of stability and peace which Italy had not experienced for a generation. Although the Germanic conquerors were Arian Christians, and thus heretical from the point of view of the majority population and of the Roman emperors at Constantinople, they maintained relatively good relations with the Orthodox population and clergy.

Theoderic died in 526 and was succeeded by his grandson Athalaric under the tutelage of his daughter Amalasuntha. The latter pursued an openly pro-Roman politics, including measures to protect the interests of the indigenous population against the depredations and oppression of Ostrogothic lords and to maintain a close association with the imperial court at Constantinople. This aroused the hostility of the traditional Ostrogothic nobility and when Athalaric died in 534, Amalasuntha was compelled to marry her cousin Theodahad, who became co-ruler and in 535 had Amalasuntha assassinated. This was Justinian's opportunity to intervene in Italy. With

Africa now firmly in Roman hands and an excellent base from which to support operations there, Belisarius was placed in command of an expeditionary force of 7,500 men. In the summer of 535 he departed from Constantinople and by the end of the year had taken Sicily with virtually no opposition. In the following years he was able to gain control of southern Italy; by December 536 he had entered Rome. The situation was complicated in part by hostilities between the Goths and the Franks, who to begin with saw the situation as one which could be exploited to their advantage. The war initially went well for the Romans. But in 539 the emperor sent the eunuch Narses with more troops to assist Belisarius – and with a brief to keep an eye on the latter. The mistrust and dissension which followed resulted in a series of setbacks for the Romans; but after Narses had been withdrawn Belisarius was able finally to take Ravenna in 540.

At this point the recovery of Italy looked secure. But Belisarius was now recalled to command on the Persian front, and under a new leader, Totila, the Goths were able to defeat the Romans in a series of encounters, recovering much of the territory and most of the fortresses and towns lost before 540. In spite of Belisarius's return to the Italian front in 544 things did not improve. Rome fell to the Goths in 546, was briefly recovered in 548 and was lost again in 550. Totila expelled the Romans from several other fortresses and began building a fleet, with which he was able to occupy Sicily and threaten both Sardinia and, on the opposite side of the peninsula, Dalmatia. Justinian was distracted by religious affairs as well as by invasions of Huns and Bulgars in the Balkans, threatening Constantinople itself. But in 551 events began to favour the Romans once more. The Gothic fleet was defeated by the senior Roman commanders off Ancona and Sicily was recovered by the general Artabanes. Justinian meanwhile, in spite of peaceful overtures from Totila, had in April 551 despatched the aged, but very able, general Narses with a substantial force to try to re-establish the Roman position. He landed his troops, covered by the Roman fleet, at Salona in the autumn. His march southwards along the Venetic coast was hampered by both the Franks, who had occupied much of northern Italy, and by the Gothic forces themselves. But Narses was able to push ahead quickly and at the end of June 552 met the Gothic army under Totila, who was marching northwards as quickly as he could, near Tadinae, a short distance to the east of the Via Flaminia.

The Battle of Tadinae (Busta Gallorum) 551/2

The army Narses commanded in 552 numbered some 20,000-25,000 altogether. This included substantial numbers of allied troops, for the Lombard king Auduin had sent a force of nearly 6,000 men to help the empire. There were in addition some 4,000 Heruls under their commanders Philemuth and Aruth, who complemented the regular imperial cavalry and infantry, as well as new units recruited from Thrace and Illyricum by Narses himself and even a small unit of Persian cavalry commanded by a relative of the Persian Great King. Knowing that Totila would be compelled to seek him out in order to drive the Roman forces away from the remaining territory held by the Goths, Narses decided to adopt a defensive position and await the Gothic attack. He selected a site straddling a local route into the Appenines from the Via Flaminia in the valley of the small river Bono, well defended by a small hill on his left, on slightly raised ground and with precipitous and very rough terrain behind and around the plain across which the Gothic force would have to pass in order to attack him. His dispositions demonstrate the strength of his position: the Lombard, Herul and Gepid allies – perhaps 9-10,000 men in all – were placed in the centre, dismounted and on a slope which gave them a defensive advantage; on either wing was a cavalry force made up of troops armed with both bows and lances, the right under the commander Valerian, the left under Narses himself. In front of each cavalry wing a strong force of some 4,000 archers was positioned. Behind the left wing a further reserve of 1,500 cavalry were placed. According to Procopius, 500 were to act as a rapid reserve for the centre, the remainder as a flanking force should the Gothic infantry attack the Roman centre or flank.

Totila's forces encamped at a site some 14 Roman miles to the south, at the place now called Fossato (no doubt from the Latin *fossatum*, the camp). In view of the fact that the Gothic army was outnumbered, Narses made overtures for a peaceful settlement or, if not, then a time for the encounter. Totila rejected any talk of a settlement, however, and suggested that the two armies meet to decide their fate in eight days time. Narses realized that this was a ploy and drew his forces up in their positions; and indeed, at dawn the next day the Gothic forces were reported to be nearing the Roman positions. Since a track through a gully around the small hill to the left of the Roman line was the only means of access to a position from which the Roman line could be outflanked, Narses had occupied the ravine with a small but adequate force of some fifty men during the night. The Goths, who had apparently drawn up their forces in roughly the same way – infantry in the centre, cavalry on the wings – spent most of the morning attempting to dislodge this force, and mounted several fierce assaults on the Roman position. But the narrowness of the gully and the extremely broken nature of the terrain made any attack easy to beat off, the more so since the Goths employed only cavalry in the attempts, all of which failed with minimal losses to the Roman troop. The opening phase of the battle was then prolonged by a series of displays of horsemanship on the part of Totila himself before both armies, preceded by a challenge to single combat on the part of one of the Gothic warriors, ending in his defeat and death. Much of this seems to have been an attempt by Totila to delay the start of battle while awaiting the arrival of a further 2,000 cavalry, who had been delayed. At about midday, however, and as news of their arrival reached the Gothic army, the Goths withdrew towards their encampment.

This situation might have encouraged Narses to launch an attack on the withdrawing Goths, but he did not, chiefly because of the strong defensive position which he would have been unwilling to relinquish but perhaps also because the Goths would have been moving back across prepared ground, about which Narses would have had only uncertain information. According to Procopius, on the other hand, Totila certainly hoped that his withdrawal would cause the Romans to relax their guard and enable him to mount a surprise attack before they had been able to resume their positions. Narses was fully conscious of this possibility, however, and ordered the army to take a sparing lunch in their lines, removing neither armour nor saddles. When, shortly thereafter, the reinforced Gothic force returned, they found the Romans ready for them.

Totila had changed his formation in the hope that his plan would work, however, and had massed his cavalry in a single body across his whole front, with the infantry in the rear. It becomes clear during Procopius's account of the battle that most of the Gothic army must in fact have consisted of cavalry and that their infantry, if they were proper soldiers at all and not peasants drafted in to make up numbers, were regarded as either insignificant or unreliable. It would have been far more sensible, for example, to try to force the gully around the hill on the Roman left with infantry rather than cavalry. In accordance with this change and with the fact that the Goths were obviously intending to launch a massive attack on his centre, Narses moved the archers on each wing out on to the flanks, where they took up position on high ground – and thus out of immediate reach of a Gothic mounted assault – ready to enfillade the Gothic cavalry as they advanced.

The battle itself cannot have lasted long. Totila had ordered all his troops to fight with the lance only, and in a single massed charge the Gothic line swept forward against the Roman centre, taking some casualties on the way from the enfillading archery. But the well-placed spearmen in the centre held their position, and after a short action the Gothic cavalry began to fall back. It is not clear at this point whether the flanking units of cavalry on the Roman left were thrown in to decide the issue but in any case the whole Roman line was given the order to advance. The Goths seemingly had no chance to fall back and regroup and under the pressure from this general advance began to break up in disorder. Rather than retreating to the safety of their infantry, they ploughed straight through them, causing further casualties and panic, with the result that the whole army now dissolved into an uncontrollable rout. The Roman cavalry pursued with ferocity and slew many – Procopius claims as many as 6,000 were slain, which in the conditions described is perhaps not unlikely – including the Gothic leader himself. The Romans had achieved a resounding victory.

One of the most important points to come out of Procopius's account is the order and discipline which the Roman forces displayed, motley though they were in their composition, and this remains a significant aspect of Roman military operations throughout the sixth century and beyond, frequently contrasted favourably not only with the empire's 'barbarian' foes but also with those who had a much higher degree of military administration and organization, such as the Persians. A similar point is apparent in the account of the next battle we will describe, fought again under the leadership of Narses against the Franks in Italy.

The Battle of the Casilinus (Volturnus) River 554

Totila died of his wounds after the battle of Tadinae and the leadership of the remaining Gothic forces was taken by his second-in-command, Teias. But he was killed in battle with Narses shortly afterwards, and it seemed that the war for Italy was finally over. The Frankish king, Theudibald, however, who had failed to come to the assistance of the Goths in their hour of need, now gave permission for two chieftains of the Alemanni, Leutharis and Butilin, to lead an expedition into Italy – aimed as much, it would seem, at the seizure of booty and prisoners as with the intention of helping the Goths. But many of the latter joined them in the hope of defeating Narses and reversing the situation. Their armies – estimated by contemporary sources at some 75,000, undoubtedly greatly exaggerated – entered the Po valley towards the beginning of June 553. Narses despatched several of his commanders at the head of a substantial force into the province of Aemilia with orders to hold the Frankish-Alemannic forces until he could prepare his position. But a combination of poor judgement on the part of one of the Herul commanders fighting on the Roman side, resulting in a signal defeat at Parma, and poor logistical support from the civil authorities of the region forced the Romans to retire in haste towards Faenza. Narses had in the meantime been able to reduce Lucca, which still held out against him, while he was greatly helped by the decision of Aligern, brother of Teias and commander of Cumae, to offer his services to the Roman emperor rather than support the Franks. In view of the Roman defeat at Parma Narses decided to withdraw and to winter his troops in preparation for a spring campaign to decide the issue.

This turned out to be a sensible decision. The combined Frankish-Alemannic armies penetrated central Italy without opposition putting all to fire and sword, but in Samnium decided to divide their forces. Butilin continued with his forces towards Campania, Lucania and Bruttium, while Leutharis marched across Apulia and Calabria as far as Otranto. During the summer of 554 this army began its return march, laden with booty, much of which was lost following an ambush laid by the Roman commander of Pisaurum (Pesaro). By the time they had reached Frankish Venetia disease had struck, and many, including Leutharis, died. The army trickled away and presented no further danger. In contrast, the forces under Butilin, although similarly affected by disease, probably dysentery, continued their advance and marched towards Rome, where Narses had set up his base of operations. Exploiting the situation in the Frankish forces, Narses continued to delay matters, until in the autumn of 554 he felt that his soldiers, among them a substantial number of barbarian allies and federate troops, were ready. The two armies met near Capua on the banks of the Casilinus, also known as the Vulturnus (mod. Volturno) river.

Narses had about 18,000 men in his army, including both Roman units of archer-lancers and heavy infantry, and a substantial force of Heruls serving under their own leaders. The Franks, who may have numbered about the same (although Agathias says that there were originally some 30,000, reduced by disease and desertion), were encamped on the banks of the river itself, which formed one side of their encampment, and Butilin created a perimeter for the rest of the camp using the wheels of the numerous carts and wagons which accompanied his army, which were dug into the earth up to the hubs in a continuous line. The bridge over the river, not far from the entrance to the camp, was defended by the construction of a wooden watch-tower which was strongly manned and intended to beat off any attack from the Romans, since this provided one possible route away from the enemy. The absence of any substantial Roman presence on the Frankish side of the river enabled Butilin's army to extract whatever supplies they required without difficulty from the surrounding villages.

As soon as Narses drew close to the Frankish encampment he moved to prevent this casual pillaging, and despatched a cavalry force under an Armenian officer named Chanaranges. He was able without difficulty to put a stop to the Franks' efforts to forage, capturing several wagons and setting one carrying hay on fire up against the watch-tower built to guard the bridge, which was destroyed. The small garrison just managed to escape.

This action proved to be the prelude to battle. As the Franks immediately began to issue forth from their encampment ready armed and eager to challenge the Roman force, Narses ordered his forces to form up in battle order outside his own camp, presumably according to well-established Roman practice for such a manoeuvre. All did not go according to plan, however. One of the Herul leaders had killed a servant in a rage over some minor infraction, and when this was reported by Roman officers to Narses the man was brought before him. According to Agathias Narses was anxious not to allow such an unpropitious event to bring misfortune to the Romans, and felt obliged therefore to punish the man. Since the latter was entirely unrepentant, claiming that masters were quite at liberty to deal with their slaves in this way, Narses ordered that he be summarily executed. The Heruls immediately refused to continue their deployment, and so Narses had necessarily to continue without them. Fortunately they were persuaded to join the rest of the army by their leader, Sindual, who asked Narses to delay the deployment until his men were ready. Narses was unwilling to do this, but reserved a position for the Heruls in the centre of the Roman line, which they were to occupy as soon as they could.

His order of battle was traditional, with cavalry armed with lance, bow and shield on either wing, some, perhaps, heavily armoured cataphracts armed with longer pikes. Narses himself took up his position with the right wing. The cavalry on the left flank were partly concealed in woods, with orders to remain concealed until they could take the enemy infantry in the flank. The Roman centre consisted entirely of infantry, the front ranks heavily armed with archers and spearmen behind them in a classic Roman battle-order described by the fifth-century strategic writer Vegetius. The Heruls were to occupy the centre of this line, immediately behind the foremost units.

The Frankish attack was given further stimulus by reports, delivered by two Herul deserters, that the Heruls themselves had withdrawn and would take no part in the battle, and that Roman morale was very low as a result. Heartened by this, the Franks quickly adopted the typical Germanic attack formation known to the Romans as the *cuneus*, the wedge or boar's head, made up essentially of two deep columns which converged at the head. The *cuneus* thus presented a narrow front protected by a wall of shields and intended to punch through the enemy line, allowing the remainder of the columns to engage the rest of the enemy line while the 'head' could then turn to take it in the rear.

In the event, the barbarian wedge achieved its aim, and was able without much opposition to smash through the Roman line and even into and through the reserve or rearguard stationed a little behind them. Some charged on regardless, heading for the Roman camp; the majority were locked in combat with that portion of the Roman centre which they had pushed back with them. But there their plans went awry. While the rest of the Roman infantry now began to engage directly with the remainder of the column as the two sides came up to one another, Narses ordered the cavalry on the wings to reverse their formation and move back and around the rear of their own infantry to contain the head of the enemy column by training their bows on them. The Franks were now being shot at from the flank and from behind, and at this point were met by the orderly advance of the Heruls who charged into them and rapidly pushed them back. The attrition from the Roman mounted archery was considerable, and caused all the more confusion because the Franks were unable in the mêlée to see where exactly the missiles were coming from. The leading elements of the Frankish column soon broke up and began to flee behind the main Roman battle line and towards the river, where some drowned and the majority of the remainder were killed or captured. The main body of the Heruls now closed up and moved into their originally designated position, and as the Roman line was now solid once more, the cavalry on the wings re-occupied their original positions and began to lap around the main body of the enemy columns. Although it is not explicitly stated, the cavalry concealed in the woods were almost certainly engaged at this point, since Agathias describes the Franks as being effectively surrounded in the final stages of the conflict, a situation most readily achieved if the Roman cavalry had now come out of their position and attacked the rear sections of the Frankish troops. The Franks had no reserve, and the two columns, now pushed into a single mass, lost all cohesion and impetus. Within a few minutes the Frankish soldiers began to turn to the rear and a complete rout began. The Roman line then surged forward and, since the Franks had no clear route of escape, the slaughter was enormous – according to Agathias only five barbarians escaped! Even if this is clearly a considerable exaggeration, it clearly signals a massive defeat and very heavy casualties. Narses had achieved a complete victory, and thoroughly vindicated his patience and his strategy of not attempting to take on both the barbarian forces at the same time.

The battle of the Casilinus illustrates the fact that well-ordered infantry, drawn up in the traditional fashion and properly supported by cavalry, were still an important and highly effective force in the Roman armies of the period. It also suggests that discipline remained the essential ingredient and that the absence of this element, rather than any sudden revolution in tactics, was the real cause of so many problems faced by Roman commanders in this period. In general, the battles described by Procopius and Agathias for the reign of Justinian make it clear that while infantry remained a key element of most armies, cavalry were playing an increasingly important and often more versatile role and, when employed appropriately – as seems to have been the case for at least some of Narses's cavalry at Tadinae – could even replace infantry in the battle line. These developments were to become increasingly pronounced in the warfare of the later sixth century.

3

After Justinian: The Later Sixth and Seventh Centuries and the Rise of Islam

Tactical and Strategic Developments

In terms of tactics the major feature to note for this period is that already explored in the previous Chapter, namely the heightened importance of cavalry. A late sixth-century treatise, the so-called *Strategikon*, goes into some detail in this respect, describing the arms, equipment and tactical training of cavalry units, as well as a range of orders of battle for cavalry with only limited infantry support. While infantry are by no means ignored, it is clearly for a commander of cavalry units that the author writes. But apart from this gradual shift in emphasis, the evidence suggests that there was little change. One important innovation seems to have been the adoption of stirrups, almost certainly from the Turkic Avars.

Strategically, the major problem faced by the emperors after Justinian was that at the end of his reign, and as a direct consequence of his successes, the spread of active troops across the empire was extremely thin. The extended armies had to defend a vast frontier, respond to sudden incursions, and deal with internal unrest in many areas. Yet they were able to defend the integrity of the imperial frontiers, and to restore them when they were breached, until the collapse of imperial defensive arrangements during the first years of the reign of Heraclius. The explanation for this success lies in the effective and efficiently co-ordinated system of logistical support which the Roman state maintained, as well as competent leadership and the ability of the Romans to field well-motivated and tactically cohesive and disciplined armies. The lack of strategic co-ordination and relatively limited numbers of the enemy forces also played an important role. Roman campaign strategy placed heavy emphasis on delaying tactics, depriving the enemy of supplies and fodder for horses, fomenting anxiety and discontent among his troops, and similar strategems to wear down the enemy, well-tried methods which were particularly important in a time of limited resources and an overstretched economy. Roman arms were complemented by diplomacy, of course, which generally relied on the use of 'subsidies' in cash or bullion to potential enemy leaders.

It should be remembered, however, that 'frontiers' are somewhat artificial constructs. Romans certainly believed that frontiers marked a line between 'them' and 'us'; but the archaeology of the later Roman world in both the Balkans and the East has shown that they remained highly notional constructs. There is plenty of evidence that 'barbarians' of one sort or another were well established on Roman territory throughout the Balkans during much of the later sixth century, for example, usually in small subsistence groups whose autonomy depended upon being able to forage and raid for provisions, blackmail local communities (by offering 'protection') and avoid imperial troops. When the latter appeared, these groups generally had to submit, and were often moved on. But the degree of control exercised over such groups was often minimal; gradually a situation arose in which the imperial presence itself became entirely notional. Thus although the Danube, for example, was held as a 'frontier' well into the seventh century, much of the Balkan hinterland was already entirely out of imperial administrative reach.

For those areas most frequently affected by the army's presence as well as by enemy activity, the regular disruption of economic activity led to depopulation and the abandonment of agricultural land, with the result that the army could barely supply itself adequately. This was already the case in northern Thrace in the later fifth century, for example, which led the emperor Anastasius to enact special measures to cater for the forces based there. It applied equally to the provinces of Moesia and Scythia in Justinian's reign. The establishment of the *quaestura*, a special command set up to deal with such problems, with armies based along and behind the Danube being supplied from the Aegean by sea, was an intelligent solution to such a problem.

The strategic basis of the armies remained much as it had done at the end of Justinian's reign, until the middle years of the reign of Heraclius, that is, until the 620s. But there were two exceptions. In Italy and Africa new commands entitled 'exarchates' were established, the former with its headquarters at Ravenna, the latter with its headquarters at Carthage. These new commands united military and civil authority in the hands of a single official and represented a response to a perceived threat – in Italy the invasion of the Lombards in 568 and their subsequent establishment in the Po valley and the central regions of the peninsula; in Africa the challenge to imperial authority presented by the constant raids of Berber tribes into the coastal plain of the North African provinces.

Further changes took place during the reign of Heraclius. The two imperial field reserve armies in Thrace and in Bithynia were amalgamated. The two divisions of the *magistri militum per Orientem* and *per Armeniam* continued to exist, as did that of the *magister militum per Thracias* – all three were later involved in fighting the Arabs in the 630s – but the division of the *magister militum per Illyricum* disappears from the record. The slender evidence makes it likely that this corps had broken up, and that the surviving elements were absorbed into the other field armies, a result of the occupation in the period 610–30 of much of the central and north Balkan region by Slav settlers under Avar hegemony.

At the end of the Persian wars (c. 628/9), therefore – and although the exarchates, the *quaestura*, the single praesental army and the disappearance of the army of Illyricum presented a rather different overall arrangement – the basic strategy remained more-or-less unaltered. The re-establishment of Arab allies along the eastern frontier seems also to have taken place, along with the restoration of the system of at least some *limitanei* posts and garrisons, while the regional command structure of the 630s and well into the 640s had hardly changed from before the time of Heraclius.

Siege Warfare in the Byzantine Period

The art of defending fortresses and cities against attack and of laying siege to enemy strongholds was an important aspect of eastern Roman military science. As with tactics and strategy, the Byzantines inherited from Hellenistic and Roman writers a long and complex tradition, embodied in tactical treatises as well as in several works especially devoted to siege warfare. The need to protect and defend, as well as the capacity to capture, fortresses of strategic value was appreciated as a fundamental element of imperial strategy in the long term as well as being essential to the empire's short-term capacity to wage war on those who threatened or challenged it.

Yet in spite of the ancient tradition to which Byzantines looked for guidance, eastern Roman siege warfare was not particularly sophisticated. In theory, and sometimes in practice, siege artillery and various other mechanical devices were employed on a large scale: the siege train taken by Manuel I on his 1176 expedition, for example, must have included many different 'engines' or the materials for their construction, although very little hard evidence of such machines has survived. Indeed, the medieval texts rarely provide much detailed information at all, and the technical vocabulary used to describe particular types of siege catapult, for example, is often confused and contradictory.

Most accounts of Byzantine sieges show the Roman forces using tried and tested techniques to reduce a fortress or city: starving it into submission by cutting off its supplies, using psychological warfare to persuade the garrison to surrender or mining the towers and walls so that breaches could be established and the city taken by storm. As long as time allowed, it was generally seen as much better to starve the enemy out – and thus keep one's own losses to a minimum – than to engage in attacks which cost lives and materials and might in the event be unsuccessful. By the same token, counter-siege warfare involved adequately preparing the garrison by ensuring both that the defenses were in good order and that the troops were properly provisioned, especially with a good water-supply.

The advice given in the tactical handbooks emphasizes indirect rather than direct methods of subduing an enemy. Various ways of trying to tempt the enemy out of their defences, or of demoralizing or frightening the besieged population, were recommended. Fomenting discord within the besieged population or among the enemy soldiers was regarded as especially effective. Persuading the enemy garrison to come out from their defences to fight a battle in the field was likewise highly recommended, and there are several examples of this being successfully carried out by Roman commanders (and of Roman garrison commanders succumbing to similar ruses and strategems!).

Only when such ploys failed, or when the attacking commander had no options (or was under some time pressure – the approach of a relief force, for example), was an outright attack recommended, and even then only after appropriate preparations had been made. Not all generals necessarily followed this advice, but there were several well-established methods that could be put into practice. To begin with, digging saps, or tunnels under the walls, was seen as a simple but highly effective means of damaging the defensive capacity of an enemy fortress. Once the tunnels were finished, they could be filled with combustibles and, when other preparations were completed, set on fire. The fire would then burn the wooden supporting posts away, the tunnel would collapsed along with the section of wall or tower above it, and a breach in the walls would appear. Mines could be intercepted by counter-mines, of course; a vivid example of such techniques has been found during excavations of the Roman fortress at Doura Europos on the Euphrates, taken by the Sassanids in AD 256. Here, just such a mine and countermine have been found, still containing the skeletal remains of the soldiers who were caught in them when the underground mêlée broke out: a grisly testament to the nature of siege-warfare in the later Roman period. Both Byzantine and Arab historians describe sieges in which such techniques were used, and it seems that this was the usual means of reducing enemy fortresses where they could not be starved or persuaded to surrender. On the other hand, many tales recorded in the histories reflect a much simpler approach. One Byzantine fortress was taken by a simple ploy when the Bulgar Tsar Samuel sent five soldiers disguised as workers into the fortress carrying axes hidden under their cloaks. As soon as they got inside the fortress they quickly cut through the rope hinge supports on the gates, enabling the main Bulgar force to rush them before they could be dragged shut.

A late tenth-century tactical treatise, written by Nikephoros Ouranos, one of Basil II's most able and successful generals, remarks on the fact that mining the walls of a city, rather than the use of elaborate or complex siege machines, was the primary means of taking enemy strongholds. But this may relate to rapid field campaigns rather than the more carefully planned and much larger undertakings in which siege machinery seems to play an important role in the accounts of the contemporary historians. Throughout the period up to the twelfth century eastern Roman armies appear in the written sources using the complete array of siege machinery, including large wooden towers with rams and catapults or *ballistae* of various types. Many of the machines described in the Byzantine treatises or mentioned occasionally by name in the chronicles may in fact be listed merely because of literary convention, taken from ancient authors upon whom Byzantine writers drew very heavily. The tenth-century account by the historian Leo the Deacon of the siege of the Muslim stronghold of Chandax on Crete, for example, is taken directly from a similar description of a siege in the sixth-century history of Agathias. But artillery did play an important role in sieges and counter-sieges as well as in field combat, where small, wagon-mounted, tension-powered *ballistae* appear in accounts of some battles.

The details of Byzantine artillery remain unclear. Missile-projecting and stone-throwing artillery was certainly employed, but the texts are vague about their construction and means of propulsion. On the other hand, there is enough evidence to suggest that the use of torsion-powered weapons probably ceased during or slightly before the sixth century, greater reliance being placed on the simpler and more easily maintained tension machines. Thus a document of the 950s or 960s listing the equipment employed in the attack on Crete in 949 includes large and small frame-mounted or hand-held 'bow-ballistae', that is, tension-powered weapons (basically the same in principle as the crossbow) which, depending on how they were mounted, could shoot either stones or bolts. Roman armies also employed traction-powered (that is, pulled by hand) trebuchets, introduced from China via the Avars in the later sixth century and in use in Byzantium and the Arab world until the twelfth century, when the much more powerful counterweight trebuchet was developed. From the later seventh until the twelfth century Byzantine forces, especially at sea, also disposed of the dreaded 'liquid fire', an early type of napalm, consisting of crude oil (collected in the Caucasus and South Russian steppe, to one or both of which the Byzantines had regular access). This was projected from tubes mounted in the bows or amidships on the larger warships of the imperial navy. It seems to have been effective when it was actually deployed, but also worked very well as a terror-weapon. In the early tenth century, a hand-held version was developed for use on land, which one Arab account describes in graphic detail. The method of propulsion was probably as dangerous to the Byzantines as the liquid fire was to their enemies, and the details remain vague. While incendiary projectiles were a standard element of siege warfare throughout the ancient and medieval worlds (pots filled with combustibles shot from catapults, fire-arrows and so forth), these eastern Roman liquid fire projectors seem to have been essentially different; and although the Arabs even evolved special units equipped with naphtha-proof clothing, they do not appear to have been able to copy this particular device successfully.

Siege towers seem frequently to have been used when a well-defended stronghold had to be taken by storm. But many of the fortresses and cities which were fought over were on such difficult terrain that siege-engines of this type were useless or ineffective. Where the ground was suitable, however, they are often mentioned. They appear in sixth-century accounts of sieges (the siege of Amida by the Romans in 503, the siege of Martyropolis by the Persians in 530, for example); the Avars who laid siege to Constantinople in 626 are reported to have constructed twelve tall siege-towers. Accounts of sieges in the ninth to twelfth centuries often mention siege-towers, and an eleventh-century manuscript illumination shows a siege-tower from which liquid fire is projected. Robert Guiscard built one, which the Byzantines were able to sally out and burn, during his siege of Dyrrachion in 1081, and a little earlier Alexios I had had siege towers built in order to storm the fortress of Kastoria, occupied by Bryennios.

There were many other devices used in sieges, of course. Much reliance was placed upon light, portable penthouses, or *laisai*, house-shaped structures of woven branches with a steep roof and several entrances covered by matting or wicker screens. They varied in size and were designed to protect the men carrying them or working behind or beneath them. The heavier wheeled penthouse or 'tortoise' was seen as too cumbersome for most sieges, requiring transport on carts. These were wooden-framed sheds, usually but not always equipped with wheels, roofed with wood, straw or wicker and covered in goat-hair mats or other cloth soaked in water to resist fire. Designed to resist arrows and spears or slingstones as well as heavy objects dropped from the battlements, they were often equipped with battering-rams, the size, weight and capability again determined by the size of the tortoise in which it was enclosed. They were an important part of any siege train, but were employed only against the most heavily defended strongholds.

The nature and duration of a siege depended upon many factors. Apart from seasonal considerations, which affected the availability of provisions for the troops and fodder and water for animals, the terrain around a fortress or city played a key role. Many East Roman fortresses were constructed on high promontories or sites which were similarly very difficult of access for anything but soldiers on foot. Such strongholds frequently changed hands, however, and this seems nearly always to have been a result of the garrison being starved, tricked or frightened into submission, rarely of an actual bombardment and a successful storming operation. Lowland sites, or sites with relatively level ground on one or more sides, could more easily be attacked in this direct way, and the occasional detailed accounts of such all-out attacks usually concern sites like this. The fortress cities of Manzikert and Khliat in eastern Anatolia are both approachable on at least two sides, for example, and the expeditions of Romanos IV in 1071 and Manuel I in 1176 were accompanied by siege trains carrying equipment which would have been deployed against them. The fortress of Amorion can similarly be approached from several directions by wheeled siege-engines, although in all these cases the ground is rough and difficult.

It was essential to place artillery properly, since otherwise its effects would be wasted. One frequently used technique, assuming time was available, was to construct earth embankments, often reinforced by timber lacework or revetments, upon which various pieces of artillery could be positioned. There is plenty of evidence for the building of such earthen ramps from the late Roman period onwards both in written texts and in the archaeological record. At the site of Doura-Europos the Sassanid assault ramp, constructed from stamped earth and brick revetments, can still be seen, angled so that wheeled siege-engines could be moved along it. It still stands higher than the walls against which it was built. Similar ramps are described by an eleventh-century Byzantine writer in a description of the siege of the fortress of Moreia, during the wars of Basil II against the Bulgars. Such ramps could be destroyed, however: during the Persian siege of Amida in 502/3 Roman soldiers dug their way into the Persian ramp from inside the walls, removing the earth until the mound collapsed. In the siege of Moreia, already mentioned, the Bulgars similarly dug their way into the enemy mound and set the timber props on fire so that the whole edifice collapsed.

The histories of the period recount many tales of sieges successful and unsuccessful conducted by Roman commanders. Isolating the fortress or town in question and stopping supplies reaching the inhabitants is nearly always mentioned as the first stage. Entrenching and ensuring adequate supplies for one's own camp was also essential. The sieges of Tephrike and Melitene by Basil I were unsuccessful because they were warned in advance of the Roman attack and were well stocked with essentials as well as having good water-supplies. In contrast, it was the besieging army which eventually ran out of supplies, having stripped the surrounding countryside to maintain itself. The siege of Tarsos in 883 failed because the careless and inexperienced commander omitted to entrench and protect his camp or set up a proper watch, with the result that the besieged army sallied out, took the Romans by surprise and inflicted on them a serious defeat. A similar tale is told of the commander in charge of the counter-attack against the Muslims forces which had seized Crete from the Byzantines in the 820s. Initially successful in defeating the enemy forces in the field and then confining them to their fortress, he threw away his advantage by failing to set proper piquets or entrench and defend the camp appropriately. The Muslim army sallied out at night and caught the Romans unawares in the midst of their premature celebrations, utterly routing them. There are many similar stories.

The Wars in the East

Between 572 and 591 the conflict which characterized Roman-Persian relations erupted once again. In 562 Justinian and Khusru had signed an 'eternal peace', an agreement which was guaranteed by the payment by the Roman side of a substantial sum in gold on a regular basis. The 'subsidies', as they were euphemistically called, had been paid for the first ten years, but neither side appeared willing to continue the arrangement: the Romans because it was felt the arrangement was simply too discreditable to them, the Persians because they were unwilling to make any concessions. Roman claims to the territory of Suania in the Caucasus were met by Persian claims for subsidies for their Arab confederates, the Lakhmids of Hira. The situation came to a head when the Persians intervened in the Yemen, which had been occupied by the pro-Roman king of Abyssinia. The native Himyarite princes appealed to the Persian court, and with Persian help were able to expel the Abyssinians and restore the Himyarite king, Sayf. A Persian military commander, or *marzban*, was sent with troops to assist him, but the Persians soon adopted an interventionist policy which was too much for the native dynasty, which now appealed to Constantinople for help. At the same time, the Christian population of Persarmenia and its leaders, under Persian authority, also appealed to the emperor Justin for assistance against the Persians. Justin agreed to make common cause with his co-religionists. Faced with remonstrations from Khusru, he replied that he could not ignore an appeal from fellow Christians.

The final stimulus to renewed hostilities was the appearance on the historical scene of the Turks, who had replaced the Huns as the dominant power in the central and western steppe, and who had been rebuffed in their overtures to the Persians. Indeed, the Persians had poisoned some Turk emissaries who arrived to negotiate over the silk trade. The Turkish Khan now sent an embassy to Constantinople, which the emperor received hospitably, and, though the Persians attempted to waylay the Roman ambassadors who travelled to the Turkish Khan's headquarters on the steppe, a treaty was signed between the two powers. The agreement was advantageous to the Romans insofar as the Turks could now threaten both the Persians – through the Caucasus – and the Avars (who were rapidly becoming a major problem for the Romans along the Danube) and to the Turks because the Romans could distract the Persians from interfering with their northern and eastern silk trade.

In 572 Justin refused to pay the subsidies guaranteeing the peace with Persia. The war opened with minor but successful Roman raids into Persian territory in Arzanene, a major Persian incursion into Syria, with great loss of life and property to the Romans, and in 574 the successful Persian siege of Dara, a strategic disaster for the Romans. The difficulties caused by the Avars on the Danube, as well as the emperor's illness, meant that the Roman response was ineffective, and a truce on the Mesopotamian front was bought for the years 576-578. In Armenia, war continued more successfully, with the defeat of Khusru himself at the hands of the Roman general Justinian near Melitene in 576, including the capture of an immense booty. Divisions within the Roman command, unfortunately, meant that Khusru was allowed to launch a punitive attack against Melitene itself, which was taken and sacked. The Persian king then turned to face the Roman forces, but was again heavily defeated. In 577 the Persians were able to reverse the situation, defeating the Roman army in a surprise attack into Armenia. In the following year, Roman forces, now under the command of the general Maurice (who would later become emperor) succeeded in re-establishing a certain equilibrium, although the death of Khusru in 579 and accession of his son Hormisdas meant that the Persians rejected any suggestion of peace. The war continued through 580 and 581, resulting in a major Roman victory at Constantina in Osrhoene. The pattern of hostilities remained much the same for the following years – Roman victories followed by Persian counterstrokes and Roman defeats, a situation not helped by the frequent divisions and tensions within the Roman high command as well as the indiscipline of the Roman troops. The account of the battle which follows is known only from the account of Theophylact Simocatta, who was writing during the early part of the reign of Heraclius (610-641), but it is typical of the sort of confrontations which occurred between Persian and Roman armies on the eastern front at this time.

The Battle of Solachon 586

In spring 586 the Roman commander Philippicus, whose strategic situation was fairly strong, rejected Persian proposals to open negotiations for peace. Advancing south from Amida as far as Tel Bes (Bibas) on the Zergan (Arzamon) river, he crossed to the eastern bank and moved forward some 15 km into the uplands of the Tur Abdin, where he established his camp with Mount Izala covering his left flank. The Roman forces, encamped on the eastern bank of the river in the plain below Mardin, covered the passage westwards towards the waters of the river Arzamon. The nearest supply apart from this was the Bouron river, on which Dara lay somewhat to the north and which the Persian forces would leave in their rear if they advanced. This would put them at a considerable strategic disadvantage if they were unsuccessful in pushing the Roman forces away from the river Arzamon, access to which Philippicus's army effectively blocked. Having taken up his position on a Wednesday, Philippicus waited some two days for news of the Persian advance. (See Map 5)

The Persian commander, who bore the title Kardarigan ('Black Falcon'), was convinced that he outnumbered the Roman forces and prepared a substantial camel train bearing waterskins, as well as fetters of iron and wood with which to secure his prisoners! He advanced from the direction of Dara, but his intentions were revealed by captives taken by the Romans' irregular Arab forces, so that Philippicus was apprised of the Persian camps and their recent movements. By Saturday, suspecting – since the Persian forces were not far off – that they would exploit the Romans' traditional Sabbath observances and attack on the Sunday, he ordered his scouts to maintain a careful lookout. True enough, they reported the approach of the enemy forces early next morning. Although the evidence is not absolutely clear, it seems that both armies consisted entirely of mounted units, the Romans of mixed lancers and archers together with a force of allied Arab troops under their own leaders, the Persians similarly armed. Both sides may also have included heavily armoured cataphract units.

Philippicus drew up his forces on rising ground in the plain of Solachon and facing the slow incline up which the enemy would have to advance to challenge his position, the left flank being well covered by the broken and hilly ground at the foot of the mountain. The army was ordered into the usual three divisions, the left wing commanded by Eilifreda, commander of the garrison forces from Emesa, together with the Hun Apsich in charge of his own mounted archers, the centre under the field commander Heraclius (later exarch of Carthage and father of the emperor Heraclius) and the right under a certain Vitalius. Philippicus himself, originally stationed in the centre, was persuaded by his junior and senior officers to move to the rear, where he remained with the small reserve. From the slightly higher ground here he could observe the course of the battle.

The Persian forces were likewise arrayed in three divisions, the centre commanded by the Kardarigan himself, the left wing by his nephew Aphraates and the right by Mebod. Halting only briefly to leave their baggage train and form into line of battle, the Persians pushed right ahead straight at the Roman line, shooting from the saddle as they approached. The Roman divisions returned the missiles, and then met them as they came close enough with a counter-charge that brought both armies to a halt. On the Roman right, however, the commander Vitalius had used the heavy cavalry stationed under him to good effect and was able to smash into the Persian line and break its formation, pushing it back and around to the left behind its own centre division. Seeing the Persian baggage train not far behind, however, a considerable number of the Roman troopers rode off to plunder it, heedless of their officers' commands. Had the Persian commander been able to take advantage of this situation, things could have swung against the Romans at this point. But Philippicus quickly saw what was happening and, removing his helmet, passed it to one of his guards with instructions to rally the soldiers under threat of punishment from the commander-in-chief himself, a ruse which succeeded when the soldiers recognized the helmet of their general.

In the centre, meanwhile, the broken Persian units had succeeded in regrouping and rejoining the struggle, and the pressure from the massed Persian ranks began to force the Roman line to retreat. At this point it seems that the Roman centre was able to withdraw a little, and Philippicus gave the order to dismount and form a wall of shields with spears projecting hedgehog-like to the front, in order to resist the enemy cavalry on foot. What happened next remains unclear, but an order appears to have been given to shoot at the Persian horses, and this tactic saw the tide of battle turn in the Romans' favour. As the Persian centre was brought once more to a halt, the Roman left seems to have been able successfully to mount a counter-charge, which drove the Persian right back in disarray. It quickly lost all cohesion and order and a rout began in which units of the Roman left wing pursued elements of the Persian force as far as Dara, twelve miles distant. With both flanks uncovered, the Persian centre began to waver and break up, and at this point the regrouped Roman right wing units swept in on the flank of the Persian forces, pushing them sideways over ground previously occupied by their own right wing. Most of the Persian centre also broke away in flight at this stage, but a small remnant, including the commander, the Kardarigan, took up a position on one of the outlying ridges projecting from the base of the mountain, where it resisted fiercely enough to dissuade the Romans from pressing their advantage, in spite of being cut off from both water and military assistance.

The Persian rout resulted in the complete disintegration of their army, for not only was it soundly defeated in the battle, but the Kardarigan had ordered his troops to destroy their water supplies before combat began, with the idea that this would make them fight all the more fiercely to get through to the Arzamon. Sadly for his soldiers, they were unsuccessful, and Theophylact, who reports the battle, describes how many died either from thirst or stomach cramps and infection, when they found a well or stream and gorged themselves too rapidly. The small detachment with the Kardarigan was left alone after three or four days, since the Romans were unaware that the Persian commander was present, but many were killed or caught – more than a thousand, according to Theophylact – by patrolling Roman units when they tried to make their escape. The Kardarigan himself did make good his escape.

The battle probably lasted a little over half an hour, and illustrates what a well-officered and disciplined Roman army could do against superior odds. It also illustrates the type of very mobile cavalry warfare that was typical of much of the campaigning along the eastern front in the sixth century, and which stimulated the increasingly important role of mounted units in the Roman army at this period.

The Islamic Conquests

The Roman defeat on the Yarmuk river in 636 marked the effective end of serious Roman resistance in Syria to the Islamic forces which had swept through the province in the two preceding years. The Muslim penetration of Syria began in late 633 and early 634. In February and July 634 imperial forces clashed with and were defeated by Muslim troops in Palestine, near Gaza and at Ajnadayn to the north. In late summer Scythopolis (Pella) fell, and in 635 both Damascus and Emesa were taken by the Arabs. The Byzantine defences in the region were in shreds and it was only with great effort that the emperor Heraclius was able to bring together troops from the field armies of both the East and Armenia, under the overall command of his brother Theodore and the Armenian general Vahan, to mount a counter-attack. In the face of this move Muslim forces evacuated both cities and withdrew towards the South. Having advanced south through the Beka'a valley, the imperial forces encamped near modern Kiswe, forcing the Arabs to withdraw towards Der'a, where they occupied a strong defensive line stretching across towards Dayr Ayyub. There followed several months of manoeuvring, involving clashes in July in which the fortunes of both sides fluctuated. Although the strategic intention of the Byzantine commander may have been sensible – delaying action in the hope that the Muslim forces would become discontented, suffer from an outbreak of disease in their camps, or withdraw to seek more booty – in the event it was the imperial forces which came off worst. To begin with, the local civilian authorities co-operated only very grudgingly in the supply of provisions, causing some clashes between the troops and the local populace, especially in and around Damascus. Dissension among the commanders caused further difficulties. The sources report that one of the commanders, the Armenian general Vahan, was proclaimed emperor by his soldiers, although it has been suggested that this is probably a later elaboration of an original account referring to such disagreements. The result was a lack of cohesion as well as of discipline, which contributed in turn to a series of tactical errors on the part of the imperial forces once the action commenced. The actual conflict stretched over several weeks, but culminated in a final clash in the middle of August. After some three days of manoeuvring and fighting across the locality stretching from Jabiya to the valley of the Yarmuk river, the Byzantine forces were finally split up and outflanked, the Arab cavalry exploiting a dust-storm which blew up on the final day. The end came on 20 August. Some units were cut off and succumbed to panic; others were driven into flight and suffered heavy casualties when they tried to escape over the rough terrain; many were massacred where they stood. The result was a complete victory for the Muslim army and the effective destruction of organized imperial field forces in the region. Damascus was retaken and the emperor, having received news of the defeat, ordered the evacuation of the provinces affected, the withdrawal of all forces to defended positions and the avoidance of open battle. The defeat was generally recognized throughout the Roman world as a disaster. Fifty years later a Palestinian monk, Anastasius of Sinai, wrote that this battle marked a decisive moment in the Muslim conquest of Syria and Palestine, after which any imperial recovery became impossible.

The Battles of Jabiya-Gabitha and the Yarmuk River 636

The battle opened in the region of Gabitha or Jabiya on the eastern slopes of the Golan, a district about three miles to the north-east of the modern township of Nawa. Jabiya was an important base and camping area for the Ghassanids, a confederacy of Christian Arabs who had long been a mainstay of Roman power in the East, acting both as allied troops against the Sassanids and their own Arab supporters, and as a useful bolster for Roman security within the eastern provinces, especially in Palestine. Jabiya and its surrounding pastureland provided fodder and supplies and was a good base from which to conduct military operations. It was also strategically important because from it an army could control the route south from Damascus, and dominate the regions to the south and east. It is understandable, therefore, why both sides in the conflict were prepared to commit a great deal to controlling it. Having approached from the north-west, the imperial troops were disposed over a considerable distance along the line of the Roman road which ran north-eastwards to Damascus, parallel to the wadi'l Ruqqad, the dry riverbed which ran up from the Yarmuk. The road turned east and crossed this wadi to the south of Jabiya, before turning north-east again. In order to avoid either flank being turned by the widely spread and partly concealed Muslim forces, the Byzantine lines were spread widely over the broken terrain, making communications between the different wings difficult. One base camp was established near modern Yaqusa, about 15 miles south of Jabiya, probably that of the Byzantine right wing, another at Jilliq (mod. Kiswe) north of Jabiya, which was the base for the troops under Theodore Trithurios (see below); while Jabiya itself was almost certainly the site of another encampment, probably that of the Ghassanid forces.

The Byzantine commander-in-chief was Vahan (Baanes), supported by Theodore Trithurios, *magister militum per Orientem* (general of the Eastern field army) and George, general of the Armenian field army, together with Jabala ibn al-Ayham, chieftain of the Ghassanid forces. Also present was Niketas, son of the Persian king Shahrbaraz who had been placed on the throne with Byzantine help before being assassinated. Vahan seems to have accompanied the forces of the master of soldiers for Armenia (*magister militum per Armeniam*) and camped with them at Yaqusa, while Theodore's forces established their base somewhat to the north of Jabiya. On the first day of the final clash, the Byzantine forces were ordered into the usual three divisions, with George commanding the right wing and an unnamed officer with the rank of *drungarius* the left. Presumably Vahan or Theodore Trithurios retained command of the centre. However, despite this typical structure, it is apparent from the sometimes garbled and often conflicting accounts of the battle that the confrontation actually consisted of several separate but linked clashes, and it is most likely that each of the main Byzantine divisions operated more or less independently in terms of its tactical battle order, with independent left and right wings and centre.

The numbers fighting on each side are impossible to determine. On the imperial side, sizeable detachments from the field armies of the East and of Armenia were involved, but it is unlikely either that these forces were up to full strength or that all of the units belonging to them were withdrawn for action on this single front. Rough estimates of the eastern field army suggest a nominal strength of about 15,000, and for that of the Armenian front about 12,000. Assuming 50% of each army were involved, a total of not more than 15,000 including the Arab allies, with a further 2,000–5,000 for extra units drafted in (from the *limitanei* based at Emesa, for example) is plausible. A total imperial force of about 20,000 would, therefore, be not unreasonable, although this remains a guess. That the Muslim forces were as numerous as this is unlikely and indeed the tactics followed by the Muslim command would strongly suggest an inferior force, compelling them to deal with the imperial armies piecemeal while employing delaying or harrying tactics over the rest of the field. Both sides included substantial contingents of both infantry and cavalry, although the exact composition of the Roman armies remains entirely unknown.

The precise order of events is difficult to determine. It seems that the command for a general advance across the whole front was issued on 18 or 19 August, provoked by Muslim sorties and missile attacks from their main line and commencing at about midday. This time seems to have been deliberately chosen by the Arab commanders as a time at which the Byzantine forces would suffer most from the heat. While the Byzantine forces were in a strategically relatively good position, tactically they were faced with several problems, notably the broken terrain in the central and southern sectors of the area over which both forces were extended and the necessary fragmentation of their forces by the two wadis across which they were moving. More crucial still was the fact that there was only one bridge across the wadi'l Ruqqad, and that as long as troops were placed between the wadi'l Ruqqad and the wadi'l Allan, to the east, they were in danger of being isolated and dealt with piecemeal.

In an initial attack in the northern sector the Byzantine left wing forces were able to push back the enemy troops opposing them and move towards the Muslim camp. Prominent in this push were the Byzantine infantry units of the left wing; but their eagerness was cleverly exploited by the Muslim troops, who feigned a disorderly retreat and began noisily breaking up their camp, as though in panic. At the same time, considerable numbers of soldiers were able to hide in the rocky terrain and await an opportunity to counter-attack, and it is highly likely that this tactic had been planned for just this sort of situation in advance. In the process of the pursuit, infantry and cavalry became separated, allowing a force of Muslim cavalry under the command of Khalid ibn al-Walid to penetrate the Byzantine line and turn on the cavalry on the wing. In concert with the concealed troops who were now behind the Byzantine cavalry's line of advance this broke the Byzantine mounted units and they fled in confusion. The withdrawing Muslim infantry forces then counter-attacked the now exhausted Byzantine infantry, apparently in the early evening. With their cavalry support eliminated, enemy horse to one side and infantry in their rear, the Byzantine troops rapidly broke up and a full-scale rout began. This had especially unfortunate consequences, for it permitted the Muslims to seize control of the only bridge over the wadi'l Ruqqad. At about the same time, the Ghassanid troops, who had been left to defend this position, seem to have panicked, some deserting to the other side and others abandoning their posts. The cavalry under Khalid ibn al-Walid then swung around to attack the Byzantine base camp at Jilliq, which they were able to storm with only token resistance. In little more than four or five hours, the whole Byzantine left wing had dissolved.

The first day's action thus drew to a close. After some initial success, and very fierce fighting recorded in both the Muslim and Byzantine sources, the opening phase of the battle had ended with the imperial forces driven in on their northern or left wing and a wedge of Muslim troops occupying the space between these units and the Byzantine centre. It seems clear that the tactics followed by the Muslim forces around their camp on the northern part of the field were carefully planned in advance to lure the imperial troops forward and enable their order and cohesion to be broken. In this, the Muslim commander, Abu 'Ubayda ibn al-Jarrah, made excellent use of the terrain, and scored a clear victory over his opposite number in terms of overall strategy. The southern, or right wing, and the central divisions of the imperial forces had in the meantime been deployed around the camp at Yaqusa and, more importantly, had advanced across the wadi'l Ruqqad to occupy the area between it and the wadi'l Allan to its east. From this position they had advanced and pushed back what Muslim forces were deployed there to cover the Muslim centre and right (and their main encampment), but appear to have stopped at the wadi'l Allan. As news of the Ghassanid defection spread, morale among this section of the army began to be affected. The situation worsened when, in a surprise night-attack, the Muslim forces were able to storm and capture the imperial camp at Yaqusa, driving those detachments positioned around it to flight in the broken terrain of the wadis, or north-eastwards along the route of the road to Damascus.

The loss of this camp, on the southern or right flank, and of the bridge over the wadi'l Ruqqad now meant that the main divisions of the imperial army were cut off both from the left wing (which they may have assumed was still in position), and from any hope of an orderly withdrawal, since they were now boxed into the area between the wadi'l Ruqqad and the wadi'l Allan to the west and east, and the wadi'l Yarmuk to the south. On the morning of 20 August, and with the approach of a strong Muslim contingent from the north, from a location supposedly occupied by imperial troops, as well as the advance of the Muslim troops which had taken their main camp at Yaqusa, the main divisions were rapidly driven to panic, and there began a complete rout. At some point, possibly as the Muslim formations from the north began to close with the left of the Byzantine centre, a sand storm blew up, and it was in this situation that all semblance of cohesion was lost. In a desperate effort to flee, many men and animals were lost in attempts to leap down and cross the steep-sided and very broken terrain along the wadi'l Ruqqad on their west and the Yarmuk to the south. Many soldiers along with their officers simply cast down their arms and sat down waiting to be captured, but tragically it would seem that the Muslim commanders had issued orders that no prisoners be taken, so those who followed this course of action were simply cut down where they were.

By now it must long have been clear that the imperial forces were broken and that no further attack could be mounted. The difficulty for the remaining Byzantine commanders was, how to extricate their forces in some sort of order. In the event, this proved to be impossible; and although substantial numbers of men were able to escape in the direction of Damascus, many having crossed the bridge over the wadi'l Ruqqad before it was taken by the Muslim cavalry on the 19th, all reports agree on the very heavy losses suffered by the imperial forces, both at the hands of the victorious Muslim troops and as a consequence of their own efforts to escape.

The pursuit of the defeated forces was merciless, and although many managed to escape the scene of the catastrophe, there are reliable reports in several sources of Muslim units chasing and cutting down Byzantine troops as far as Damascus and well beyond, even as far as Emesa to the north. The imperial army effectively ceased to exist, and while it is likely that the imperial field armies which had contributed units to this force – those of the Armenian and Eastern military zones – remained intact, if very much reduced in numbers, it seems clear that the Muslim victory was such that no further opposition to the Islamic armies in Syria and Palestine could be mounted effectively. Only individual garrisons and fortress towns could hold out, and indeed Heraclius issued a general order shortly thereafter to the effect that direct battle with Muslim troops was henceforth to be avoided.

Although the reports of the battle are confusing and laced with semi-legendary detail added as the stories about the Byzantine defeat grew over the years, it is possible to glean an idea of the basic pattern of the fighting. And it becomes fairly clear that the imperial army suffered from two major disadvantages. In the first place, the command of this composite army was fragmented. Even though the overall commander, Vahan, was in charge, there were clear disagreements and a good deal of factional squabbling among the Byzantine generals. The co-ordination of the imperial divisions with one another seems to have been very poor, and indeed it seems as though the northern division and the central and southern divisions fought effectively as three, and certainly two, separate armies. The crucial bridge over the wadi'l Ruqqad, for example, was held by a force that was both potentially unreliable – desertions to the Muslim side, or simply away from the field of battle, seem to have begun from the start – and clearly not strong enough to resist a determined onslaught. The camps, while correctly adhering to standard Byzantine practice, as outlined in the military handbooks of the period, were well back from the main battle, yet in a context in which the highly mobile, hit-and-run tactics of the Arab Muslim forces were to be expected (and the Byzantines were quite familiar with such fighting), they remained surprisingly exposed. This last point is especially important, for it seems that the Byzantine command substantially underestimated Muslim mobility and speed of movement. One result was that their obvious attempts to establish a 'front' were sadly misplaced, since Muslim forces were clearly able to move across and through the 'front' at various key moments in the battle with little hindrance. This further weakened the cohesion of the imperial forces, and meant that the battle of Jabiya-Yarmuk in reality took the form of several separate but linked clashes, in which the outcome of each would affect that of the others, but in which the tactical relationship of one to the other remained extremely loose.

In the second place, the Muslim high command was clearly fully aware of the tactical possibilities of the broken and very rugged terrain, and had obviously planned in several cases to employ tactics which would make the most of the possibilities. Feigned withdrawals and, especially, the concealment of units among features which would permit them to remain in hiding until called upon to attack were especially effective. It is also probable that the Muslim commanders had decided in advance that the battle would have to be handled as several related conflicts, so that individual commanders had a good deal of freedom of action within the overall plan to exploit particular situations as they arose. The initiative thus remained almost entirely on the Muslim side, with the Byzantines attempting both to hold some sort of single front, and, except in the opening clashes in the northern sector, operating exclusively defensively.

But the effectiveness of the imperial forces was jeopardized by several other factors. In the first place, a substantial portion of the troops was either of raw recruits or entirely unfamiliar with the type of fighting and the nature of the enemy they were called upon to deal with. One report mentions that George, commander of the Armenian field troops, established his camp at Yaqusa with the intention of spending some days in training his men to deal with the enemy's tactics and in familiarizing them with their appearance and fighting habits. Other reports refer to the breakdown in discipline among the rank and file of some sections of the army, and the very low morale that prevailed.

The governor of Damascus had fallen out with the overall commander, Vahan, over the issue of provisioning the army from local resources. He was able to instill panic among some of the troops on their way to the battlefield by getting groups of citizens to bang cymbals and make loud noises at night, and drive them away from the city. Such nervous and timid behaviour on the part of supposedly regular field troops did not bode well for their reaction to battle itself.

Much of this would appear to reflect the general state of the imperial armies in the East after the final defeat of the Persians in 626-627. For although the administrative infrastructure of the field armies and frontier or garrison forces seems to have been re-established, the fighting capacity, discipline and training of the soldiers in these armies at least seems to have been wanting. Although there is no reason to doubt that the Byzantine defeat was the result of excellent strategic and tactical planning on the Muslim side, it is clear that a split command, lack of cohesion and lack of morale among much of the regular soldiery played a key role, too. This legacy was to be one which the empire made good only with great difficulty, and over an extended period during the period up to the middle of the eighth century, and which was certainly a major contributory factor to the loss of the remaining eastern provinces and Egypt.

Consequences: The Transformation of Strategy

The Arab Islamic conquests radically altered the strategic and political geography of the whole East Mediterranean region. The complete failure of attempts to meet and drive back the invaders in open battle induced a major shift in strategy whereby open confrontations with the Muslim armies were avoided. As a result of the disastrous defeat of 636, the field armies were withdrawn first to North Syria and Mesopotamia, and shortly thereafter back to the line of the Taurus and Anti-Taurus ranges. The field armies which had operated in Syria, Palestine and Mesopotamia were withdrawn into Anatolia, and re-established within a greatly changed economic and strategic framework. The regions across which they were based were determined by the ability of these districts to provide for the soldiers in terms of supplies and other requirements. The imperial field army was pulled back to its original bases in north-west Asia Minor and Thrace, where it becomes known as the *Opsikion* division. That of the *magister militum per Orientem* (or 'Master of soldiers of the East'), occupied southern central Asia Minor, and became known as the *Anatolikon* army; and that of the Master of soldiers of Armenia, now known as the *Armeniakon*, occupied the eastern and northern districts of Asia Minor. The army of the Master of soldiers of Thrace, which had apparently been transferred to the eastern theatre in the mid-630s, and had been employed unsuccessfully to defend Egypt, was established in the rich provinces of central western Anatolia, and known thenceforth as the *Thrakesion* army. By the last decades of the seventh century, the districts across which these armies were garrisoned were known collectively by the name of the army based there. While the distribution of the various units of the field armies across the provinces in this way was certainly connected with logistical demands, it had obvious strategic implications, since it meant that Roman counter-attacks were relatively slow to organize, and that defence was fragmented and organized locally on a somewhat piecemeal basis.

The provinces which had belonged to the *quaestura exercitus* established by Justinian did not survive the Slav and Avar invasions of the Balkan provinces (although the empire still controlled much of the Danube itself, through isolated fortresses on the Danube delta and along the coast of the Black Sea); but the Aegean regions continued to function as a source for men, ships and resources, and a maritime corps, known in the later seventh century as the 'ship troops', or *karabisianoi*, seems to have been based to begin with on Rhodes. In the light of the considerably increased threat posed to the empire's exposed coastline and its hinterlands, brought about by the rapid development of Arab seapower from the 660s, these 'ship troops' were to develop into the core of middle Byzantine provincial naval power. The armies of the *magistri militum* or exarchs of Italy, and Africa (which included Sardinia) continued to function, although the latter disappeared with the completion of the Arab conquest of North Africa in the 690s, the army of Italy surviving, on an ever more localized basis, until the demise of the Exarchate of Ravenna in the middle of the eighth century.

4
Bulgars and Arabs: The Eighth and Ninth Centuries

The history of Byzantine warfare during much of the eighth and ninth centuries is a rather depressing one, for the empire often seems to have lost far more battles than it won. Several of the encounters in this chapter were defeats, some of them important ones. Yet in general and, perhaps, paradoxically, this was a period of imperial revival or recovery, a demonstration of the old adage that one does not need to win all the battles to win the war. Defeats reflected, on the whole, short-term difficulties and problems, while the longer-term recovery reflected an increasingly stable strategic situation, a growing economy and, just as importantly, the increasing weakness of the empire's most dangerous and persistent enemy during the seventh and most of the eighth century, the Caliphate. Internal factionalism and political fragmentation played the key role here and, greatly to the empire's advantage, brought about a dissipation of Muslim military power and an overall weakening of the strategic situation of the Caliphate in northern Syria and Iraq.

Strategy

As we have seen, the East Roman empire was left with a rump of its former lands: central and northern Asia Minor, the southern Balkan coastal regions, the Aegean islands including Crete (Cyprus was attacked several times, but in the 680s an agreement was reached with the Caliphate that no military forces would be based there, of either side), and in the west, parts of

Italy, Sardinia and the central and western North African provinces. North Africa was lost by 700, while imperial territory in Italy was constantly shrinking.

The system of maintaining, supplying and recruiting armies which developed during the later seventh and early eighth centuries has been dubbed the 'theme system', after the new Greek term *thema* applied to the armies and the districts across which they were based. To begin with, from the 640s, the army attempted to control the major passes through the mountain barrier running from the sea north-west towards the Armenian highlands. The abandonment of Cilicia at the end of the seventh century forced changes to this approach. Rather than attempting to maintain a clearly defined frontier, the field armies followed a strategy of attempting to throw invading armies back following a pitched battle and, from the later part of the seventh century after this approach had met with virtually no success, harassing and dogging invaders once they had entered imperial territory and completed their attack. This strategy meant, however, that the economic hinterland of the frontier incurred substantial damage, subject as it was to regular devastation. The result was the appearance, by the first half of the eighth century, of what was in effect a 'no-man's land' between the settled and economically safer regions on both sides. But the new arrangements do seem to have prevented the establishment by the Arabs of permanent bases to the north or west of the Taurus and Anti-Taurus ranges. And while these developments were taking place on land, the naval command of the Kibyrrhaiotai (named after the coastal town of Kibyrrha in Caria) had come into existence, probably by the 690s, made up from the older Karabisianoi and with some extra territories taken in western and south-western coastal Anatolia, thus establishing a sea-borne defence for the western Anatolian coast and Aegean region.

The *themata* or themes were at first merely groupings of provinces across which different armies were based. By 730 or thereabouts they had acquired a clear geographical identity; and by the later eighth century some elements of fiscal as well as military administration were set up on a thematic basis, although the late Roman provinces continued to subsist. The number of *themata* expanded as the empire's economic and political situation improved, partly through the original large military divisions being split up into different 'provincial' armies, and partly through the recovery in the last years of the eighth century and the re-imposition of imperial authority over lands once held in the southern Balkans.

The distribution of the field armies across Asia Minor encouraged a localization of military recruitment and identities, and there evolved in consequence a distinction between the regular elements – full-time soldiers – and the less competent or well-supplied militia-like elements in each *thema*. The emperor Constantine V (741-775) established a small elite force, known as the *tagmata* ('the regiments'), which soon became the elite field division of campaign armies. While never very large, it had better pay and discipline than regular and part-time provincial units, and served as a valuable nucleus of picked troops on campaign. This was, in fact, the first step in a rapidly growing tendency to recruit mercenary forces, both foreign and indigenous, to form special units and to serve for the duration of a particular campaign or group of campaigns. As imperial might recovered and grew, so the empire was able to re-assert its military strength in the East during the ninth century, and so the role and the proportion of such full-time units became ever more important.

A number of key elements contributed to Byzantine strategy. Initially, and if at all possible, raiding forces were to be held and turned back at the Taurus and Anti-Taurus passes. On occasion this policy worked quite well, as when, at the very end of the seventh century, Herakleios, the brother of the emperor Tiberios Apsimar (698-705), was made *monostrategos* ('sole general') of the frontier cavalry forces and was able to mark up a run of spectacular victories, including a series of successful counter-raids deep into Syria. Where this policy of meeting and repulsing hostile attacks at the frontier did not work (which was frequently the case), local forces should harass and dog the invading forces, making sure to follow their every movement so that the location of each party or group was known. This strategy was successful partly due to the garrisoning of numerous small forts and fortresses along the major routes, on cross-roads and locations where supplies might be stored, and above and behind the frontier passes through which enemy forces had to pass to gain access to the Byzantine hinterland. Such posts were a constant threat to any invading force, although to hold up the advance or the raiding party to lay siege to them was more trouble than it was worth, and as long as they were occupied by the imperial forces the enemy raiders could be tracked and eventually brought to battle or ambushed.

A third aspect consisted in the series of special frontier districts which, from the later eighth and early ninth century, constituted independent commands along the frontier, complementing the armies of the themes. These units were called kleisourarchies (*kleisourarchiai*), and reflect very closely the strategy followed by the imperial government, focused on a highly localized pattern of defence, entailing a strategy of harassment and ambushes, designed to hold up and limit the damage inflicted by all but the largest forces. Although the first clear evidence for such a policy appears at the end of the eighth century, there is no reason to doubt that it had been practiced for some time before this.

Tactics and Tactical Organization

In responding to the threat from the victorious Islamic armies after the initial conquests, Byzantine tactics and strategy from the 640s had to adapt quickly to a new situation. The fact that those contingents from the main field armies of the second half of the seventh and the eighth century were referred to as *kaballarika themata* – 'cavalry armies' – illustrates the fact that light cavalry now came to dominate the border warfare, skirmishing and hit-and-run raids of the period. Infantry continued to play an important role in the battles fought against the armies of early Islam during the middle of the seventh century, if only because the Arabs were themselves mostly infantry, although their extensive use of camels and horses to improve their mobility enabled them to travel far more quickly than most of their enemies, and the highly mobile nature of the warfare thereafter gave the Arab mounted infantry an advantage over traditionally outfitted Roman infantry. While infantry continued to be needed, therefore, playing an important part in several campaigns, as well as in the guerrilla warfare along the eastern frontier in the later ninth and tenth centuries, it seems that their value slowly declined, perhaps because they were drawn largely from the poorest and least well-equipped of the provincial soldiery. Hardly any of the descriptive sources for the wars against Bulgars and Arabs during the campaigns of the eighth and ninth centuries give any details. The increasingly seasonal campaigning and localized recruitment in the theme armies, combined with a lack of professional training, and with the physical dispersal of the soldiers and the type of warfare waged, meant that while infantry soldiers could fulfil garrison duties and irregular, skirmishing warfare in broken country, or lie in wait for hostile forces, they would not be reliable under regular battlefield conditions. The development of infantry tactics after the period of the first Islamic conquests as well as the higher profile of mounted warfare thus reflected quite closely the general strategic situation in which the empire found itself.

During the period from the later seventh to the ninth or early tenth century, the differences which once existed between *limitanei* and *comitatenses* disappeared, and most units came to have a local or regional appellation; although some of the late Roman names of units did survive, applied to the later Byzantine divisions. There was also a general levelling out of the different arms, into light cavalry and infantry. Only the *tagmata* at Constantinople seem to have provided a heavy cavalry force. It seems to have been the responsibility of local officers in the provinces to establish field units and to arm them as each specific occasion required.

The provincial armies were organized into divisions called *tourmai*, *drouggoi* and *banda*: very roughly, divisions, brigades and regiments. The first and last of these had a territorial identity, and each *tourma* had a headquarters or base, a fortified town or fortress. Each *bandon* was identified with a clearly defined locality, from which it drew its soldiers. The middle level of this structure, the brigade, always remained a tactical unit, without any territorial identity. Each *tourmarches* had his base in a fortress town, and was an important figure in the military administration of his theme. He was responsible for the fortresses and strongpoints in his district, as well as for the safety of the local population and their goods and chattels. He was responsible also for dealing with raids into his territory and for informing his superior of enemy movements.

The sizes of units on the battlefield varied according to tactical need, and there was no neat equivalence between the territorial and administrative districts and the size of the units drawn from them. Several administrative *tourmai* could appear on campaign as a single large division, for example, or vice versa: the fact that a theme had two *tourmai* did not mean that they were each made up of the same number of smaller units, or indeed that they were the same size as the divisions in a neighbouring military province. Most themes had two or three divisions or *tourmai*, but this does not mean that they were the same size or could muster the same number of soldiers. The numbers in a *bandon* also varied, and figures ranging from 50 to 400 are recorded. Calculating the size of Byzantine armies from this sort of information is, in consequence, rather tricky.

Security on the March

One of the distinguishing features of Roman and Byzantine warfare, according to Byzantine as well as non-Byzantine observers, was the habit of constructing marching camps to protect the army, especially when in hostile territory. It was taken for granted by all the military handbooks and by many observers and commentators that armies would encamp and entrench whenever they had to stop. The handbooks go into great detail on the procedures for choosing, laying out and fortifying the encampment, including the duties of the scouts responsible for identifying appropriate locations and for laying out the camp in advance of the main force. A defensible situation, good water supply and forage for the horses and pack animals were key requirements. Tenth-century treatises also offer guidance on the order in which the different units were to pitch their tents, as well as matters such as picket-lines, passwords and so forth.

Camps were protected by ditches and fences or palisades, sometimes cut from wood available at the site, sometimes made from the spears of the soldiers, and the entrances were situated so that they could be covered by archers and not easily rushed. The handbooks also describe various manoeuvres which would allow a force under attack to march out against the enemy, to retreat into the camp, or to set up a camp while under attack. Byzantine marching camps evolved from late Roman patterns, usually rectangular in plan, divided into four quadrants separated by centrally crossing paths leading to entrances in the middle of each side. This pattern is described in the handbooks of the sixth to tenth centuries.

Contemporary writers often mention specifically occasions when careless or ignorant generals failed in their responsibilities in respect of encampments. Some established a camp but failed to defend it or set proper watches and piquets. Others simply did not entrench their camps, and from ignorance or overconfidence opened their forces to night-attacks or ambushes. Such failings were often seen as more blameworthy than poor tactics on the battlefield, since they could easily be rectified and required no special skill.

The Battle of Pliska 811

The Balkan front was always an area of concern for the imperial government at Constantinople. Technically, the Danube remained the border even in the 660s and '70s, although in reality only the presence of an imperial army could bring the local Slav chieftains to heel, and then only very briefly. (The Danube itself remained in fact largely under Byzantine control because it was navigable, and the imperial fleet could patrol it.) In 679, however, the situation was transformed by the arrival of the Turkic Bulgars, a nomadic people who had been forced out of their homelands and pastures around the Volga by the encroachments of the Chazars from the East. They petitioned the emperor Constantine IV for permission to seek refuge and protection south of the Danube on 'Roman' territory, but were refused. Having crossed over anyway, they were then met by an imperial army under Constantine himself. Unfortunately, due to poor discipline, a lack of cohesion and mistaken signals, the imperial army fell into panic and was defeated by the Bulgars, who over the next twenty years consolidated their hold over the region and established a loose hegemony over the indigenous Slav and other peoples in the region. By 700, the Bulgar Khanate was an important political and military power threatening Byzantine Thrace, and was to remain so for the next three centuries. The emperor Constantine V conducted a series of campaigns over some twenty years into the heartland of Bulgarian territory in his efforts to render it subject to the empire. He came near to destroying the Bulgar khanate entirely, but the Bulgars offered a tenacious and fierce resistance, and showed a remarkable capacity for recovery. By the end of the eighth century they were once more a serious threat to the empire's territory in Thrace and to the plans, begun under Eirene and Constantine VI, to recover southern and central Greece.

The emperor Nikephoros I, who had been the chief finance officer of the empress Eirene, came to the throne in 802 and seems to have planned to defeat the Bulgars so decisively that he would be able to reincorporate the Balkan territories of the Bulgar khanate into the empire. An expedition in 809 reached the Bulgar capital at Pliska, near modern Aboba in north-east Bulgaria, and sacked it; the expedition of 811 was planned on a grander scale, and was intended to establish a more permanent Roman presence in the region. A large force was assembled, made up from contingents from the Asia Minor armies, or *themata*, supplemented by troops from the European *themata* and the imperial guards units, the *tagmata*. The expedition had a ceremonial aspect, and the emperor clearly took victory – after the easy win in 809 – for granted. For, as well as the soldiers of the different thematic contingents, a large number of courtiers and palace officials also accompanied the army: the emperor's son Staurakios, who was also junior emperor, his son-in-law the *kouropalates*, the senior minister Theoktistos, and the prefect, or governor, of Constantinople, as well as tens of other high-ranking officials.

Preparations for the campaign began in late May, and continued into the first days of July. By 10 July the army is reported to have encamped on the frontier, at Markellai, partly, it would seem, to induce some panic among the Bulgars and to mislead them as to the exact intentions of the emperor – several feint thrusts were made at different points along the frontier, for example. Unfortunately, this delay also gave the Bulgars time to ascertain the numbers and composition of the imperial army, information which they were helped to acquire by the desertion of an imperial household servant. In spite of this, when the emperor did eventually launch his main attack on 19 or 20 July, it seems to have taken the Bulgars by surprise. The army was divided into several columns, each of which marched across the frontier by different routes, one column perhaps following the coastal route up around the eastern edge of the Sredna Gora, another moving directly across the mountains through the Shipka pass, the two re-uniting at Pliska. Within three days he was able to reach Pliska, overwhelm and destroy the garrison as well as a relief force of about the same size and on 23 July report his victory to the capital. Having made a thorough search of Pliska, Nikephoros discovered the khan's treasure, and proceeded to assign shares in the booty to his troops. The palace and associated buildings were burned and the surrounding countryside devastated – crops put to the torch, livestock slaughtered, settlements razed. Although the Bulgar Khan, Krum, sued for peace, Nikephoros wanted to eradicate the Bulgar threat to imperial power once and for all. He marched now south-west and westwards in the direction of Serdica (mod. Sofia) in pursuit of the remaining Bulgar forces and continued the policy of devastation. On 24 July the column entered one of the many wooded valleys through which flow the rivers and streams that have their sources in the Balkan range itself. All reports agree that the army was grossly over-confident about its successes thus far, that discipline was relaxed or non-existent in some corps, and that the senior commanders were beginning to doubt the wisdom of the emperor's policy of pursuing an enemy they had barely seen since the initial clashes ever deeper into his own territory. The emperor remained shut away in his tent, refusing to be counselled, even by his son Staurakios, and seems to have paid no heed to the pleas of his leading officers to advance more cautiously.

In advance of the Byzantine invasion, the Bulgars had taken certain measures designed to prevent access to their lands. Most importantly, this involved the construction across the mouth of several of the most important passes through the Sredna Gora mountains of heavy palisades fronted by a ditch which, although they might not detain an army for long, would leave it exposed to attack from above and the flanks while waiting for the obstacles to be removed. The imperial forces had clearly been able to avoid these obstacles on their inward march (or the sources do not mention their removal). But on 25 July the forward scouts reported that the exit of the valley along which the army was marching in a south-westerly direction had been blocked by one such palisade. The emperor and his officers realized that they had marched into a trap, and Nikephoros himself is reported to have panicked and fallen into a depression when the news was reported to him. For he had foolishly assumed that, having defeated the Bulgar forces attempting to block his way to Pliska, Bulgar resistance had been crushed and Krum had no troops left. It is also evident from the sources that insufficient attention had been paid to scouting the line of march. In fact, Krum had not only been able to scratch together enough soldiers to oppose the imperial advance, but the request he must have made in late May or June for help from the Avars and the allied Slav peoples had by now been answered. He now had at his disposal Slav as well as Avar troops (the latter being the remnants of a Turco-Mongol people, until the middle of the seventh century the dominant group in a great steppe empire, who now dwelt in the south-western region of the plain of Hungary).

The army could at this point have attempted to retrace its steps north-eastwards, since there is no evidence that the other end of the valley had also been blocked after the imperial forces had passed through. Since the day was drawing on, however, the order was given to halt for the night, and the column encamped by thematic divisions, each field army in its own encampment and spaced at some distance one from another, on the southern side of a stream and marsh which ran a winding course through the valley, affording a good supply of water for the horses and men. The emperor's encampment included all the dignitaries who had accompanied him, together with the imperial guards, the *tagmata*. The provincial troops continued to plunder the valley around them, although there seems to have been a number of desertions from among the officers, who doubted that the army could extricate itself.

Shortly before dawn on Saturday 26 July, the Bulgar khan launched a full-scale assault, directed specifically at the imperial encampment, which Bulgar scouts in the hills around the Byzantine forces had clearly recognized. The troops were asleep and in spite of the watch that must have been set were taken completely by surprise. The Bulgar troops rapidly penetrated the perimeter and began indiscriminately slaughtering all they found. Within a few minutes the guard units, which had attempted to form up and to organize a more effective resistance, had begun to fight back and were able to impose some casualties on the attackers. But resistance was short-lived, and in the chaos and noise of a night attack the defenders quickly lost order and were soon cut to pieces in the confusion. Most of their officers were killed or put to flight, including the commander of the emperor's personal guard, the *drouggarios* of the Watch and many other senior officers and dignitaries. The fate of the emperor himself is unclear, but he was certainly killed in the first moments of the attack, and it was perhaps at the news of his death that the guards broke.

At this point the nearest thematic divisions had clearly been alerted to what was happening, but in the darkness, of course, it would have been impossible to tell exactly what was going on. As units from the different divisions formed up and hurriedly marched towards the imperial encampment, they were met by fleeing guardsmen, news of the emperor's death and the sight of the imperial encampment being sacked by the Bulgars. With apparently no resistance at all these units panicked and ran, so that the whole valley south of the stream and marsh was filled with men desperately trying to get away from the massacre of their comrades. With Bulgar soldiers in their midst cutting down those they could reach, the whole army rapidly dissolved. The accounts of the battle, partly based on eye-witness statements made within a few years of the disaster, go on to describe how many men and horses drowned in the marshes as they desperately tried to get around the stream and ride north out of harm's way – so many, indeed, that the Bulgars were able to cross both marsh and stream safely on the bodies of those who had been crushed or drowned in the flight. On the other side of the imperial encampment those soldiers who had fled to the south found themselves up against the wooden palisade and trench built by the Bulgars. Many abandoned their mounts and tried to climb over, only to fall and fatally injure themselves in the ditch on the other side. Some then set fire to the wooden supports of the timbers, causing a section of the palisade to fall outwards over the ditch. But when men and horses tried to cross it, the charred and weakened timbers gave way beneath them and they too fell into the ditch, to be burned alive in the conflagration which had now taken hold.

Although it is clear that many did manage to make good their escape – including a certain Theodore Salibaras, a leading imperial officer and confidant of the emperor, to whose report much of the detail in the accounts of the disaster are due – large numbers clearly perished, and the slaughter was immense. The defeat near Pliska in 811 went down in the annals of Byzantium as one of the blackest days of imperial history, no less of a catastrophe than the battle of Adrianople in 378 at which the emperor Valens had died fighting the Goths. Khan Krum became for the next three years the most dangerous enemy the empire had to face, pushing on two occasions as far as Constantinople itself and besieging the city in 813. The threat was only ended by his death in the following year.

The defeat near Pliska is interesting because it illustrates both the campaigning efficiency of Byzantine armies when well led, and their dependence on competent and intelligent leadership. Indeed, the quality of the commanding generals was one of the most important aspects of Byzantine warfare, for under a good commander the imperial armies were frequently able to achieve extraordinary feats of war, whereas under poor leadership even the best-trained forces suffered a huge disadvantage. Unlike the Roman legions of the first and second centuries AD, for example, the Byzantine forces did not have a reliable, tried and tested,self-aware corps of what we might today refer to as 'non-commissioned officers', able to manage and organize the discipline of their units and sub-units and often to redress the failings of senior officers in tactical situations. The quality of leadership was crucial, therefore, for upon the commander-in-chief's attitudes depended everything from morale and discipline to effective logistical arrangements. The events of 811 show, for example, that the corps commanders had made sensible arrangements for the encampments of their different divisions; yet this counted for nothing when morale was low and leadership lacking, especially when the army had marched into what was clearly and for all to see a tactically very difficult situation. The history of Byzantine warfare demonstrates this point time and again.

Quality of leadership was one of several qualities which determined the performance of an army and the outcome of the battles it fought. Friction between the commanders of the different corps that made up an army was also a significant element, as was seen at the battle of Jabiya-Yarmuk and on several occasions during the sixth century, as well as in the period thereafter. But treachery and betrayal, for whatever reason, also played a role. Manzikert in 1071 is possibly best known for the betrayal of the emperor Romanos IV by some of his divisional commanders, but there are other examples.

Another important aspect of campaigning was the need to keep the troops active and occupied. East Roman military handbooks frequently impress upon the general the dangers of permitting troops to remain together for too long, since this produces disorder, lack of discipline, insubordination and harm to the local population which has to support the soldiers, and can be as effective as the enemy in destroying an army. The Roman defeat in the battle of Versinikia in 813 is almost certainly due to this, rather than – as was claimed by later chroniclers – to the treachery and ambition of the general Leo, later the emperor Leo V.

The Battle of Versinikia 813

Following the defeat and death of Nikephoros, his son Staurakios, who had been badly wounded at the battle, became emperor, but was soon deposed, entering a monastery and dying shortly thereafter. He was succeeded by his brother-in-law Michael Rhaggabe, who ruled as Michael I. His failure to oppose the Bulgars effectively in 812 led to mass abandonment of the fortresses and other settlements behind the frontier, and the Bulgars were able to expand their territory by moving into these districts. In 813 Michael, whose position on the throne he owed to the support of the soldiers at Constantinople and the leading officers of state and Church, felt obliged to mount a major expedition to check the victorious Bulgars and to rescue his rapidly ailing reputation. A minor victory in the early Spring encouraged him in this scheme, and once again provincial forces from Asia Minor, the remaining European forces and the *tagmata* were assembled for an expedition. The provincial forces, however, were brought across too early, and spent most of May idly in Thrace awaiting the imperial division and *tagmata*, causing much hardship for the local population through their heavy demands for provisions. Having joined up with the provincial *themata* in early May, the emperor, who clearly lacked the support and confidence of most of the army, marched as far as Adrianople, where the army established a camp near Versinikia not far away. When Krum and his army arrived on 7 June, he established a camp in the same district, some 25 miles from the imperial forces, and waited, since it was clear that his army was substantially outnumbered. Although no doubt exaggerating, John Aplakes, the general of the Macedonian forces, claimed that the Romans outnumbered their foe by ten to one. As the armies waited, disagreement raged among the Byzantine commanders, some urging an attack, others urging caution. Those preferring to attack pointed out to the emperor that here they had the Bulgarian forces before them, on lower ground and in the open, and that it was well-known that Roman order and discipline always gave them an advantage over the Bulgars in such a situation.

After some two weeks during which the respective armies faced one another inconclusively, both men and animals suffered from the heat of midsummer. Indiscipline was rife in the imperial army, and low morale and disease began seriously to undermine the army's effectiveness. Many of the troops in the Asia Minor units which had been brought over were inexperienced recruits or conscripts, and were resentful and sullen about being taken far from their home territory. Eventually the *strategos* of Macedonia, Aplakes, lost his patience, and sent a message to the emperor informing him that he could delay no longer but would attack and would expect the centre and the other wing to follow.

Whether Aplakes commanded the left or the right wing is unclear, but he had under him the contingents from Thrace and Macedonia, perhaps 8,000 men in all. The emperor commanded the centre, made up of the *tagmata*, numbering perhaps 4,000, along with the forces from the Thrakesion and Opsikion regions, perhaps as many as 10,000 men altogether; while the general Leo, commander of the Anatolikon region, had his own troops and those of Cappadocia, probably some 8,000 again. On the Bulgar side Krum had perhaps some 12,000, although there is no clear figure in the sources, merely the report that his forces were anxious not to make the first move in view of the superior numbers on the imperial side.

Aplakes seems initially to have attacked with the Macedonian troops under his personal command, and launched his assault down the slopes of the ridge along which the imperial forces were drawn against the Bulgars. In the initial impact the Bulgars were pushed back, but rallied and counter-charged. At this point the Thracian units crashed into the Bulgar forces and together the two contingents began to force the Bulgars back on their own reserves and camp. Unfortunately for Aplakes, however, the emperor did not give the order to follow up this attack, and so the centre and remaining wing stood and watched as the forces under Aplakes, at first successful, began to meet stiffer resistance from the Bulgar centre which, observing the lack of movement on the part of the forces opposite, rallied to the support of the troops on their flank. At this point, the troops on the other Roman wing, most prominently those from the Anatolikon theme under general Leo, suddenly began to withdraw, leaving the field of battle in some disorder, a development which then caused the centre divisions to lose heart. And as they watched the massacre of Aplakes's division below them and the fleeing troops on their other wing, they too broke and abandoned their positions, leaving the emperor and his entourage to make their way in haste back towards Constantinople as best they could.

The Bulgar Khan thought at first that this was a trick, a feigned retreat to draw his troops out in disorder. But the Bulgars soon realized that this could not be the case and, taking heart from the collapse of the Roman attack and the isolation of Aplakes's command, began vigorously to pursue the fleeing imperial troops. The troops under Aplakes were either killed or, according to one of the two main sources, able to make their escape and flee the field. Aplakes himself, along with several senior officers, fell in the fray. In the meanwhile panic overtook the now dissolving centre and flank formations, and the terror which afflicted many of the soldiers is described in great detail in one source – every time they heard the hooves or feet of their fleeing comrades behind them they thought it was the Bulgars, inciting them to run even faster. Many men and horses died in the pursuit; others took refuge in the fortresses along the route back into Roman territory. Overall, losses were less than they might have been, since the Bulgars were also tired from the long confrontation and besides were fully engaged in collecting the vast bonanza of abandoned weapons and armour cast aside by the panicking imperial forces.

Such an ignominious defeat is difficult to explain. Although later sources suggest that the blame lay with the general Leo himself, accusing him of deliberate treachery, the evidence of the more contemporary texts does not support this notion. On the other hand, Leo's division included, it seems, substantial numbers of raw recruits, and their long wait in Thrace, lack of discipline, poor conditions and alien terrain and conditions may have affected them especially strongly. Anatolikon units appear to have been able to retire as far as Constantinople unscathed, and upon their arrival rebelled against the emperor Michael, acclaiming in his stead their general Leo as emperor. Michael himself, in despair at his failure as a leader and in respect of his political programme generally, abdicated without further ado, and the city of Constantinople, the patriarch and the remaining troops accepted Leo. Whatever the causes of the withdrawal, non-participation or panic of the Roman units at Versinikia, the cost was the massacre of the western provincial units, the loss of Aplakes, clearly an able and fearless officer, and a considerable blow to Roman prestige and military confidence.

The Battle of Anzen, near Dazimon, 838

In 837 the emperor Theophilos had mounted a major expedition against the region of Melitene (mod. Malatya), taking the towns of Sozopetra and Arsamosata and forcing the city of Melitene to pay him off. The expedition was an important propaganda success, although its military and strategic significance was limited. But the Caliph Mu'tasim vowed to avenge this humiliation, and in 838 retaliated with an even more extensive and, for the Byzantines, far more harmful campaign. His chief objectives were Ankyra and Amorion (mod. Hisar on the Emirdad), the latter of symbolic value because it was the emperor's birthplace. Apprised of the invasion plan in advance, Theophilos himself set out in June with the *tagmata* and, probably, units of the

European *themata* of Thrace and Macedonia. Also accompanying the army was a force of Kurdish rebels who had deserted to the Byzantines under their leader, Theophobos, some time before, and had been re-equipped by the emperor as regular imperial troops. At Dorylaion (mod. Eskişehir) the emperor divided his forces, sending a large reinforcement to assist the garrison of Amorion, taking the rest of the army himself, perhaps as many as 25,000 men, to Cappadocia, where he blocked the route from the Cilician Gates to Ankyra.

The Muslim forces, meanwhile, waiting until the middle of the month before starting out, had split into three columns, the first marching to Malatya and then pushing into the district of the Armeniak army while the second and third columns advanced along the main road towards Ankyra, as Theophilos had anticipated. The first objective was Ankyra itself, where the three columns were to join before proceeding to Amorion. Byzantine intelligence of Mu'tasim's movements seems to have been poor, whereas the Muslim leader was able to capture some Byzantine scouts and learn of the emperor's position blocking his route on the Halys. This information was passed on to Afshin, the commander of the first, eastern column, numbering possibly 20,000, perhaps fewer, and including a very substantial force of Turkish horse archers, as many as 10,000 strong according to some accounts. This division advanced as far as the important Byzantine military assembly point at Dazimon (mod. Dazmana, between Tokat and Amasya) in the theme of the Armeniakon, a fortress constructed on an eminence at the eastern end of the like-named plain, Dazimonitis. The terrain consists for the most part of rolling uplands intersected by occasional depressions with marshes and mud-flats, and little woodland.

In mid-July Theophilos was informed of the presence of this force and, leaving a detachment to cover the road to Ankyra, led his troops eastwards to drive the enemy army out. Once again, however, Muslim scouts had ranged widely across the regions through which the imperial forces were expected to pass and soon learned of the emperor's approach, while maintaining their own strength and position secure. On 21 July the imperial forces came into visual contact with the Muslim force, which had occupied a defensive position.

The emperor's forces took up position somewhat to the south, near an unidentified hill called Anzen from which the enemy positions could be observed.

Theophilos received varying advice from his officers: some urged him to attack that night and use his superior numbers to drive the enemy force from their position. Theophilos rejected this advice, and launched his attack at dawn on 22 July. The imperial forces were immediately successful on one wing, driving the enemy forces from their positions within a short time, and inflicting some 3,000 casualties. At some point during this process the emperor decided to reinforce his other wing from the troops under his own command, and with some 2,000 men of the *tagmata* and the Kurds rode across the rear of his own lines accordingly. After this initial success, however, and perhaps towards noon, the Muslim commander launched a strong counter-attack led by his contingent of Turkish horse archers, whose effective shooting halted the Roman advance and gave the withdrawing Arab forces time to regroup and reform their lines. Unfortunately, however, it was at this point that the troops on the wing and centre remarked the absence of the emperor and his standard and, assuming that he had fallen, began to waver. Under the continuous hail of missiles from the Turkish mounted archers, they began to fall back in some disorder, and shortly thereafter the Roman battle line quickly dissolved. Grasping the opportunity, the Muslim forces surged forward and drove the Roman troops from the battlefield. Although some units broke up in complete disorder, and some soldiers even reached Constantinople (where they spread rumours of the emperor's death in battle), it would seem that many were able to withdraw in some order and regroup somewhat to the North, in the district of Chiliokomon.

The enemy forces were now able to surround the units that remained with the emperor – the *tagmata* and their commanders, and the Kurdish units – and isolate them on the hill of Anzen, where they took up a strong defensive position. The fierce onslaught of the mounted archers posed a real threat to the emperor, but fortunately, a sudden and very heavy shower of rain prevented the enemy from pushing home their attack, for the tension of the Turkish bowstrings was loosened by the rain. This gave the Roman forces in turn some time in which to reform and reorganize themselves.

According to some of the sources, one of the emperor's leading officers (the name varies according to the source) now noticed that the Kurdish soldiers were trying to talk with soldiers on the other side in their own tongue, and feared that they would desert and hand the emperor over to the enemy in return for a pardon for their earlier desertion. While this was going on, and in view of the fact that his Turkish archers were temporarily unable to operate as before, Afshin brought up siege catapults from his baggage train in an effort to drive the Roman units from their cover.

While his body of 2,000 continued to resist, however, the emperor had been persuaded that his duty was to extricate himself from this predicament as quickly as possible and so, together with a small band of officers and men, he proceeded to cut his way through the attacking forces and make good his escape. Many of the men with him were seriously wounded. The remainder of the surrounded force was eventually forced to surrender, though their subsequent fate is unknown.

The emperor reached the region of Chiliokomon to the west (near Amaseia), where he was able to rejoin the troops who had abandoned him, whence he eventually joined up with the force he had left to cover the road to Ankyra. In the face of vastly superior numbers, this corps had withdrawn north-westwards, stripping the countryside as it went and leaving Ankyra to fend for itself. A force sent to assist in the defence of this town found it abandoned, and was ordered instead to proceed to assist Amorion. While the emperor waited at Dorylaion before returning to Constantinople to quell rumours of his death in battle, the first Muslim force reached Ankyra on about 27 July and sacked the town before moving on to besiege Amorion at the beginning of August. After a two-week siege, Muslim and Turkish troops succeeded in gaining entry to the city, which was quickly taken, sacked, and the garrison slaughtered. This was one of the most significant defeats of the ninth century, although it had far greater symbolic and ideological significance than strategic importance, since the Caliph soon withdrew his armies from Asia Minor to deal with a rebellion at home.

The battle of Anzen was itself strategically important, of

course, for had the emperor won, he might well have been able to force the Caliph to alter his plans or withdraw before he was able to reach either Ankyra or Amorion. But it was also important in being the first encounter mentioned in the sources between Byzantine troops and the central Asian Turkish warriors, who were now being employed on a large scale by the Caliph as a reliable and totally loyal military force, upon whom he could depend both for his own political security and as an effective fighting force.

The evidence suggests that archery had declined considerably among eastern Roman soldiers as a discipline of real tactical importance since the sixth and early seventh centuries. The use of the bow did not disappear entirely, since there always seem to have been some mounted archers and provincial infantry troops probably included some soldiers armed with bows. Nevertheless, the limited evidence makes almost no mention of archery, the standard armament for the middle Byzantine soldier consisting of sword, lance, shield and helmet, sometimes including also a *lorikion* or body-armour of some type.

The evidence from the eastern wars fought by the empire as well as that from the Balkans shows that the enemies of the Roman empire relied upon the same panoply – indeed, the sources mention the sling as often as they mention the bow. And as the battle of Anzen appears to show, the Byzantines experienced great difficulties when confronted by effective archery, especially in the form of the powerful composite reflex bow wielded by the steppe nomads. The reason is almost certainly to do with the fact that this type of weapon was not native to the empire's lands, and military and tactical organization was not up to enforcing regular training and practice of the sort possible in the context of late Roman military structures. In the sixth and seventh centuries, the Byzantine forces had used Hunnic mercenaries and allies, and from this basis had trained their own mounted archers accordingly. Thereafter, the possibilities for this sort of training declined. In the later ninth and early tenth century such soldiers were once again recruited from the steppes – Chazars, Magyars and others, for example – and when the emperor Leo VI (886-912) wrote his military handbook, the *Tactica*, noting the decline that Roman archery had suffered and the many defeats which were a result, he commended that all

Roman recruits practice with the bow.

The Later Ninth Century: The Battles of Marj al-Usquf ('Bishop's Meadow') and Lalakaon 863, and Bathys Ryax 878

With the outbreak of civil war in the Caliphate in 842 upon the death of the Caliph Mu'tasim, Byzantium was able to take advantage of the situation to begin once again a reassertion of imperial military power on the eastern front. The main enemies in this region were no longer centrally led Caliphal armies, however, but the forces of the many emirs who governed the frontier fortress towns such as Tarsos in Cilicia or Melitene further East. The struggle was evenly balanced throughout the rest of the century, although the imperial armies were able to achieve several resounding victories and force the Arabs onto the defensive. The defensive strategy employed by the empire throughout this period was that which had failed in 838 but which was, on the whole, successful in preventing hostile occupation of Byzantine territory and inflicting anything more than short-term damage to the economy of the regions traversed. During the later eighth century, indeed, Muslim raids into Byzantine territory had begun increasingly to take on a ritual character, for the Romans represented the major non-Islamic enemy of the Caliphate, and became in consequence the primary target for *jihâd*, or holy war. The collection of booty and the fact of having made the raid became the key objectives, rather than any longer-term strategic gains. As the ninth century wore on, so the balance slowly tipped in favour of the eastern Roman forces, until a full-scale offensive could be inaugurated in the tenth century.

A good example of the imperial strategy comes from the campaign of 863, when the joint forces of the emirs of Tarsos and Melitene, totalling perhaps as many as 15,000-20,000 men, penetrated through the Cilician Gates, pillaging and collecting booty as it went. Warned in advance of the enemy raid, the emperor Michael III had assembled two forces to deal with the attack. For reasons which are not clear, the larger part of the invading force turned back once it had reached Cappadocia, and the emir of Malatya (Melitene) Omar, and his force of some 8,000, were given permission to continue deeper into Roman territory. In the region between Nazianzos and Nyssa, known in the Arabic sources as Marj al-Usquf or 'Bishop's Meadow' – a plateau on which the episcopal seat of Doara (mod. Duvarlı) was located, on the road from Tyana (mod. Kemarhisar) to Koloneia (Aksaray) – they were confronted by a small Byzantine force of about the same size, possibly smaller, under the command of the emperor Michael himself. This force was probably made up of the imperial *tagmata* and the thematic forces from Cappadocia and Charsianon. After a short but fierce fight in which many fell on both sides the invaders were able to push the imperial force aside and continue their raid northwards, where they eventually pushed through to the region of the city of Amisos on the Black Sea coast.

In the meantime, however, they had been shadowed by the emperor's troops, and at a location near the river Lalakaon (probably mod. Şehirmeydanı Çayı) in the border region between the themes of Paphlagonia and Armeniakon, the commander of the imperial *tagmata*, Petronas, who had command of the second, much larger army, was able to surround the corps under Omar. The site of the ensuing battle, about 130 km from Amisos (mod. Samsun), was on the rolling meadowlands, surrounded by the cliffs and rocky foothills of the Deveci Da through which the river flowed. Petronas had a total of thirteen different corps, which had marched by separate routes to meet near the point at which the action took place. The *themata* of Thrakesion, Thrace and Macedonia together with the four imperial *tagmata* under Petronas's direct command approached from the west; those of Anatolikon, Opsikion, and Cappadocia, along with the smaller corps from the *kleisourai* of Charsianon and Seleukeia arrived from the south; and those of Koloneia, Paphlagonia, Armeniakon and Boukellarion came in from the north. The forces which arrived from the south had presumably been those who had fought earlier under the emperor – who seems to have returned to Constantinople – and these now effectively blocked Omar's route home. In spite of the advice of his officers that he should abandon any thought of fighting and make good his own escape, Omar was determined to fight and battle was joined. The greatly superior imperial forces, which must have outnumbered Omar's troops by at least three to one, fell on the invaders mercilessly, and Omar's force was virtually annihilated. Omar himself was killed, and although his son with a small column managed to escape the trap, this force too was caught shortly afterwards by the forces of Charsianon and destroyed.

This encounter, although involving relatively limited numbers of invaders, marked a substantial imperial victory, both in military as well as in symbolic terms. It also showed that the strategy operated by the imperial forces could succeed, when the armies were well-led and adequate intelligence of enemy movements was available.

A similarly successful encounter took place a few years later, this time against the Paulicians, dualist heretics from central eastern Anatolia who had allied themselves with the emirs of Melitene in their fight against what they saw as imperial oppression of their religion. The origins of the sect and its beliefs are unclear, but they first appear in the sources in the seventh century, since when they had grown in strength and numbers. The emperors of the ninth century in particular went on the offensive against them, and they responded to these attempts to eliminate their communities and beliefs with well-organized military action. It was under the emperor Basil I (867-886) that, after several hard campaigns, they were finally defeated, and he transferred many by forced relocation to the Balkan provinces.

In the campaign of the spring and summer of 878 against the Paulicians, the commander of the *tagmata* (the *domestikos* of the *scholai*) was in overall command of the provincial and tagmatic forces, and had marched east to try to confront and bring to battle the rebel leader, Chrysocheir, and his army. The latter had managed to avoid a fight, but had also failed to penetrate the Roman forces, which pursued and harried his army as it marched, preventing Chrysocheir from raiding Roman territory and carrying off any booty. Towards the end of the campaigning season the Paulician leader encamped at Agranes (near mod. Mu alem Kale) in the Charsianon region, with the *domestikos* and his force a short distance away at Siboron (mod. Karamadara). From there Chrysocheir marched north-east towards Bathys Ryax, the modern Kalinirmak Gap on the north-eastern edge of the Ak Da , close to the point at which the road from Sebasteia (Sivas) divides some 28 km. to the north west, one branch going west, the other northwards. It was an important strategic location and an established meeting-place for the Byzantine forces of eastern Anatolia when campaigning in the region or further to the east. The Byzantine commander detached two thematic contingents under their *strategoi*, those of Charsianon and Armeniakon – perhaps 4,000-5,000 men — to follow him as far as Bathys Ryax. There they were to report on his movements and whether or not he detached a division to attack the Roman regions to the west, or whether he decided to march homewards, in which case he would meet the domestikos. In the event of the Paulicians adopting the latter plan, the two *strategoi* were to rejoin the *domestikos* at Siboron.

In the event, Chrysocheir seems to have been unaware that he was being shadowed, and after a short march pitched camp towards evening in the plain at the foot of the mountains which form the head of the valley of Bathys Ryax. The pursuing forces took up their position behind the enemy host and on the saddle between the two hills above them. Here the sources record a debate broke out between the soldiers and officers of the two thematic armies as to who were the braver. In the end, it was decided that only an attack upon the enemy force would determine this and so – against the orders issued by the commander-in-chief – it was agreed that a select force of some 600 men from both divisions would mount a dawn attack, supported by the remaining forces who would create a great clamour, with trumpets and beating of drums, to panic the enemy soldiers into believing that the whole combined thematic army under the *domestikos* had fallen upon them.

The plan worked perfectly. The enemy host fell into a complete panic, some leaping on their horses and fleeing, other cutting the loads off the pack-animals and trying to escape on them. Their baggage train and all the booty they had been able to collect was taken, Chrysocheir himself fled with a few bodyguards but was killed during the flight, and the pursuit of the broken army, many of whom then ran into the much larger force under the *domestikos*, stretched across some 30 miles of the province. The battle marked the effective end of the independent Paulicians and their resistance, for Tephrike held out for only a short while thereafter.

The Battle of Acheloos 917

The situation in the Balkans seemed to have improved under

Basil I with the conversion to Christianity of the Bulgar Khan Boris, who took the Christian name Michael (852-889) and the title of Tsar (Caesar), and some of his entourage; a strong Christian, pro-Byzantine party developed at the Bulgar court. But during the reign of Symeon (893-927), who was brought up in the imperial court at Constantinople and evolved his own imperial pretensions, war broke out once more, a war which, with pauses, lasted until the 920s and which at one point saw Constantinople besieged by a powerful Bulgar army. The record of the imperial armies is, on the whole, not particularly impressive in this period, which can be ascribed to poor organization and administration as well as to indiscipline and sometimes incompetent leadership. But the battle of Acheloos is a good example of the role of chance in battle, for an otherwise well-prepared and well-led army managed to lose because of a misunderstanding half-way through the fight and the ensuing panic which set in.

In 916-917 the empire prepared for a major expedition against Bulgaria, specifically with the intention of crushing Tsar Symeon and ridding the Romans forever of his demands to marry an imperial princess and become the ruler of a united Byzantine-Bulgarian state. The plans included winning the support of the nomadic Pechenegs north of the Danube, who were to be transported over that river by Byzantine ships and then fall on the Bulgars from the rear, accompanied by a major land invasion up the coastal route into Bulgar territory, again supported by the imperial fleet. By August the imperial army, under the command of the general Leo Phokas, had penetrated as far as the region of the Acheloos river (mod. Aheloj), not far from Anchialos (mod. Pomorie), but Symeon, having been informed of the attack at the last minute, managed to gather his forces and march down towards the Byzantine army, where he took up a position in the hills overlooking the coastal plain where the imperial troops were encamped. (See Map 9)

The number of troops in the Bulgarian forces in unknown. On the eastern Roman side were the imperial *tagmata* as well as several divisions from Asia Minor brought across for the campaign, together with the armies of Thrace and Macedonia – an army of as many as 30,000, perhaps. The exact course of events is unclear, but it seems that Symeon launched his attack after the army was fully deployed. In the opening phases of the battle, the imperial army had the upper hand, and the Bulgarians seem to have suffered heavy casualties. As the battle was going reasonably well, the commander is reported to have dismounted at a stream to refresh himself. Unfortunately, his horse took fright and bolted and, seeing the riderless horse careering along behind the lines and through the imperial camp, some soldiers nearby mistakenly set up the cry that he had been killed. This caused some panic among the troops preparing to press forward the attack on the retreating Bulgars, and Symeon, who was watching events from a nearby eminence and had been able to conduct an orderly withdrawal towards a more defensive position, saw his chance. He ordered his troops to halt their retreat and turn suddenly on the pursuing Roman forces. Combined with the cry that the commander-in-chief had fallen, this sudden move sufficed to bring the whole advance to a halt and start a disorderly retreat from the field along the length of the Roman positions. The retreat turned into a rout and panic set in, and the Bulgarians, seeing the turn of events, pursued their enemy without respite.

The resulting casualties were extremely high on the Roman side, several senior officers, including those in charge of some of the *tagmata*, being cut down. Leo Phokas was himself able to reach Mesembria on the coast (mod. Nesebur). The unseemly panic and ensuing rout were largely the cause of the heavy losses, and it was reported some sixty years later that heaps of skulls and the whitened bones of the fallen could still be seen strewn across the battlefield and along the banks of the Acheloos river. Indeed, the nearby placename Kokalos – 'bones' – may be a memory of the disaster.

The defeat at Acheloos was one of the worst defeats suffered by an eastern Roman army since that at Pliska a century before. But importantly, it marks a dramatic end to a period stretching from the middle of the eighth to the early tenth century in which indiscipline and chance played such an important role in Roman military fortunes. Even though the armies of the empire had largely succeeded in their overall mission of defending its territorial integrity and establishing a balance of strategic power in the East, in the Balkans the situation had certainly deteriorated since the defeat of 811, and the Bulgar state had expanded southwards and south-westwards to become a major Balkan power to rival Constantinople in the following century. The christianization of the Bulgar elite after the 860s had introduced a stabilizing element, but also brought with it certain dangers – as the plans of the Tsar Symeon, whose ambition to establish a Christian Bulgaro-Byzantine empire only ended with his death in 927, amply demonstrated. The century which followed was to see a complete transformation in the strategic situation on both fronts.

5
Warfare in the Age of Reconquest

Raids and Razzias

As well as being characterized by the sort of larger-scale offensive and defensive strategy exemplified in the campaigns of, for example, 838 or 863 described already, the period up to the middle of the tenth century saw a style of frontier fighting and skirmishing, of guerrilla tactics and raiding, that had developed over the centuries from the period when the frontiers became more-or-less stable in the first part of the eighth century. Quite a lot is known about this style of fighting both from historians' accounts of campaigns and battles, as well as from a number of military handbooks, some of them written by serving soldiers. The late ninth- or early tenth-century *Tactica* of the emperor Leo VI, for example, shows that warfare along the eastern front followed a well-established pattern. By the 950s and 960s, this was changing, as imperial successes in pushing forward the frontier rendered the traditional system of defensive warfare more or less redundant.

The eastern frontier was guarded by a chain of lookout posts, with small units of irregulars acting as scouts and informants along the frontier, particularly covering the various points of ingress into imperial territory. The frontier was a broad band of territory, and the location of such lookout posts seems to have changed according to the situation, while raids and counter-raids intended to destroy enemy outposts or more important local fortresses and bases frequently altered the pattern of local strategy.

An anonymous treatise written in the 960s sets out the key aspects of this type of warfare. First, the local commanders should make sure that the networks of watch-posts and look-outs are in order. Scouts should be recruited from among the local population, men with experience, a good knowledge of local routes and the different qualities they possess. They should work on a fifteen-day rotation, and be dispatched in small groups to watch the roads and routes that might be used by the enemy. Local commanders should make extensive use of spies, including merchants and others on genuine business in the enemy's land – a long tradition in Byzantine strategic thinking. The call-up of registered soldiers should be strictly observed, and the scouting parties should be checked by an officer from time to time. They should also change their location in order to avoid capture. There were pre-planned schemes for evacuating the non-military population of the regions through which an enemy raiding party would pass, once its route had been ascertained, in order to preserve the local population and at the same time to deprive the enemy of the chance to collect provisions and easy booty.

The most important aspect of this frontier defensive strategy was 'shadowing'. Following and harassing the enemy by exploiting one's own knowledge of the local terrain was one aspect; keeping a close watch on his column and especially his encampment, in order to attempt ambushes on forage parties and other isolated groups, was another. Crucial to all operations was the idea of bringing together several smaller forces, leading eventually either to a full-scale confrontation, but with the imperial forces at a numerical advantage, or to a pincer movement, designed to encourage the enemy force to give up and return home. In this case, it was usually planned for imperial troops to have occupied the passes or exit routes which the enemy commander would follow. The subsequent surprise attack or ambush, which could result in the recovery of all or most of the booty, and certainly with the destruction and rout of the enemy army, was the ultimate aim. The possibility that his own forces might themselves become the victims of shadowing and ambush was ever-present, however, and the Byzantine commander was urged to use scouts and outriders in order to prevent this from happening.

One of the distinguishing features of this treatise is the focus on the judgement and independence of the local commanders. Not only should they themselves organize regular, small-scale raids over the border (unless the empire had made a formal truce with the Arab emirs or the Caliphate itself); they should be prepared to attack an invading force whenever an appropriate opportunity arose, and not necessarily wait for the arrival of reinforcements or the local senior commander.

The author of the treatise distinguishes three types of enemy raid, differentiated by size or by timing. Small, rapid raiding parties of cavalry, which might invade Roman territory at any time, and whose entry should be communicated to the local commanders as quickly as possible by the border scouts and watch-posts, should be shadowed, met, ambushed or hemmed in, and turned back, and if possible without any substantial gains in booty. Secondly, there were major raids, generally in August and September, consisting of substantial forces made up of volunteers for the *jihâd* as well as regular troops from the Arab borderlands – Malatya, Aleppo, Tarsos and Antioch. Such raids had both an economic and an ideological function, first in terms of the desire for booty, and to damage the Roman economy, and second in respect of the desire of many Muslims to participate in the *jihâd*. The local commander was enjoined to use every means at his disposal to find out when such raids would begin, by which route, and how numerous the enemy host would be. The invading force should be shadowed, along with any accompanying raiding parties which were sent out once the main force had reached Roman territory. The invaders' logistical difficulties should be maximized by the removal of livestock and crops, or even their destruction in extreme cases. The enemy force should be subject to constant harassment as it moved, foraged for supplies, set up camp, or attempted to collect booty. The passes through which it would return should be occupied and ambushes laid; the water-supplies should be held by Byzantine forces. The enemy should be attacked as they returned, laden with booty. Naturally, the Romans were not always able to respond successfully to such attacks, and there are many examples where Roman preparations failed to produce the desired results, or where the Roman commanders were unable to outwit and out-general their adversary.

The local commander also had to be on his guard against surprise raids, launched before the local population had been evacuated or any sort of ambush or shadowing-party sent out. In an effort to delay the enemy, various measures could be applied, such as a feint attack to distract the enemy from pillaging the villages while they were being hastily evacuated. Once the local troops were in the field, the strategy of harassment and ambush, by day and by night, came into play. While he was one of the empire's most successful antagonists, the emir of Aleppo was ambushed on at least three occasions using this strategy, barely escaping with his life on one occasion.

This sort of warfare could also be offensive. Local commanders were advised to maintain bands of raiders, whose task it was to raid deep into enemy territory in order to foment insecurity and uncertainty. One of their most important tasks was to take prisoners, so that Byzantine commanders might learn of enemy troop movements and intentions. Similar arrangements seem to have operated in the Balkans at times, although these were not always regular soldiers, but drawn from semi-independent peoples whose marginal situation between the two cultures suited them ideally for this task. Such sources also provided some of the regular light cavalry, in view of their detailed knowledge both of regular routes as well as side-paths and concealed tracks, watering- and camping-places in the mountains.

In the following, a typical penetrative raid into eastern Asia Minor by a medium-sized Arab army is described. The account comes from an eyewitness and contemporary of the leader of the expedition, the famous warrior emir of Aleppo, Sa'if ad-Daulah, and provides a wealth of topographical detail which neatly complements the information and the description of the Byzantine strategic response to such raids found in the tenth-century military handbooks.

Sa'if ad-Daulah's Raid of 956

The raid in question was launched in early spring of that year, intended as a booty-collecting expedition, as an attack on the Roman frontier provinces, and as a distraction intended to draw off the Roman forces that had been sent to raid the lands to the east of Sa'if's own base at Aleppo. Its object was the district of Anzitene, recently conquered by the eastern Roman armies and incorporated into the *thema* of Mesopotamia. This was a rich district and had always been of strategic importance, both in the wars between east Rome and the Persians and later in those between Romans and Arabs. Its strategic location attracted attention, for it commanded access to Armenia from the south and south-west and across the Euphrates. Whoever held Anzitene had a springboard for attacks in either direction, and the Romans were now using it for precisely that purpose, as their campaigns to roll back the Islamic emirates along their south-eastern flank progressed. Sa'if had received information that the military governor of Anzitene, based at the fortress town of Harput (mod. Elaziz), had set out to raid the upper Tigris region, part of Sa'if's domain, leaving his home territory more-or-less undefended, presumably because Sa'if was himself still far to the south-west in his capital at Aleppo. (See Map 10)

Gathering his forces of both cavalry and infantry (who nonetheless, as was customary with Muslim raiders throughout this period, were mounted so that they could keep up with the fast pace set by the cavalry units), Sa'if set out on Monday 28 April first for the town of Harran, where he negotiated the support of the local Beduin, the Banu Numair. Rather than marching east to deal with the Byzantine raiders in and around Amida, however, he then turned north and marching past several of his own fortresses, entered enemy territory north of the fortress of Hisn Arqanin (mod. Ergani) – the marches of Anzitene – some twelve days after leaving Aleppo, on Saturday 10 May. The castle controls the southern end of the Ergani pass, and it is likely that Sa'if's forces controlled the rest of the pass, which cuts through the mountains to enter the plain of Anzitene near the lake now known as Hazar Gölü (anc. Lake Thospitis). Upon receiving news of the Muslim raid, the eastern Roman commander and his forces withdrew from Amida, and began the march back to their own territory. Sa'if's raid had clearly taken them by surprise.

Sa'if set up camp on the shores of the lake. The nearest major Byzantine base was at Arsamosata (mod. Haraba), some distance to the north-east at the end of the valley of the Arsanias river,

1 The emperor Justinian with guards and members of the clergy, sixth-century mosaic, San Vitale, Ravenna.

Left: 2 Gold coin of the emperor Theophilos (829-842).

Right: 3 Gold coin of the emperor Leo VI (886-912) with his youngest son Constantine VII (913-959).

4 Gold coin of the emperor Constantine VII (913-959).

5 Gold coin of the emperor Alexios I (1081-1118).

6 Gold coin of the emperor Manuel I (1143-1180).

7 The Yarmuk region looking east from the Damascus road.

8 Hill country south of Jabiya/Yarmuk.

9 Amida (mod. Diyarbekir).

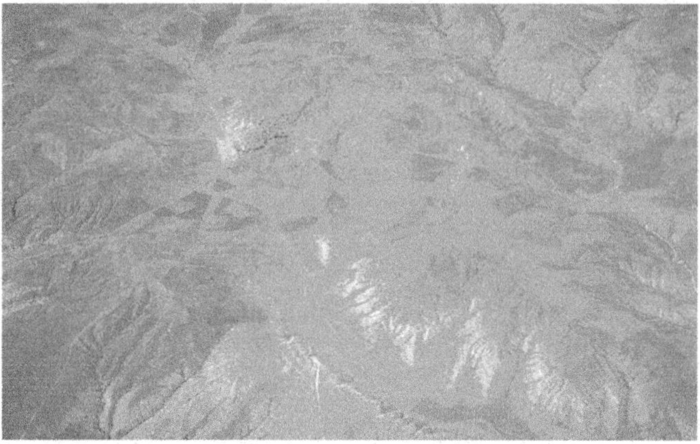

10 The central Anatolian plateau east of Ankara.

11 The fortress of Harput (Elaziz).

12 The citadel of Acrocorinth, guarding the entrance to the Peloponnese.

13 The Byzantine fortress of Koloneia (modern ebinkarahisar).

14 Amasya (Byzantine Amaseia).

15 Sardis, western Asia Minor. In the background is the citadel.

16 Medieval walls of Ani, Armenia.

17 The Balkans, looking north. This view epitomizes the rugged, wooded nature of the Balkan highlands, which made – and indeed still makes – communication difficult.

18 The Of Da and valley of the Of river (anc. Ophis), in north-east Anatolia.

Above: 19 The Pazar river gorge in north-east Anatolia south of the Black Sea coast.

Right: 20 The 'Cilician Gates', a crucial pass into Asia Minor.

21 Gold coin from the reign of the emperor Justinian I (527-565).

23 Gold coin of the emperor Maurice (582-602).

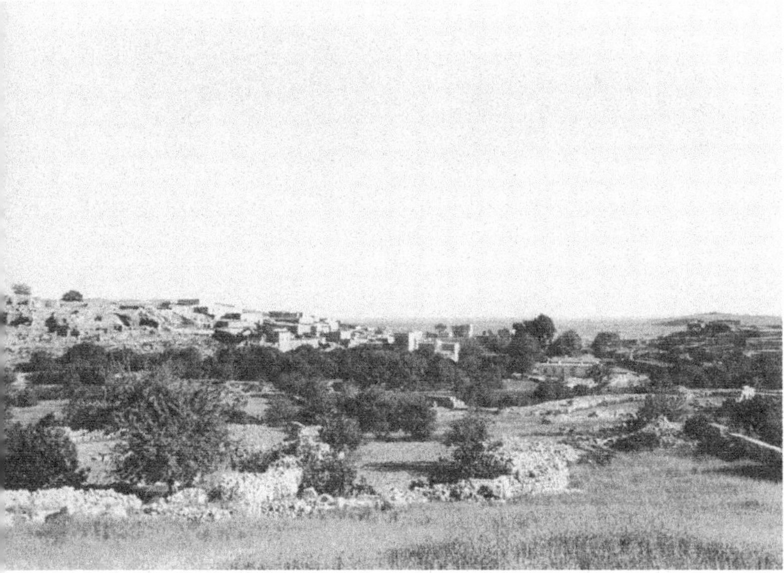

22 The plain of Dara with the village in the distance.

24 The Anatolian plateau looking south-east from the fortress at Euchaita.

25 Hill country east of Ankara.

26 The central Anatolian plateau, south of Ankara.

27 The region around A ın/Keban, north-east of Melitene.

28 The Byzantine thematic fortress of Charsianon Kastron (mod. Mu alim Kalesi)

29 The citadel of Tephrike (mod. Divri i), capital of the Paulicians in the 850s-870s.

30 General view of the region north of the Tigris, looking towards the Kurdish Taurus.

31 The valley of the Hozat Su, a tributary of the Euphrates, north of Harput (Elaziz).

32 Site of the citadel of Arsamosata (mod. Haraba).

33 The plain of the Halys (Kızılırmak), east of Sebasteia (mod. Sivas).

34 The road through the Pontic Alps from Trabzon to Erzurum (Theodosioupolis).

Above: 35 The pass through the Kurdish Taurus north to Lake Van.

Right: 36 Western shore of Lake Van, south of Khliat.

37 Medieval walls of the city of Manzikert.

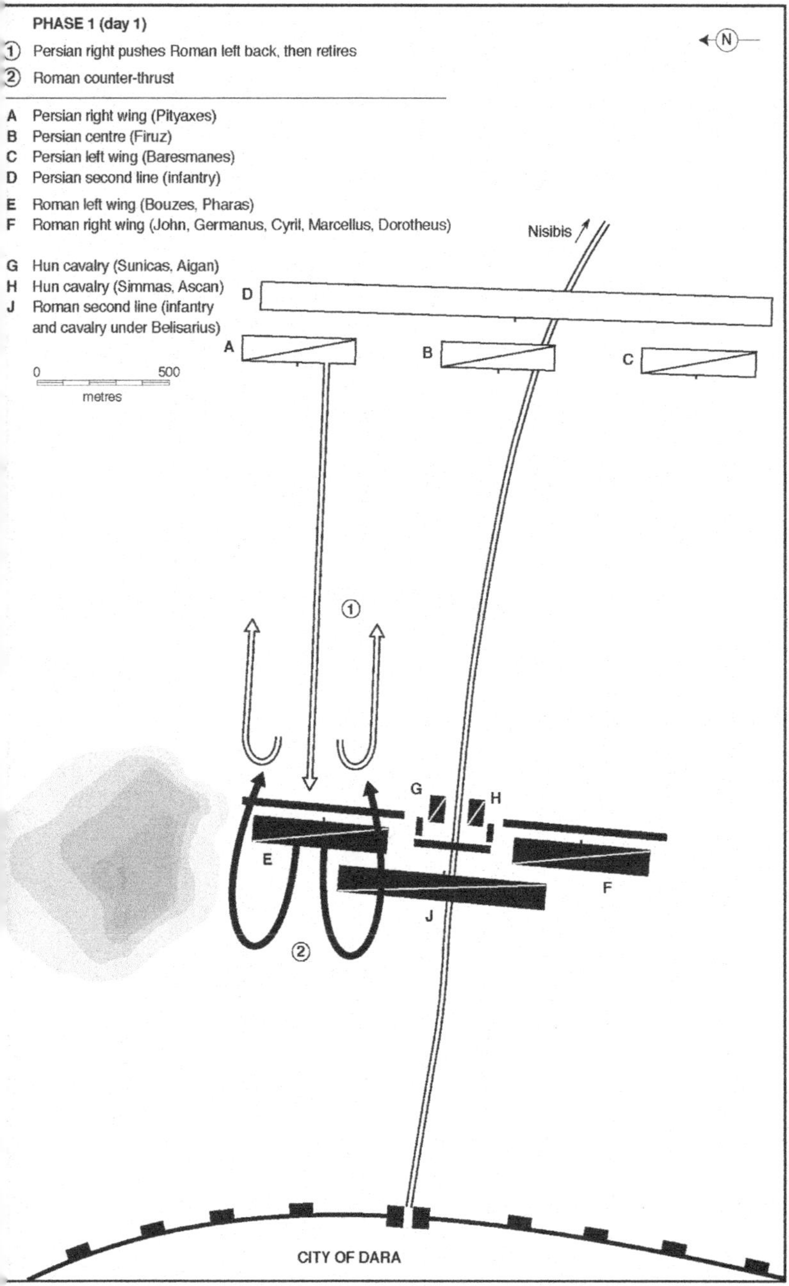

38 Plan of the battle of Dara 530, day 1.

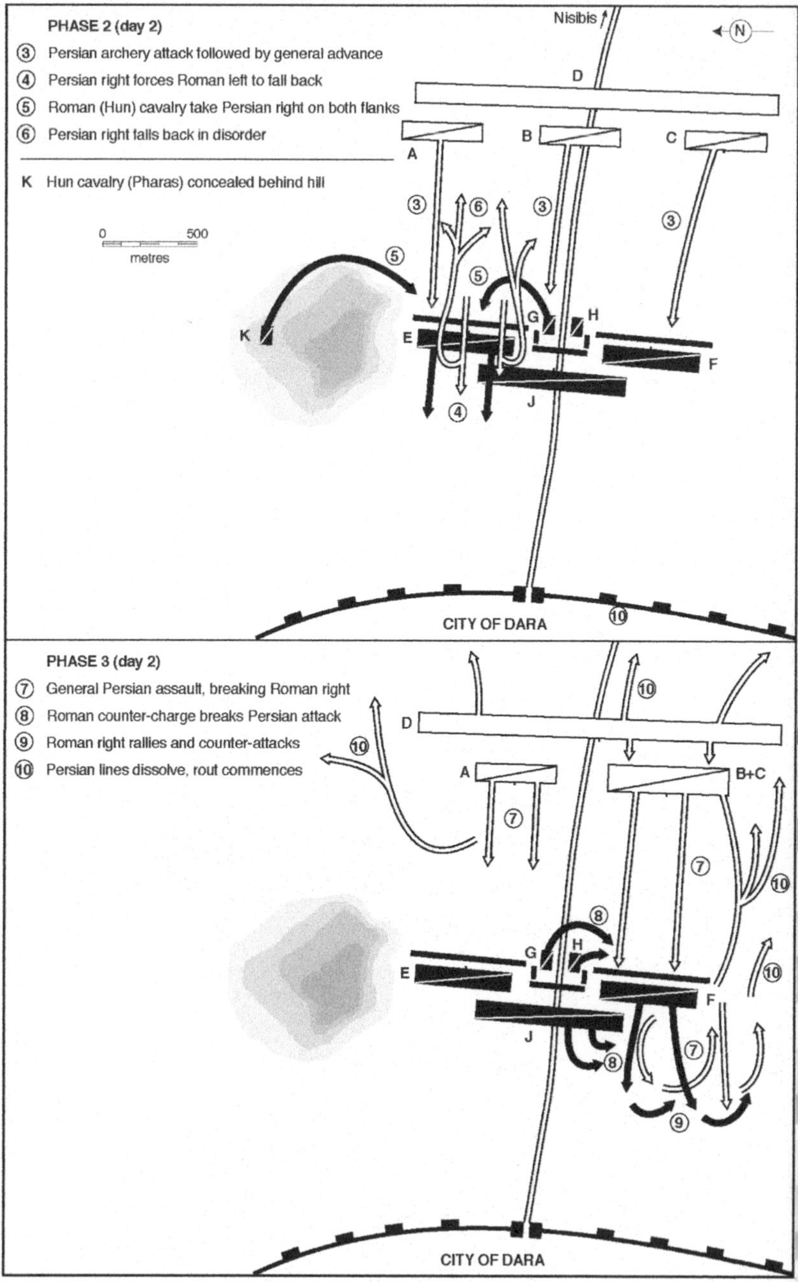

39 Plan of the battle of Dara 530, day 2.

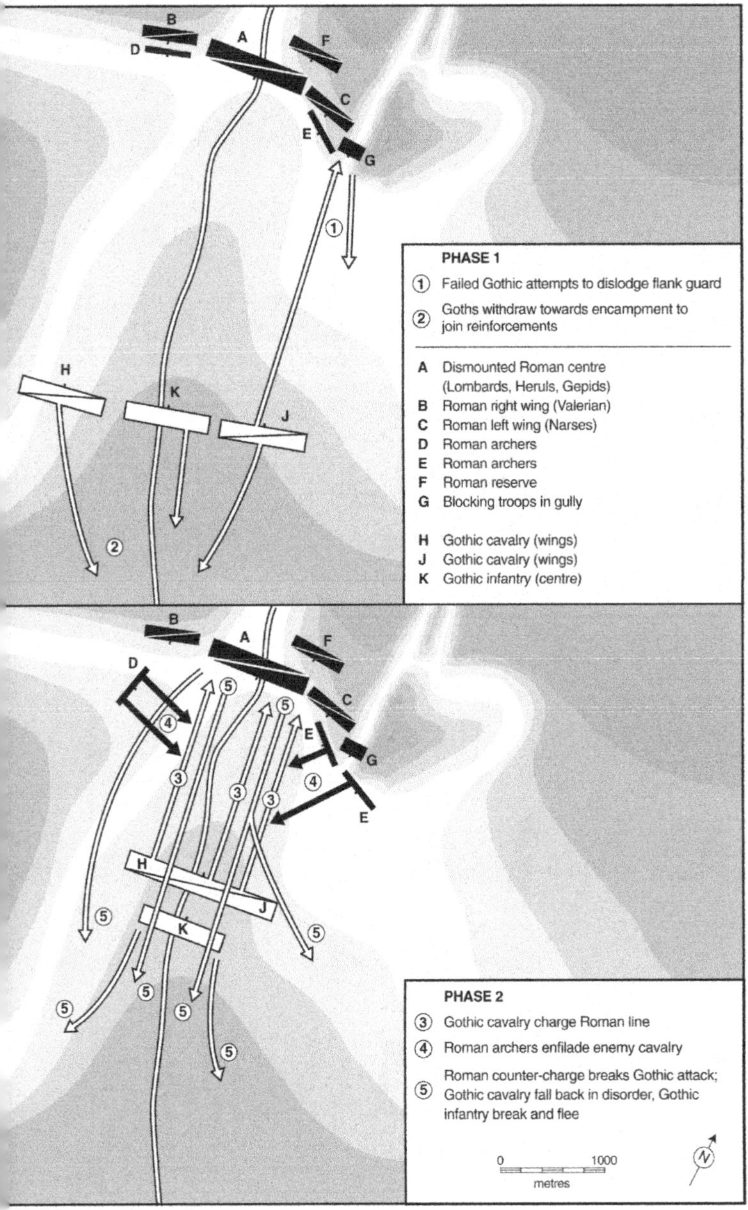

40 Plan of the battle of Tadinae.

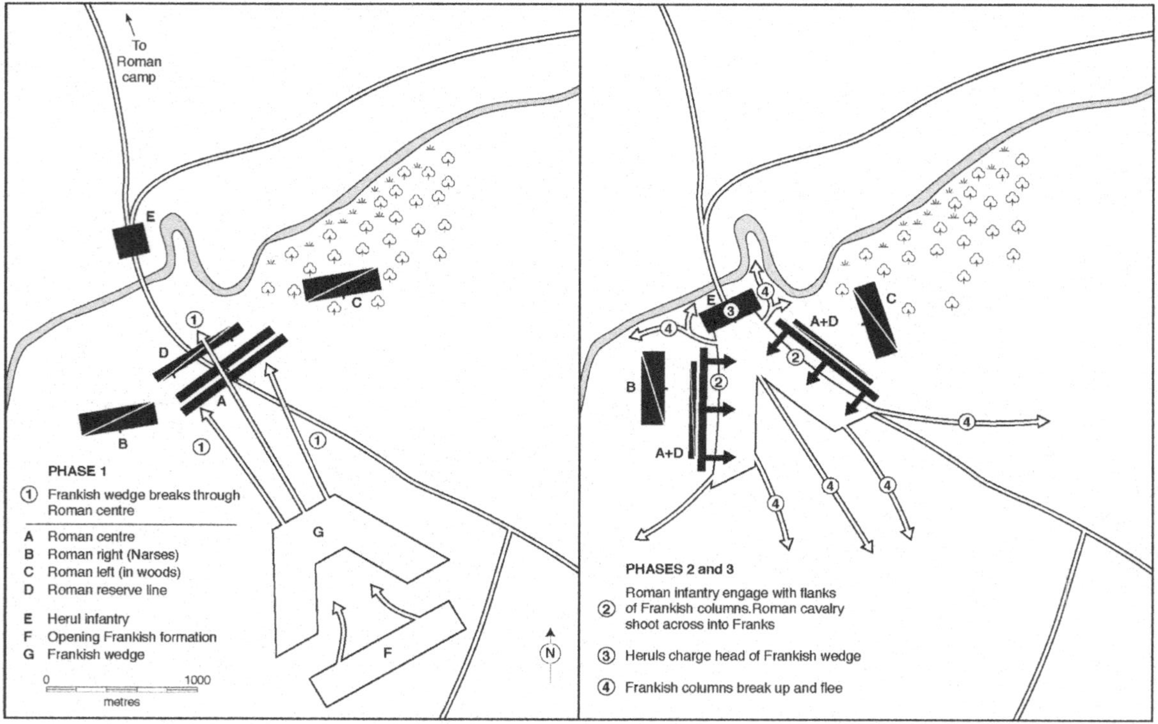

41 Plan of the battle of Casilinus.

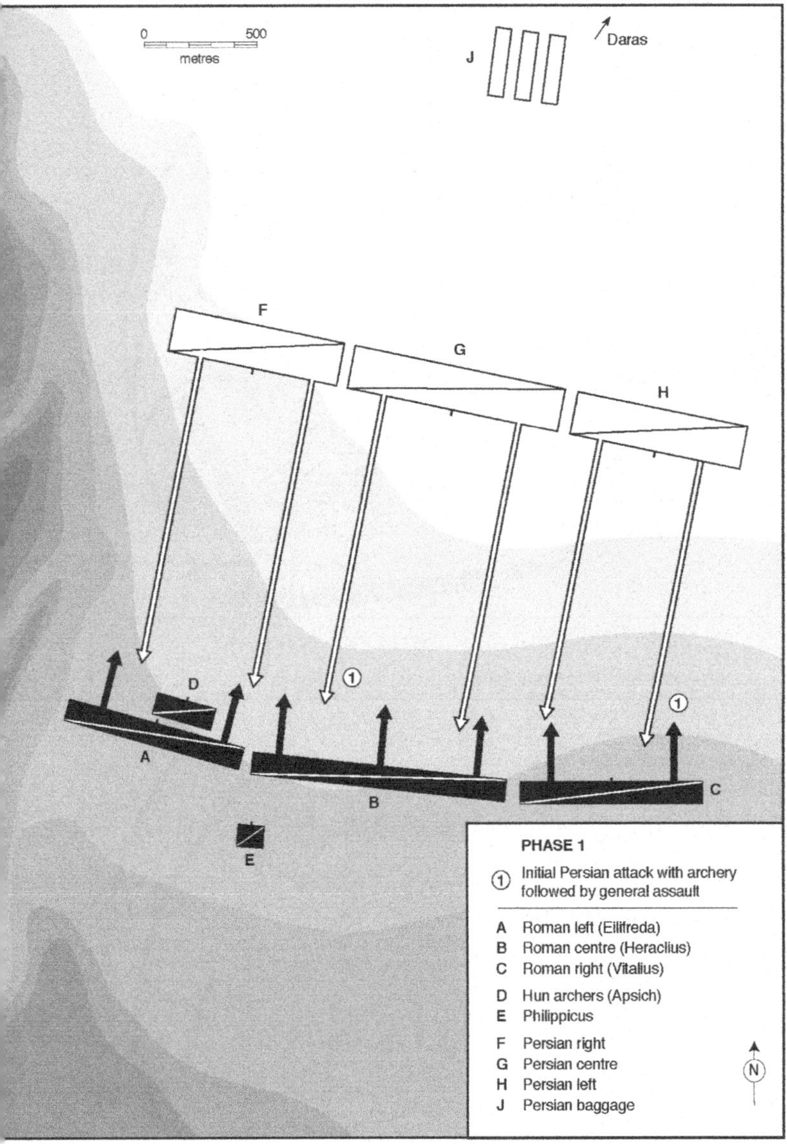

42 Plan of the battle of Solachon, phase 1.

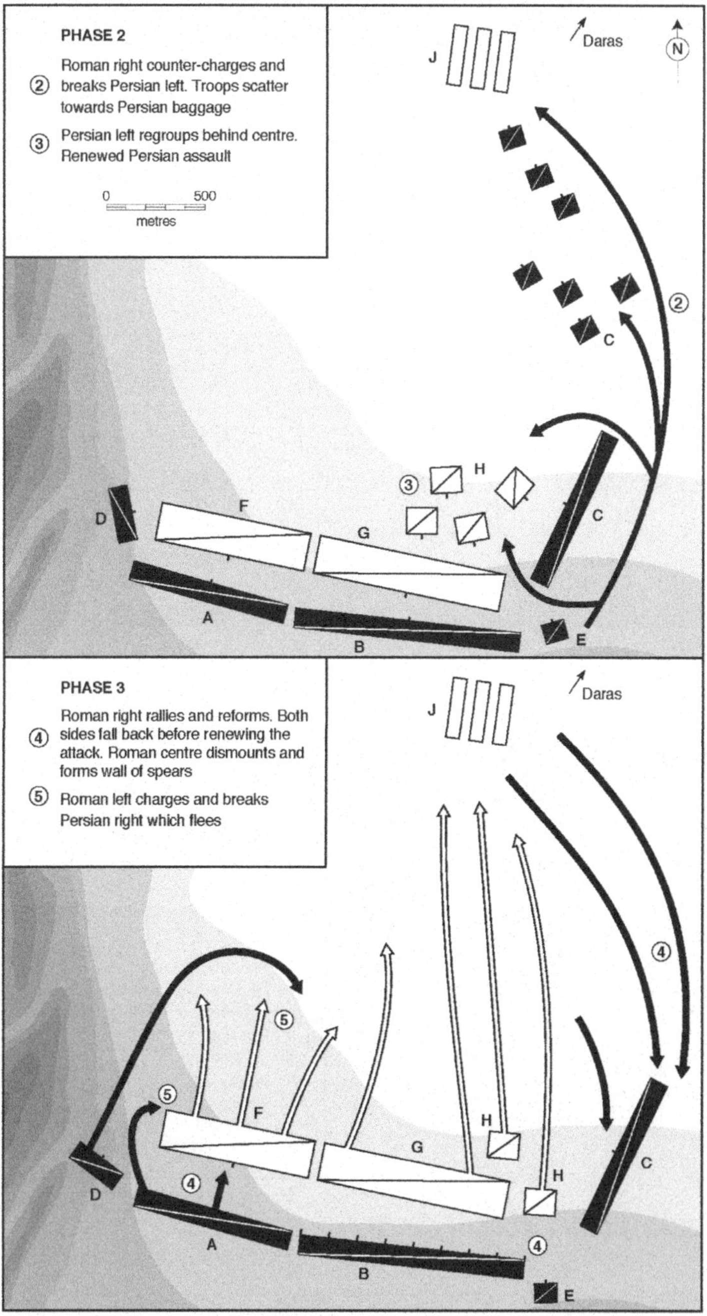

43 Plan of the battle of Solachon, phases 2 & 3.

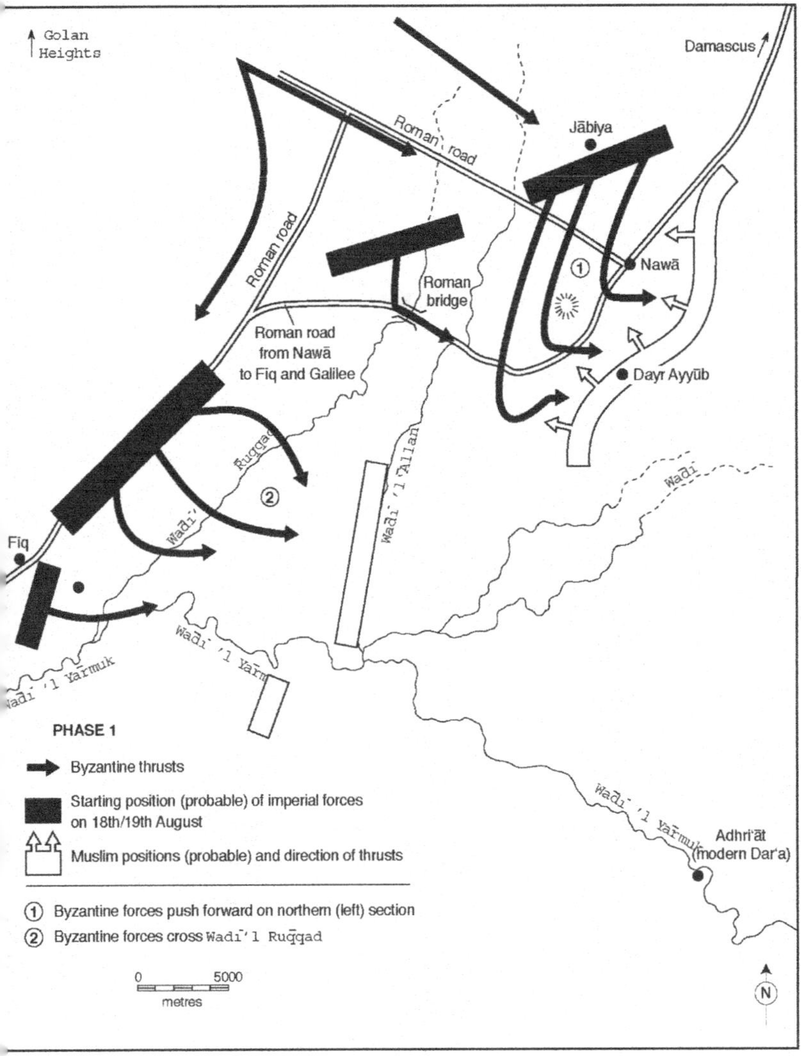

44 Plan of the battle of Jabiya-Gabitha, phase 1.

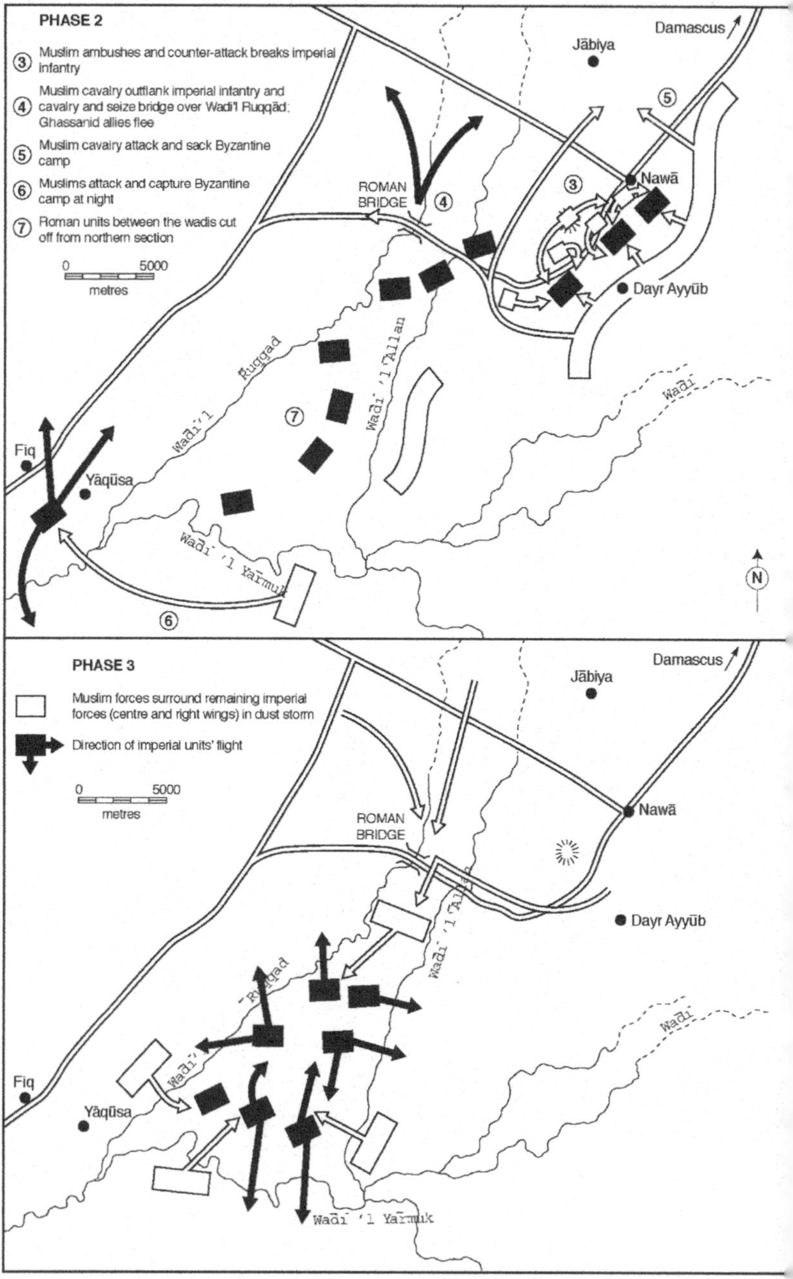

45 Plan of the battle of Jabiya-Gabitha, phases 2 & 3.

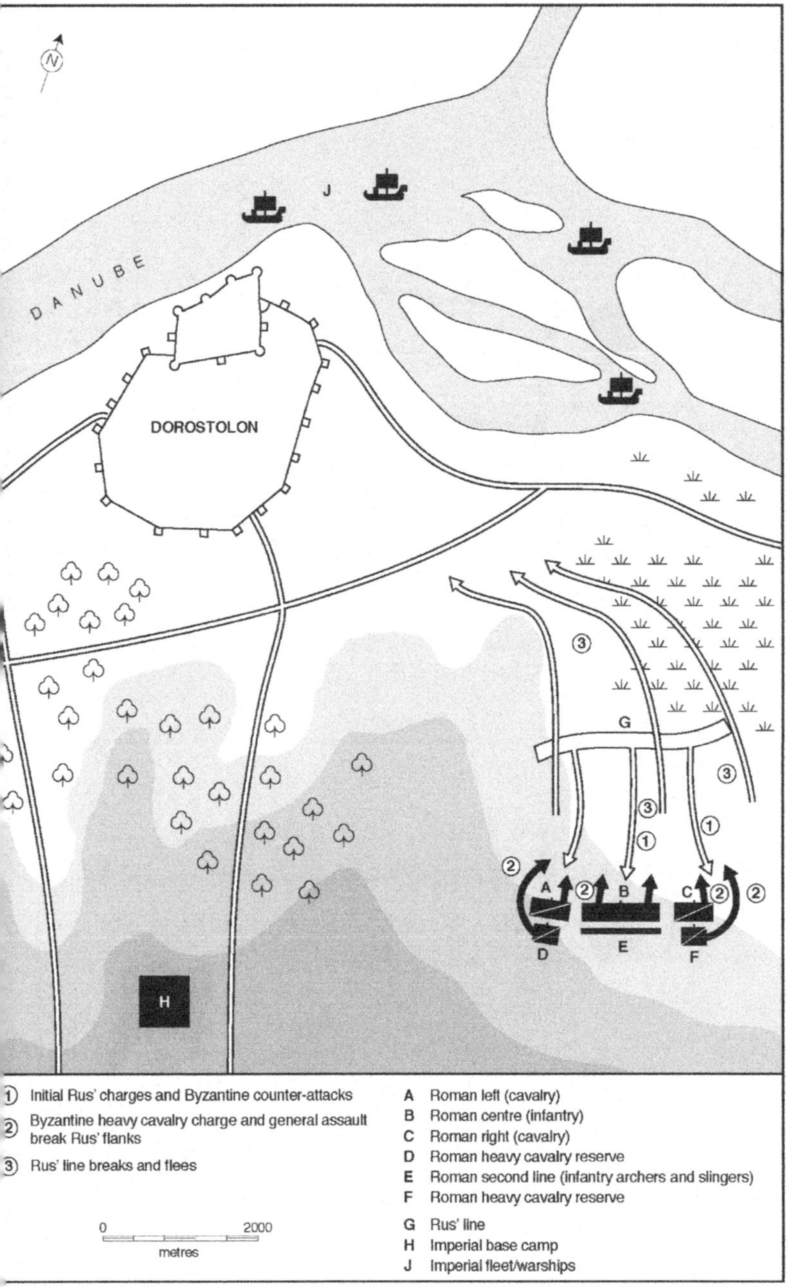

46 Plan of the battle of Dorostolon.

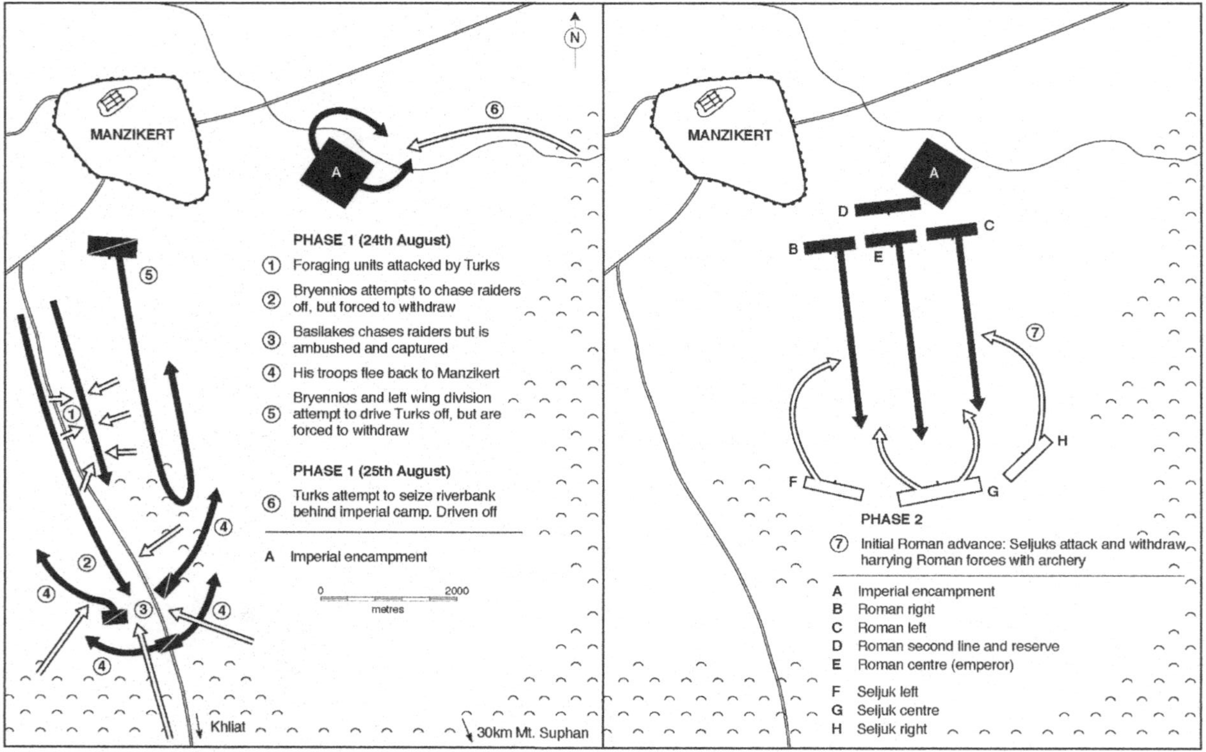

47 Plan of the battle of Manzikert, phases 1 & 2

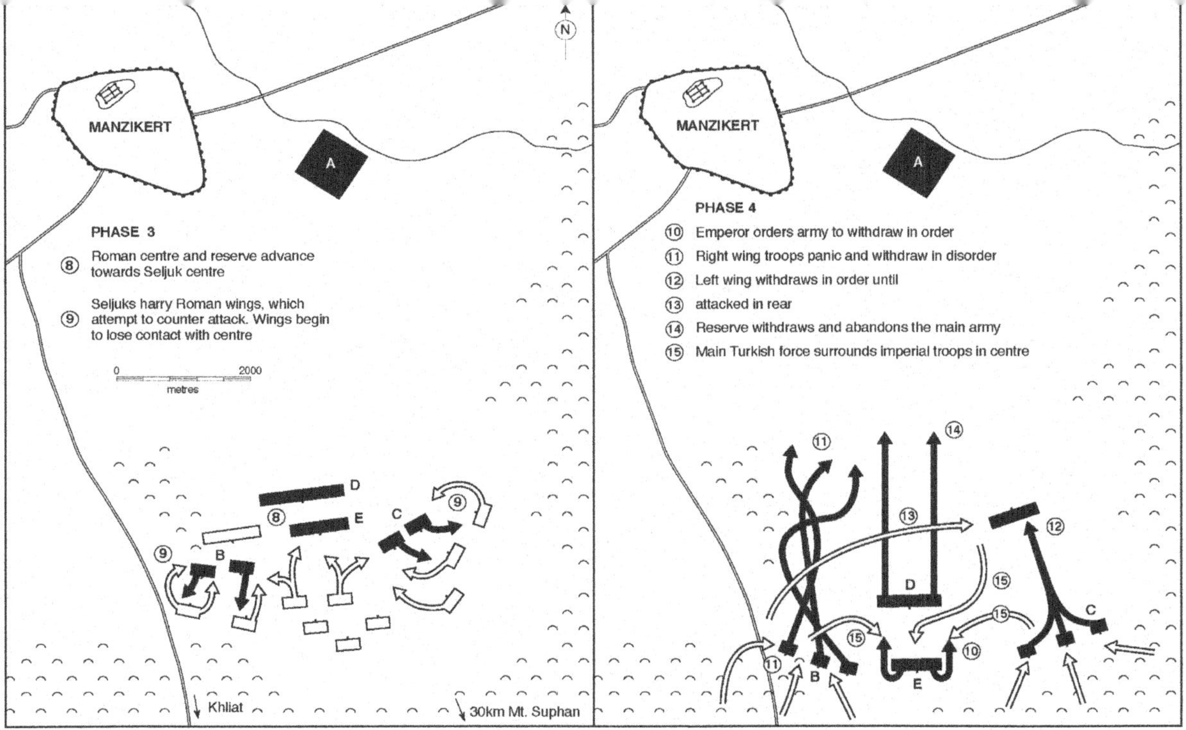

48 Plan of the battle of Manzikert, phases 3 & 4.

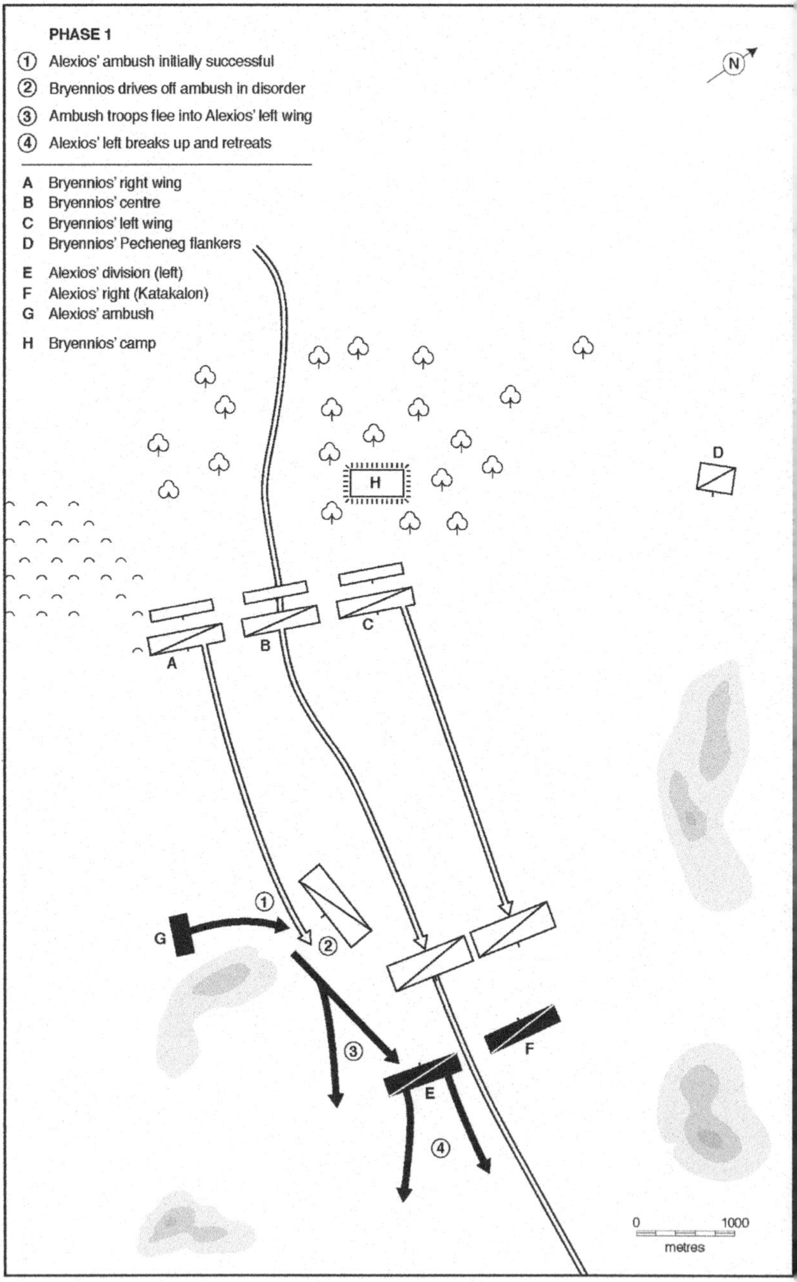

49 Plan of the battle of Kalavryai, phase 1.

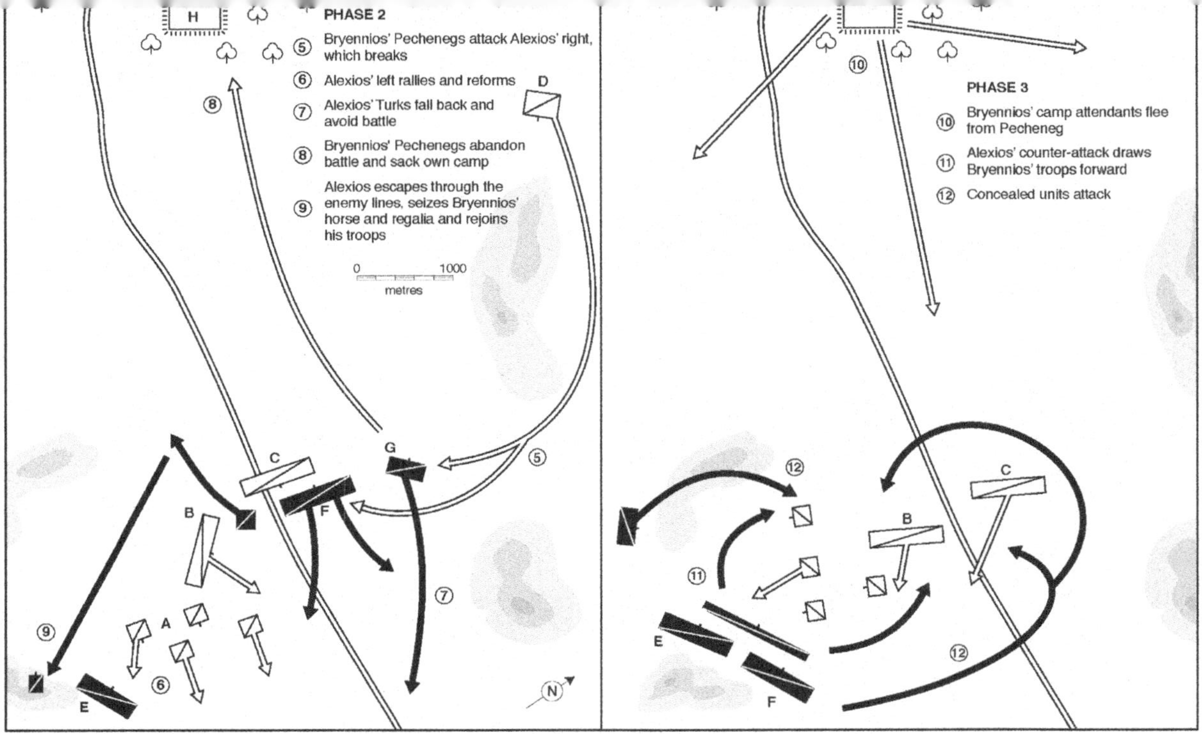

50 Plan of the battle of Kalavryai, phases 2 & 3.

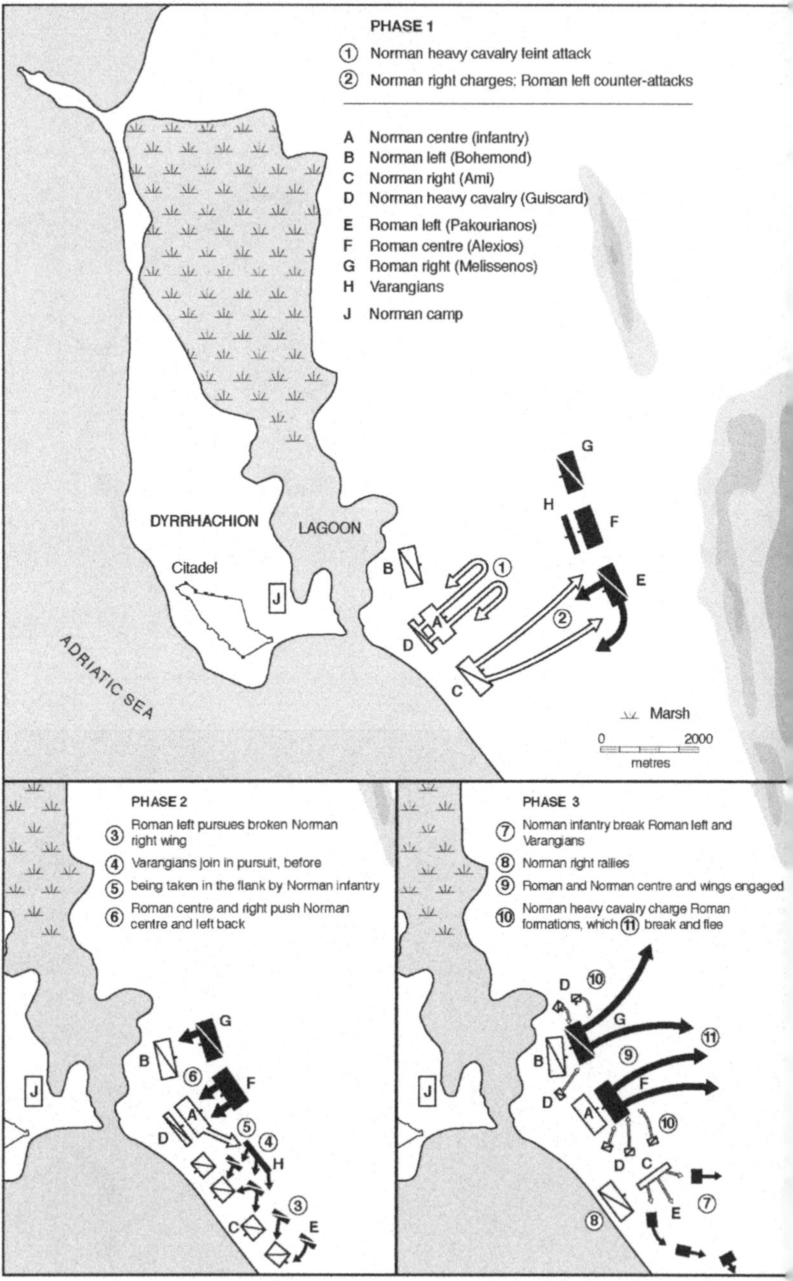

51 Plan of the battle of Dyrrachion

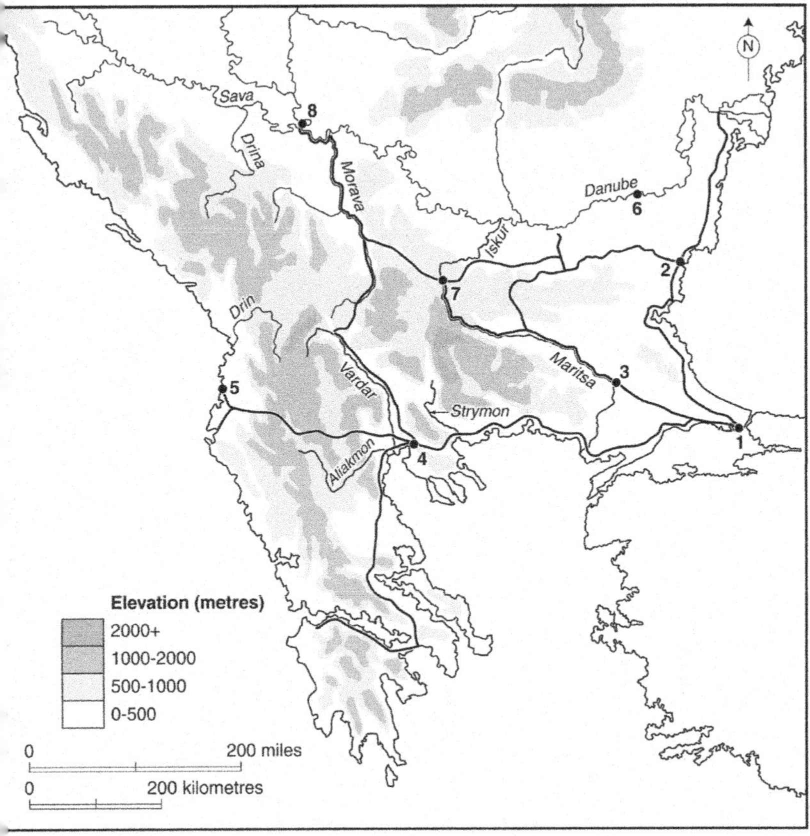

1 – Constantinople; 2 – Varna; 3 – Adrianople; 4 – Thessaloniki; 5 – Dyrrachium (Dürreš); 6 – Dorostolum; 7 – Serdica (Sofia); 8 – Singidunum (Belgrade)

Map 1: The Balkans

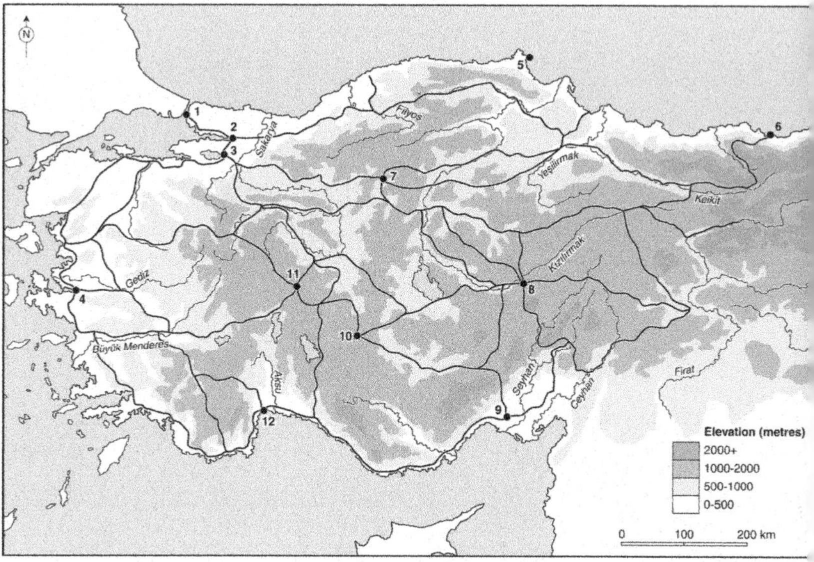

	Places	Modern river names	Byzantine river names
1	*Chalcedon*	*Sakarya*	*Sangarios*
2	*Nikomedeia*	*Filyos*	*Billaios*
3	*Nicaea*	*Yeşilirmak*	*Iris*
4	*Smyrna*	*Kelkit*	*Lykos*
5	*Sinope*	*Kızılırmak*	*Halys*
6	*Trebizond*	*Gediz*	*Hermos*
7	*Ankyra*	*Büyük Menderes*	*Maiandros (Maeander)*
8	*Caesarea*	*Aksu*	*Eurymedon*
9	*Tarsos*	*Seyhan*	*Saros*
10	*Ikonion*	*Ceyhan*	*Pyramos*
11	*Akroinon*	*Firat*	*Euphrates*
12	*Attaleia*		

Map 2: Asia Minor.

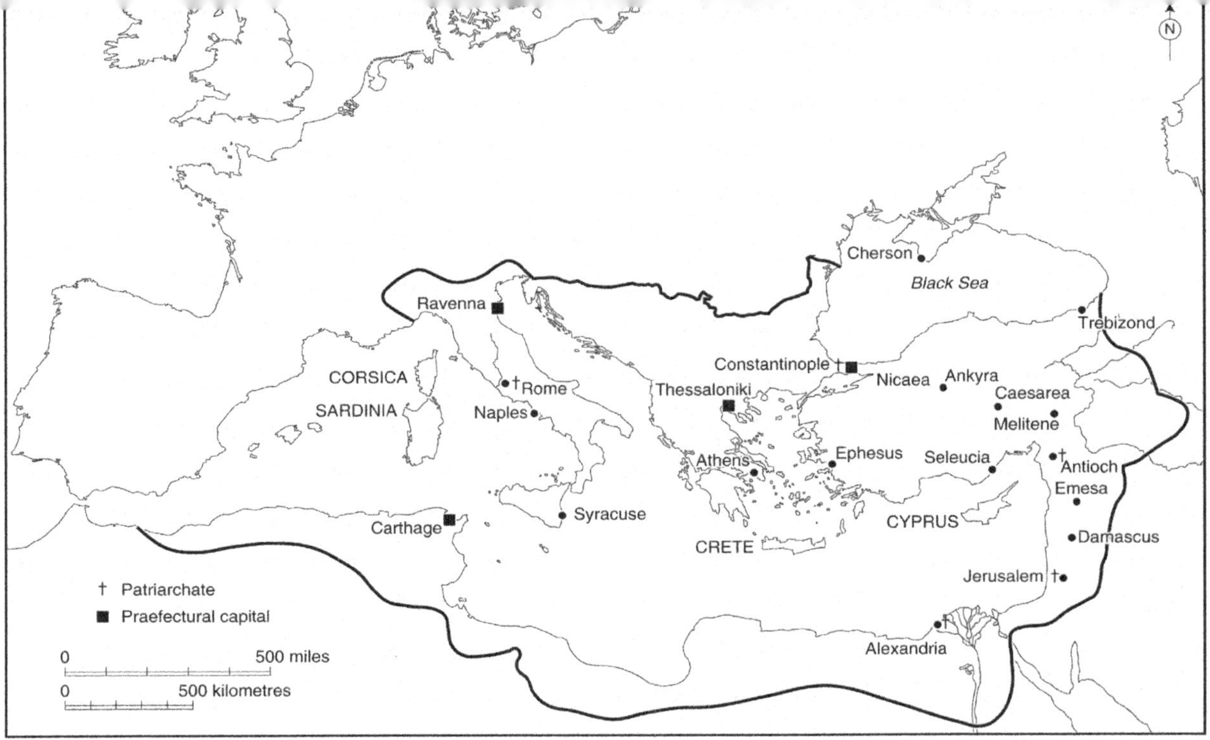

Map 3: The eastern Roman Empire in AD 565.

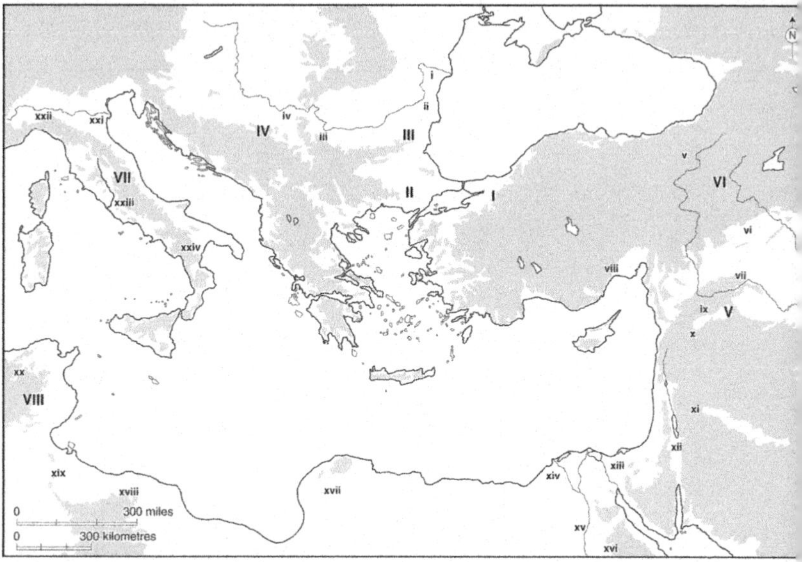

Field armies (comitatenses) under the Masters of Soldiers (magistri militum):

I	*Magister militum praesentalis I*
II	*Magister militum praesentalis II*
III	*Magister militum per Thracias*
IV	*Magister militum per Illyricum*
V	*Magister militum per Orientem*
VI	*Magister militum per Armeniam*
VII	*Magister militum per Italiam (Exarchus Italiae)*
VIII	*Magister militum per Africam (Exarchus Africae)*

Frontier or garrison forces (limitanei):

i	*Scythia*	*ix*	*Syria*	*xvii*	*Libya*
ii	*Moesia II*	*x*	*Phoenice*	*xviii*	*Tripolitania*
iii	*Dacia*	*xi*	*Arabia*	*xix*	*Byzacena*
iv	*Moesia I*	*xii*	*Palaestina*	*xx*	*Numidia*
v	*Armenia*	*xiii*	*Augustamnica*	*xxi*	*Ravenna*
vi	*Mesopotamia*	*xiv*	*Aegyptus*	*xxii*	*Liguria*
vii	*Osrhoene*	*xv*	*Arcadia*	*xxiii*	*Roma*
viii	*Isauria*	*xvi*	*Thebais*	*xxiv*	*Neapolis*

Map 4: Distribution of field armies and garrisons in the mid-sixth century.

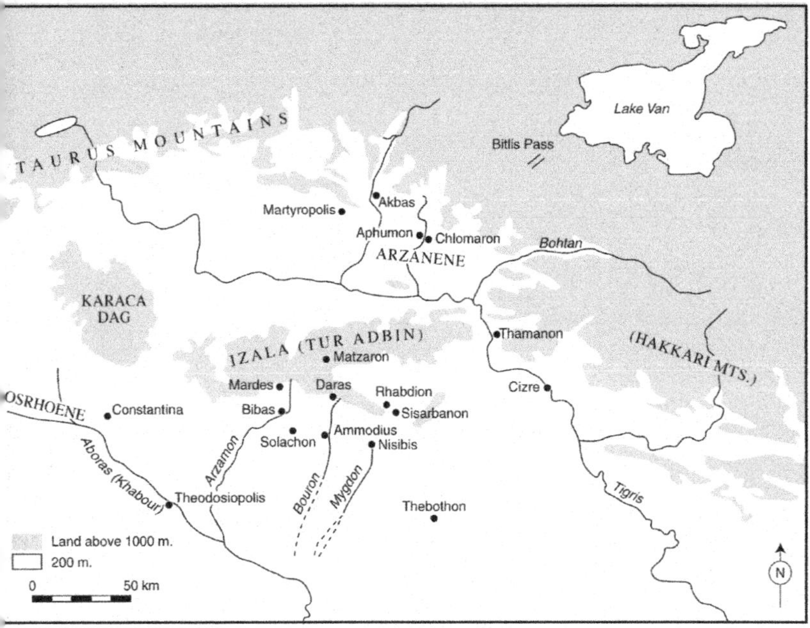

Map 5: The eastern frontier in northern Iraq/Mesopotamia in the sixth century.

Map 6: Byzantine Italy c.550.

Map 7: Palestine and southern Syria c.636 AD (after Kaegi, *Byzantium and the Islamic Conquests*, p.4

Map 8: The early *themata* and empire after the Islamic conquests.

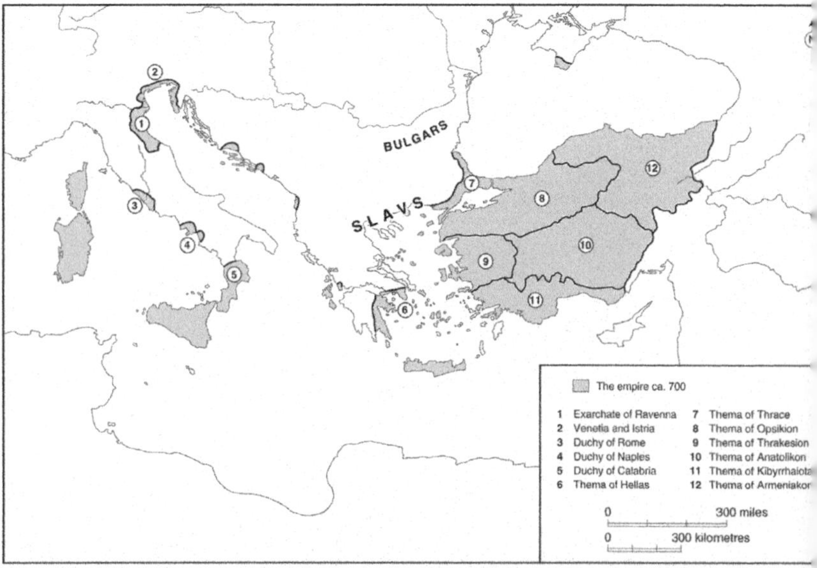

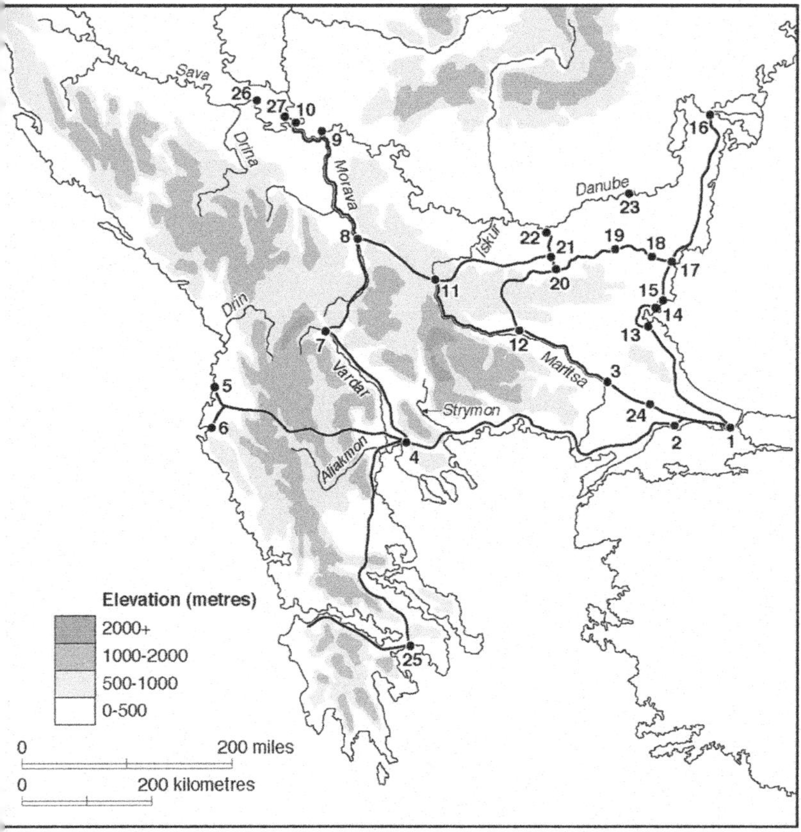

1	*Constantinople*	10	*Singidunum (Belgrade)*	19	*Pliska*
2	*Heracleia*	11	*Serdica (Sofia)*	20	*Trnovo*
3	*Adrianople*	12	*Philippoupolis*	21	*Nicopolis*
4	*Thessaloniki*	13	*Develtus*	22	*Novae*
5	*Dyrrachium (Dürreš)*	14	*Anchialus*	23	*Dorostolum*
6	*Avlona*	15	*Mesembria*	24	*Arcadioupolis*
7	*Skopje*	16	*Noviodunum*	25	*Corinth*
8	*Naissus (Nis)*	17	*Varna*	26	*Sirmium*
9	*Viminacium*	18	*Marcianoupolis*	27	*Semlin*

Map 9: The Balkans in the eighth to eleventh centuries.

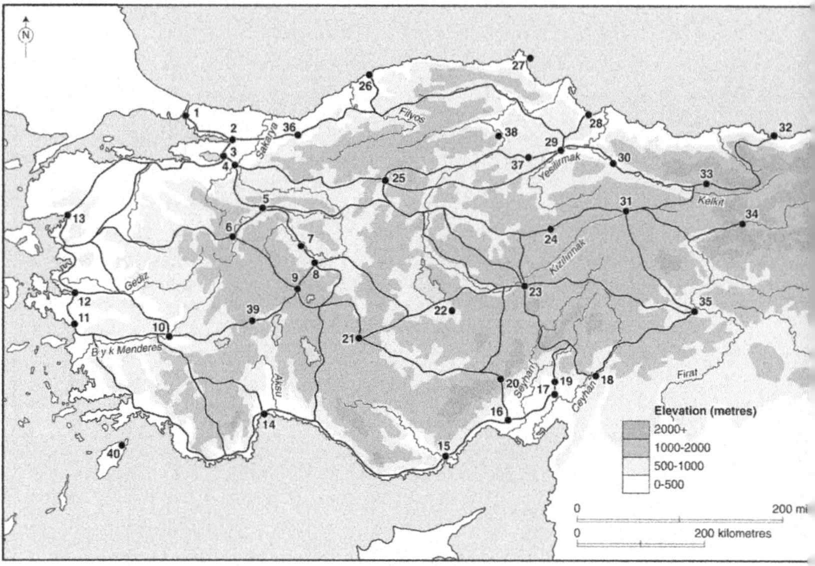

1	*Chalkedon*	*15*	*Seleukeia*	*29*	*Amaseia*
2	*Nikomedeia*	*16*	*Tarsos*	*30*	*Dazimon*
3	*Nikaia*	*17*	*Anazarbos*	*31*	*Sebasteia*
4	*Malagina*	*18*	*Germanikeia*	*32*	*Trapezous*
5	*Dorylaion*	*19*	*Sision*	*33*	*Koloneia*
6	*Kotyaion*	*20*	*Podandos*	*34*	*Kamacha*
7	*Kaborkion*	*21*	*Ikonion*	*35*	*Melitene*
8	*Amorion*	*22*	*Koron*	*36*	*Kaludioupolis*
9	*Akroinon*	*23*	*Kaisareia*	*37*	*Euchaita*
10	*Chonai*	*24*	*Charsianon*	*38*	*Gangra*
11	*Ephesos*	*25*	*Ankyra*	*39*	*Sozopolis*
12	*Smyrna*	*26*	*Amastris*	*40*	*Rhodos*
13	*Adramyttion*	*27*	*Sinope*		
14	*Attaleia*	*28*	*Amisos*		

Map 10: Asia Minor in the eighth to tenth centuries. River names as given in Map 2

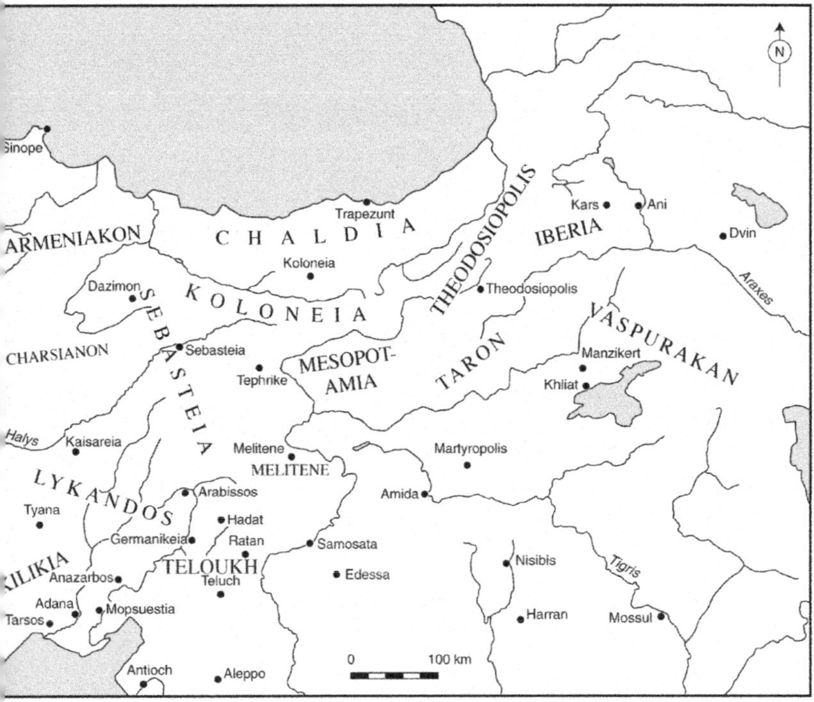

Map 11: Eastern Asia Minor in the eleventh century.

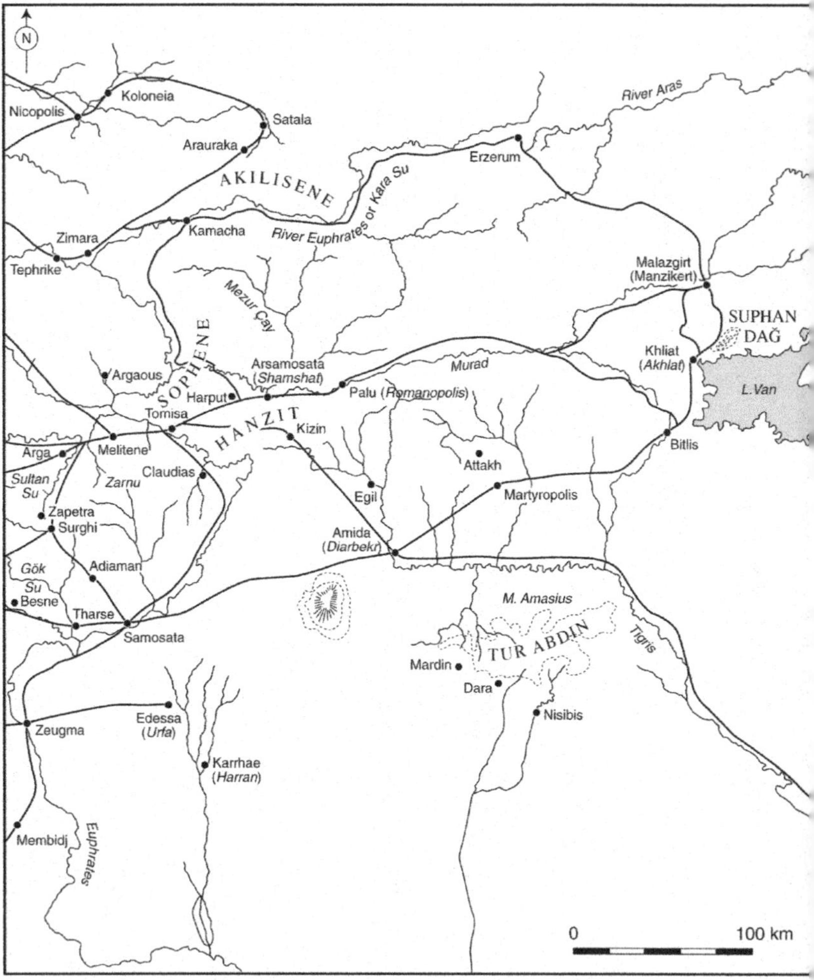

Map 12: Eastern Asia Minor in the eleventh century – detail.

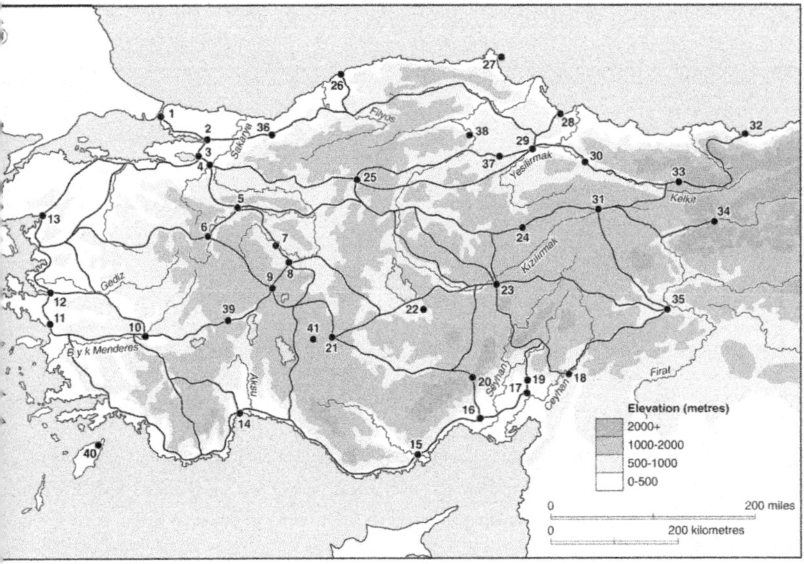

1 *Chalkedon*
2 *Nikomedeia*
3 *Nikaia*
4 *Malagina*
5 *Dorylaion*
6 *Kotyaion*
7 *Kaborkion*
8 *Amorion*
9 *Akroinon*
10 *Chonai*
11 *Ephesos*
12 *Smyrna*
13 *Adramyttion*
14 *Attaleia*
15 *Seleukeia*
16 *Tarsos*
17 *Anazarbos*
18 *Germanikeia*
19 *Sision*
20 *Podandos*
21 *Ikonion*
22 *Koron*
23 *Kaisareia*
24 *Charsianon*
25 *Ankyra*
26 *Amastris*
27 *Sinope*
28 *Amisos*
29 *Amaseia*
30 *Dazimon*
31 *Sebasteia*
32 *Trapezous*
33 *Koloneia*
34 *Kamacha*
35 *Melitene*
36 *Kaludioupolis*
37 *Euchaita*
38 *Gangra*
39 *Sozopolis*
40 *Rhodos*
41 *Myriokephalon*

Map 13: Asia Minor in the twelfth century. River names as given in Map 2.

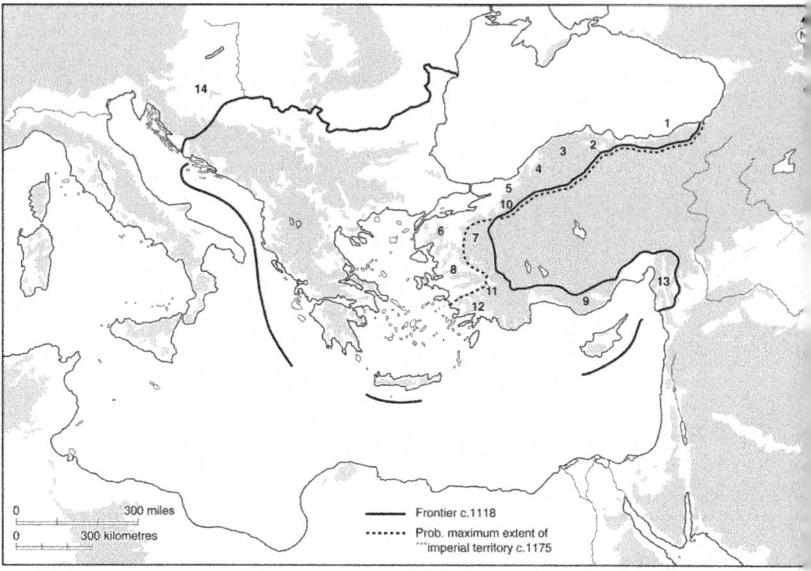

1 *Trapezous/Chaldia*
2 *Oinaion/Sinope*
3 *Paphlagonia*
4 *Boukellarion*
5 *Optimaton/Mesothynia*
6 *Opsikion*
7 *Achyraous/Neokastra*
8 *Thrakesion*
9 *Attaleia/Seleukeia*
10 *Malagina*
11 *Laodikeia/Maeander*
12 *Mylasa/Melanoudion*
13 *Principality of Antioch*
14 *Serbia/Rascia (vassal status)*

Map 14: The Byzantine empire c.1100–1180.

which flows westwards down to the Euphrates. Sa'if's force was, therefore, safe from attack for a while. Here the Arab cavalry ravaged the surrounding countryside, carrying off much booty and many captives. The next day – Sunday 11 May – Sa'if himself sent a small raiding force to scout ahead as far as the Arsanias, following himself once it had been deemed safe, and encamped in a small village at the base of the hill on which the provincial capital of Harput was situated – the absence of most of the local forces gave him essentially a free hand in the region. The area was thoroughly ravaged, before he set forth again marching this time to the north-west, where he bridged the river with materials he had carried with him (dismantled rafts and boats) and, having sent across a small cavalry vanguard in advance to secure the bridgehead, crossed with his main army three days later (on Thursday 15 May), destroying the governor's residence. This was an entirely unexpected action on Sa'if's part, and as well as burning the residence of the governor other undefended settlements were also destroyed. The whole area was thoroughly ravaged and an enormous booty in people, livestock and materials was collected.

Having completed his action on the northern bank of the river, Sa'if withdrew to his base and then marched south, pillaging as he went, until he reached the important fortress of Dadima, to which he lay siege. The garrison was quite unprepared for an attack, and would have surrendered had Sa'if not received news at this point of the occupation of the passes through which he was expected to retire by the returning Roman forces. Rather than head for the obvious exits, however, on Friday 23 May he marched south east and encamped not far from Arsamosata, whence he made his way not to the pass of Ergani, by which he had entered Anzitene, but to the pass of Baq'saya, to the south of Arsamosata and east of the Ergani pass. Here he found a small eastern Roman force blocking his way and, in a fierce battle late on Saturday 24 May, he managed to drive it off with considerable loss, seizing its baggage train and killing several prominent leaders. By the evening of Sunday (25 May) he was back in Amida, where he received, of course, a hero's welcome. In three weeks of campaigning he had penetrated deeply into the Byzantine frontier region, caused a great deal of damage and dislocation to the local population and the military command, totally outmanoeuvred his enemy, outwitted them in a short, sharp field action, and returned safely laden with booty. The raid is a classic of its kind, and also illustrates the problems faced by eastern Roman commanders when they failed to follow the strategy of shadowing warfare enunciated in the treatise we have discussed above and left their own territories inadequately protected. And although there can be little doubt that Sa'if was by far one of the most outstanding of the Muslim emirs with whom the Byzantines had to contend in the region, the account of this raid provides an excellent insight into the character of the warfare along the eastern frontier of the Roman world from the eighth until the tenth century.

Sa'if was not always so successful, however, and indeed there is enough evidence to suggest that the Byzantine tactics – permitting the enemy force to enter Roman territory but blocking their exits – proved sufficiently successful to deter all but the bravest raiders. In 950, for example, he had mounted a similar large-scale raid with a substantial force – supposedly some 30,000, although this may be exaggerated. Leaving Aleppo in the spring he had pushed up through the Taurus, marched north to cross the Halys, and ravaged the area before meeting and defeating a smaller Byzantine force. On his return, however, the Roman forces had correctly assessed which defiles he would use and, permitting the vanguard to pass their pickets unopposed, had then blocked the pass and fallen on the main body and the rearguard. The raiders panicked and fled, suffering substantial casualties, the booty was recovered more-or-less in its entirety and Sa'if, having been abandoned by all but a few of his men, barely escaped with his life. Similar tactics were employed again in both 958 and 960, when Sa'if found his way blocked and suffered a substantial and, on the last occasion, nearly fatal defeat, with the loss of all the booty and his own baggage train.

Offensive Strategy and Tactical Change

As a result of the increasingly aggressive warfare carried on by the empire from the second quarter of the tenth century, particularly on the eastern front, the need to recruit more professional soldiers, and the need to operate effectively on campaigns which demanded more than the seasonally available forces provided by the traditional thematic armies, a number of important changes appeared in the tactical structure and in the arms and armour of Byzantine troops. A number of important technical treatises on strategy and tactics were written in the middle and later tenth century, and the narrative accounts of contemporaries, both Byzantines and Arabs, corroborate much of what they say. The changes can be enumerated briefly as follows: (1) the revival of a corps of disciplined, effective heavy infantry, able to stand firm in the line of battle, confront enemy infantry and cavalry, support their own cavalry, march long distances and function as garrison troops away from their home territory on a permanent basis; (2) the introduction of a corps of heavy cavalry armed with lances and maces, which could operate effectively alongside infantry, adding weight to the Byzantine attack and thus substantially enhancing the aggressive power of the Byzantine cavalry; (3) the development of field tactics in which these arms operate in a complementary way, offering the commanding officer a flexible yet hard-hitting force which could respond appropriately to a range of different situations.

Evidence for these changes comes partly from the contemporary sources, especially the military handbooks already referred to, but also from the startling successes marked up by Byzantine armies in the process of reconquest and expansion from the 950s onwards. In a tract known as the 'Recapitulation of Tactics', a new formation of infantry soldiers is described, consisting of troops wielding thick-stocked, long-necked javelins or pikes, probably similar in form to the Roman legionary *pilum*. Their task was to confront and beat back enemy heavy cavalry attacks. According to the 'Recapitulation' there should have been about 300 soldiers equipped in this manner, arrayed in the intervals between the infantry units making up the main battle line. They were deployed in either line or wedge formation to break up an enemy attack. In a treatise known as the 'Military Precepts' compiled some twenty years later, the tactic had evolved further, so that there were in each major infantry unit of 1,000 men 100 soldiers so equipped, integrated with 400 ordinary spearmen, 300 archers and 200 light infantry (with slings and javelins). Their task remained unchanged.

This important change in the role of infantry was reflected in the changed political and military situation of the tenth century. Whereas the sixth-century *Strategikon* presents its sections on infantry drill and formations after those (more detailed) dealing with cavalry, the tenth-century texts give infantry formations equal or even preferential treatment. Infantry had now become a key element of the army both numerically and tactically, outnumbering cavalry by 2:1 or more, in contrast to the normal situation in the preceding centuries. Contemporaries note the greatly improved discipline and training which such troops displayed. The importance of infantry is demonstrated in the fact that a special commander for the infantry division in each army was appointed, the hoplitarch (*hoplitarches*), in charge of training, discipline and fighting skill. The new tactics were embodied in a new formation, in which infantry and cavalry worked together, essentially a hollow square or rectangle, depending on the terrain, designed to cope with encircling movements from hostile cavalry, as a refuge for Byzantine mounted units when forced to retreat, and as a means of strengthening infantry cohesiveness and morale.

These new formations mark a real change in the role of infantry, no longer drawn up in a deep line with only a limited offensive role, but actively integrated into the offensive heavy cavalry tactics of the period. Infantry units now represented a sort of mobile marching-camp, with a traditionally rather unreliable force given new strength as a defensive field formation on the one hand, to provide security in defence and on the march, a mobile base and refuge for lighter troops and cavalry, and on the other as a formation which could be transformed into a solid attacking formation at a few simple commands. One important aspect of this change was a focus on the recruitment of good infantry from warlike peoples within the empire, especially Armenians. The demand for uniformity in tactical function and therefore equipment and weaponry meant that the Byzantine infantry of this period were more like their classical Roman predecessors than anything in the intervening period.

The cavalry also evolved at this time. New formations of 'super heavy' cavalry appear, called *klibanophoroi*, heavy cavalry troopers armed from head to foot in lamellar, mail and quilting, whose horse was likewise protected – face, neck, flanks and forequarters were all to be covered with armour to prevent enemy missiles and blows from injuring the cavalryman's mount. Very few in number (because they were so expensive to maintain) these became the elite strike force within each field army. Drawn up in a broad-nosed wedge, their primary function was to smash through the enemy heavy cavalry or infantry line, disrupt his formation, and open up the enemy battle order to allow the supporting horse to turn the enemy's flanks. The 'Military Precepts' mentions a formation of just over 500 such troops for a large wedge, two-thirds of whom would be real *klibanarioi/kataphraktoi*, the rest equipped as lightly armed mounted archers.

Both Byzantine and Arab writers of the time comment on the impressive effects of this formation on their foes. One Arab writer notes that the horse-armour of the heavy cavalry mounts made them appear to be advancing without legs. Some of these changes were probably due to the general, later emperor, Nikephoros Phokas, who became commander-in-chief in the East in the 950s, and immediately embarked upon a programme of training and drilling the soldiers in an attempt to re-establish good discipline, fighting spirit and good battlefield skills. His success is evident in the effective warfare waged by Byzantine forces over the following fifty years or more.

A Feigned Retreat in 970

In the autumn of the year 965, shortly after the conquest by Byzantine armies of the islands of Crete and Cyprus, as well as the destruction of the Islamic power in Cilicia and its incorporation into the empire, Bulgarian envoys arrived at the court of the emperor Nikephoros II Phokas. Their purpose was to request the payment of the 'tribute' (or 'subsidy' from the imperial perspective) paid by Constantinople to the Bulgar Tsar as part of the guarantee for the long-lasting peace which had been established after the death of Tsar Symeon in 927. But the situation of the empire had changed radically in the course of the preceding half century, and rather than pay, the emperor Nikephoros, outraged by the presumptive demand of the Bulgarian ruler, had the envoys beaten and sent home in disgrace. He despatched a small force to demolish a number of Bulgarian frontier posts, and then called in his allies to the north, the Kievan Rus', to attack the Bulgars in the rear.

The steppe region stretching from the plain of Hungary eastwards through south Russia and north of the Caspian was the home of many nomadic peoples, mostly of Turkic stock. It was always a key principle of Byzantine diplomacy to keep these peoples well disposed towards the empire. Following the collapse of the Avar empire in the 630s, Constantinople had been able to establish good relations with the Chazars whose Khans, although converting to Judaism, remained a faithful ally of most Byzantine emperors. Chazar Khans often took up Byzantine invitations to attack the Bulgars from the North, for example, when war broke out in this region. And they served also to keep the imperial court informed of developments further east. The Chazar empire contracted during the later ninth century, as various peoples to the east were set in motion by the expansion of the Turkic Pechenegs. These newcomers clashed with both the Chazars and the Magyars, establishing themselves in the steppe region between the Danube and Don. Their value to the empire as a check on both the Rus' and the Magyars was obvious, particularly in the wars of the later tenth century, but they were a dangerous and frequently unreliable ally. The Magyars (Hungarians) had been established to the north-west and west of the Chazars since the middle of the ninth century, settling in what is now Hungary by about 900 AD. Both Chazars and Magyars served as mercenaries in Byzantine armies, particularly against the Bulgars, although the establishment by the later tenth century of a christianized Hungarian kingdom on the central Danube posed a potential challenge to Byzantine power in the region, which became especially acute during later centuries. But the growing power of the Kiev Rus' during the later ninth and tenth centuries introduced important changes to this situation and to Byzantine diplomacy.

The Rus' were the product of an amalgamation of Scandinavian settlers and indigenous, largely Slavic peoples, based along the rivers of central and western Russia. Their dominance over the neighbouring steppe and forest peoples had made them an important political power. By the middle of the ninth century their longships were entering the Black Sea, and by the early tenth century they had established trading agreements – not without some serious fighting between the two parties – with the empire. An alliance had been established from the middle of the tenth century; and when Nikephoros II asked for their help in 966, the warlike and ambitious Prince Svyatoslav, who had already established a considerable reputation through his successful warfare with and defeat of the Chazars, was only too willing to agree. In 968 he arrived on the Danube and easily defeated the Bulgarian forces sent against him. In 969 he had to return to Kiev to repulse an attack from the Pechenegs, but he returned later in the year and quickly occupied most of northern and eastern Bulgaria, deposing the Tsar, Boris II, and incorporating Bulgaria into his own domain. (See Map 9)

This was not part of the emperor's original plan at all. Nikephoros tried in vain to establish an alliance with the Bulgars, but late in 969 he was assassinated, leaving his successor, John I Tzimiskes, with the difficult task of removing this potentially far more dangerous foe. To add to his problems, some of the Bulgar nobility now saw a chance to recover their independence of the Byzantine state and its culture by working with the Rus'. Svyatoslav sent the new emperor an ultimatum to evacuate all the European provinces and confine the empire to Asia alone. Then, in the spring of 970 a large Rus' force invaded Thrace, sacking the fortress of Philippoupolis (mod. Plovdiv) and moving on down the road to Constantinople. John was forced to take action.

The emperor was not able to march immediately against the Rus', for the majority of the effective field units were still in the east, where they had been campaigning in the region of Antioch and beyond, consolidating Roman gains after the recent fall of that city to the forces of Nikephoros II. In response, however, John appointed Bardas Skleros, together with the *patrikios* Peter, both experienced commanders, to take command of a small force and reconnoitre the enemy dispositions in the occupied territories. Their mission was, in addition, to exercise the troops and to prevent, as far as they were able, enemy raiders committing widespread damage on imperial territory. They were also to send spies, disguised in Bulgarian and Rus' costume, deep into enemy-held territory to learn as much as possible about

Svyatoslav's intentions and movements.

It was not long before the Rus' leader was informed of the imperial army's presence, and he despatched a considerable force, consisting of both Rus' and Bulgar troops as well as a powerful detachment of Pechenegs, whom he had temporarily managed to bring onto his side with the promise of booty and pillage, to drive the Romans off. Bardas immediately collected an elite force of some 10-12,000, sending one of his officers ahead to keep an eye on the enemy army and find out how many they numbered and where they had encamped. On receipt of the information that the enemy force was quite close, in the region of Arkadioupolis (mod. Luleburgaz), Bardas divided his force into three: two divisions were concealed in the rough scrub and woodlands on either side of the track leading towards the enemy position; the remaining division he led himself, launching a furious surprise attack against the Pecheneg contingent in the enemy force. Although heavily outnumbered – Bardas can have had only 2,000-3,000 men with him – he was able to draw the enemy out of their encampment and feign a gradual withdrawal. The fortunes of the battle swung back and forth, and it seemed at times that the small Byzantine force must be overwhelmed. Yet their discipline and training told, and Skleros finally ordered the pre-arranged signal to be given for the whole force to fall back. At the same time, however, the two divisions which lay in ambush prepared themselves, and as their comrades drew level with them and then past them, they too launched themselves upon the unsuspecting enemy from both flanks and the rear. Within a few minutes the Pechenegs had received such a savage mauling that they turned and fled, while their allies, the Rus' and Bulgars, who had been hastening to catch them up in their pursuit of the supposedly defeated Romans, were caught in the panic and suffered similarly heavy casualties as the rout became general. According to a contemporary, the Romans lost some 550 men and many wounded, as well as a large number of horses, which fell to the archery of the Pechenegs. The combined enemy force, however, lost very many thousands. The action won the emperor John valuable time and also provided him with essential information about the make-up, morale and fighting prowess of his enemy, information which he put to excellent use in his campaign the following year.

This brief encounter, although the sources offer few details of the order of battle of either side, gives some idea of the possibilities for a properly trained eastern Roman force, when well-led and prepared, to defeat an enemy vastly superior in numbers. There is no doubt that the troops Bardas Skleros had under his command were well-trained and disciplined, as their careful withdrawal and feigned retreat under very difficult conditions, heavily outnumbered and under constant fire from accurate enemy archery, demonstrates. The short battle admirably reflects the *esprit de corps*, training and morale of the armies of this period.

The Battles of Dorostolon 971

Immediately following this victory the emperor ordered more units from the Asia Minor forces to cross into Thrace and prepare for the coming campaign. He also began to build up a strong siege train and amass supplies adequate for the powerful force he intended to assemble in order to drive the Rus' forces from Bulgaria entirely. The expedition was to be accompanied by a powerful naval force which was to carry troops and supplies and be ready to harry the invader from the coast or support the imperial land forces once they had reached the Danube. For this was John's intention, and his careful preparations make it clear that he was hoping to drive the Rus' forces back across the mighty river. Diplomacy also played a key role, with the defeat near Arkadioupolis being used to persuade the Pechenegs to withdraw their support, and John claiming that his intention was to replace the deposed Boris on his throne.

In April 971 the emperor's army – a reasonable estimate based on contemporary sources suggests it may have numbered as many as 30,000 – set off and passed through the Bulgarian frontier regions. The passes which had so often proved the site of Byzantine reverses were undefended – possibly because the Rus' were engaged in suppressing Bulgarian rebellion to the north – and the army passed safely through, to issue onto the plain in which the Bulgarian capital, Preslav, was located. After a series of short but vicious encounters the Russian forces were defeated and driven off, and the city was recovered, along with the important political prize of the deposed Tsar himself. The Rus' forces withdrew to the north and joined the remaining Rus' troops under Svyatoslav himself, who had established his base in the fortress of Dorostolon (Dristra, modern Silistra) on the south bank of the Danube.

The campaign proceeded with the emperor's march northward. As he went the Bulgarians began to slip away from Svyatoslav, which prompted the latter to execute a number of high-ranking Bulgars he had with him at Dorostolon and imprison many others. The emperor's advance was virtually unopposed, and the army quickly took a series of smaller fortresses and strong-points defended nominally by Bulgarian troops who, however, offered no resistance when the emperor offered them terms. Only in the approach to Dorostolon itself was there some hostile action: a small Rus' force had set an ambush in the dense woodland on the approaches to the fortress, and were able to surprise an advance party of imperial cavalry, sent ahead to scout the terrain and, possibly, locate a suitable site for the various divisions of the imperial army to set up camp. As the main body of the vanguard, together with the emperor, arrived to find the bodies of those who had been killed, troops from the imperial bodyguard were despatched to comb through the woods and eradicate the threat. A number of prisoners were taken and as a token of his policy to the enemy the emperor ordered them immediately put to the sword.

Once clear of the woodland, the imperial forces established a base camp where the baggage and siege trains were drawn up in a defensive position with a small detachment to guard them. Shortly afterwards the scouts returned to inform the emperor that the Russians were drawn up in battle order on open terrain before the fortress. Their formation was reported as a long, dense line bristling with weapons, awaiting the imperial assault and confident in their numbers. Although the figure of 60,000 given by one of the sources is an exaggeration (the area of the medieval fortifications within which the Rus' forces were quartered shows that this figure is far too large), it is clear that the Russian army was considerable, and had been built up over the three years that Svyatoslav had been active in Bulgaria. The incremental addition of more soldiers – possibly including some from beyond the Rus' lands themselves – had no doubt increased very considerably the original force that had accompanied Svyatoslav's first campaign in 968.

To oppose the long, dense line of the Rus', John drew up his force in three divisions over the same front. Both wings were reinforced by a reserve of heavy cataphract cavalry; and in a second line behind the first he placed infantry archers and slingers, who were instructed to maintain a constant hail of missiles on the enemy forces as long as they were in range. By shortly after midday the two forces were drawn up opposite one another. The Russians did not await the Roman attack, but with a long drawn-out battle roar advanced to meet the imperial forces. At the initial clash the Romans were able to halt the Rus' advance and at one or two points break through the densely packed mass of warriors; but the latter were quickly able to regroup and re-establish the shield-wall with which they now opposed the Roman thrusts. The battle lines moved back and forth for more than an hour until both sides fell back and regrouped preparatory to a fresh assault. Again the Byzantine forces halted the Russian charge, and were even able to push their line back some distance, but it could not be broken. A contemporary eye-witness, Leo the Deacon, who accompanied the imperial high command on the expedition, remarks on the Russian refusal to concede defeat when they had a reputation for invincibility to maintain, as well as their personal honour as warriors; the Roman forces, unwilling to accept defeat at the hands of a barbarian nation who, to paraphrase Leo, could not even ride, were equally unwilling to give up. By late afternoon the battle appeared to have reached a stalemate, and it was at this point that the emperor gave the command to commit the heavy cavalry on both wings. Supported by a renewed push from the heavy infantry in the centre, the wedges of heavily armoured horsemen now advanced against the enemy wings, and with a concerted war-cry from the whole Roman front the imperial forces charged into the Russian lines, the cavalry crashing through the shield-wall with irresistible force, driving the Russian wings back towards their centre. Within a few minutes the Rus' front collapsed, imperial units had penetrated the enemy line, and the Russians began to break and stream back towards the fortress for refuge. The rout was complete, and many were killed as they tried desperately to enter the fortress before the Romans caught up or the gates were shut on them.

The emperor recalled his troops, and as they began to return to their base camp, preparatory to establishing a siege of Dorostolon, Leo records that the soldiers sang a victory song. The emperor had selected for the imperial encampment a low eminence at some distance from the fortress. This was fortified by a ditch with the earth piled inside, upon which the troops were ordered to set their spears and lances and, propped against them in an unbroken wall, their shields. Leo the Deacon notes that this was the usual arrangement for a Roman encampment in hostile country.

The following day the imperial troops approached the fortress and launched attacks against various points around the defences, but were met with a hail of arrows and stones. Although they replied in kind, neither side seems to have suffered particularly badly from this exchange and, after being unable to make any headway against the defenders, the army was withdrawn to its camp, although the fortress was kept under constant surveillance. Towards evening the Rus' made a sortie from the fortress and sent a mounted detachment to harry the Roman pickets. Leo notes that this was the first time they had seen the enemy on horseback. It soon became obvious that their lack of experience in mounted fighting would tell against them, and a detachment of Roman cavalry rapidly broke their formation and sent them helter-skelter back to Dorostolon.

The emperor seems at this stage to have decided not to press the fortress too closely but rather to try to tempt the Russian forces out to meet his own army in open battle, where victory might be had much more readily and quickly than through either a direct attack against the well-defended walls and towers of Dorostolon or a prolonged siege. But he had prepared for all eventualities, and it was at this point, about the third day after the Roman forces reached the fortress, that the fleet arrived, a fleet which included both supplies and reinforcements, as well as a number of warships equipped with liquid fire projectors. This weapon – a type of medieval napalm projected from tubes mounted on the bows of the vessels in question – was already known to the Rus', for the warships of Svyatoslav's father, Igor, had been destroyed by the very same weapon some thirty years earlier. The arrival of the fleet, which now sealed the Russians on the southern bank of the Danube and removed any chance they might have had to escape, was a great boost to Roman morale but must have seriously eroded the confidence of the Rus' forces bottled up in Dorostolon.

The day after the arrival of the fleet, Svyatoslav led his forces out once again in an effort to draw the Roman forces into battle, hoping to defeating them and relieve the siege. As before, however, the two armies were evenly matched until the Roman heavy cavalry with their fearful iron maces once more drove the Russian line in on itself. Again the enemy fell back, at first in some order, then dissolving into rout and fleeing back inside the defences.

The emperor now set up his siege weapons around the fortress and began to attack both the walls and the troops within by a constant shower of missiles. In an effort to rid themselves of this annoyance, which was causing casualties and affecting morale, the Rus' mounted a series of sorties with the aim of burning the Roman siege engines and other equipment. In one such incident the detachment guarding one of the emplacements was taken almost by surprise and its leader, a certain Kourkouas, who is reported to have been slightly drunk following his midday meal, was killed. Kourkouas was renowned for his luxurious and conspicuous outfit, and the Rus' who killed him, thinking he was the emperor himself, hefted his head on a spear and mocked the Romans, though without the effect for which they had hoped. The siege machinery that they attacked remained undamaged, and the siege continued.

Pleased with this apparent success, however, the Russian army issued forth again the next day, and the emperor permitted them to draw up their line of battle. Once again the battle was joined, with the Roman forces drawn up in a single deep phalanx, the cavalry partly concealed behind the extremities on each wing and the missile troops behind the heavy infantry in the centre. On this occasion, a sharp charge by a Rus' contingent succeeded in pushing deep into the Roman line, inflicting heavy casualties. But a counter-charge by the supporting cavalry, including units of the imperial guards, thrust it back, with the loss of its leader, Svyatoslav's second-in-command, at the hand of Anemas, a member of the emperor's own bodyguard. The Romans were immediately ordered to advance and push back the demoralized Rus' line, which broke and ran, retreating once more in disorder to the safety of the fortress.

That night the Rus' soldiers and their families opened the gates and came out onto the field of battle to search for their dead, for whom they then built funeral pyres and, having carried out the appropriate rites, committed their bodies to the flames. Whether the Roman forces watching the fortress were ordered not to interfere, or whether they allowed this activity to take place without consultation, is not stated. But Svyatoslav now summoned a meeting of the leading warriors to seek counsel. Some advised an attempt to break out by boat, across the Danube, braving the Roman warships which were on constant patrol; others advised opening negotiations with the emperor in an effort to save as many lives as possible – for, as one of the Rus' leaders put it, 'we are not accustomed to facing heavily armoured cavalry, especially after the loss of so many of our foremost warriors, upon whom the men depend for their courage and leadership'.

Svyatoslav was unwilling to follow either of these courses of action, however, and with the support, apparently, of the majority, voted to fight it out to the bitter end. The Rus', he said, are not accustomed to give in, but would rather die in battle and go to Valhalla. And, as Leo the Deacon adds in his account, a Rus' soldier has never been known to fall living into the hands of their enemies.

The same night, therefore, in a desperate attempt to obtain supplies, a Rus' detachment of some 2,000 men left the fortress in small boats, and at some distance along the southern bank of the river crept ashore to begin their search for provisions. The naval detachments guarding the river should have detected this move, for the emperor had ordered that no Russian should be allowed to get out of the fortress. Instead, having succeeded in collecting some food for their beleaguered comrades, the Russian force made its way back by a different route from that which it had followed on the way from its boats, and stumbled by accident upon a small group of Byzantine cavalry soldiers sent out to water their horses and collect wood. Heavily outnumbered, the unsuspecting Roman troops were quickly put to the sword, and although the alarm was quickly raised, the Russians managed to get back with their supplies before they could be intercepted. The emperor was furious at this lapse in naval discipline, which had caused an entirely unnecessary loss of life and allowed the enemy, who were clearly in increasingly short supply, to replenish their stores. The naval commanders were threatened with execution if such a lapse recurred.

The next day was Friday 24 July, and having spent the day preparing for the battle, the whole Rus' army sallied out towards late afternoon before the fortress. They formed up in a deep, solid phalanx protected by a solid shield-wall bristling with spears. The Roman forces were drawn up in the usual three divisions with the heavy cavalry behind the wings and with the emperor himself in the centre leading his own cavalry as a reserve. The location of the conflict was slightly nearer the fortress than hitherto, however, with the result that both forces were crowded together on a narrower front, with woodland on one flank and the marshy regions stretching back from the river on the other. The Russians, in order to counter the effect of the heavy cavalry on the Roman side, placed their archers on the wings where they could do most damage should the Roman cavalry attack them there. Led now by Svyatoslav himself, the desperate Rus' warriors hurled themselves with fury against the Roman line, and soon began to push the centre back. Many cavalry mounts were injured or killed by the unusually heavy Rus' archery. The emperor, observing that while his men were holding the line they were also rapidly tiring in the heat of the day, ordered the issue of water mixed with wine to the ranks, presumably on a rotational basis so as to leave the battle-lines undisturbed, a move which refreshed the imperial troops and enabled them to withstand the constant Rus' charges.

Realizing that the overall tactical situation did not favour the Roman dispositions, however, the emperor then ordered a general withdrawal, and with admirable discipline and order the whole Roman line was able to pull back some distance from the fortress onto a broader plain which offered much greater room for manoeuvre and for more effective use of the Roman heavy cavalry. During the withdrawal one Roman officer, a certain Theodore of Misthia, was cut off and isolated from his unit – suggestive of the closeness of the Russian pursuit – and a fierce mêlée developed around him. At one point he is reported to have used a Rus' corpse, which he lifted before him by the belt, as a shield. He was eventually helped by his comrades who rushed his attackers and got him safely back to their own lines. Some time after this, Anemas, who had already distinguished himself, moved with his unit of guards (probably the *Athanatoi*, the Immortals, a unit created by the emperor John shortly after his accession in 969) to reinforce the line. Anemas himself came close enough to the Rus' leader to attack him and knock him down, but Svyatoslav's armour prevented serious injury and within seconds Anemas was himself cut down by the spears and axes of Svyatoslav's men.

Heartened by this the Rus' in the centre attacked with renewed force and the Roman line began to give way. Some of the cavalry in the rear of the line began to waver and turn, and at this crucial moment the emperor decided that he must commit his reserve, his own bodyguard, to the fray. The emperor's units, with the emperor himself in the forefront, moved to join the fray, and this sight steadied the Roman centre and allowed them to stabilize their position once more. At this critical point a strong wind blew up, accompanied by a fierce thunderstorm – not untypical of midsummer weather conditions in the region – and the Rus' had the misfortune to find the wind blowing directly in their faces. Eye witnesses reported seeing a rider on a white horse, who appeared in the centre of the Roman lines and led a charge which smashed through the Russian shield-wall. Later stories had it that this was in fact St Theodore, the emperor's own patron and a leading soldier saint in the Byzantine Church. In fact, it was almost certainly the emperor himself and his elite guards who, in a final move to open up the Russian shield-wall, led a charge of the heavy cataphract cavalry. Either way, the move was successful. The Roman centre now began to push forward once more, and the Rus' warriors themselves, partially blinded by the rain and dust, were unable to organize themselves against this new onslaught. At the same moment the Roman heavy cavalry on one wing (the reports do not specify which) under the general Bardas Skleros completed an encircling movement begun moments before, crashing into the flank of the Russian wing and driving it back onto the troops in the centre. With this sudden turn of events the Russian lines dissolved and began to flee once more towards the fortress. The slaughter was enormous as the victorious Roman cavalry fell on the routing troops. The Romans lost some 350 against over 15,000 Russian casualties, an improbable figure but indicative nevertheless of very heavy losses. Some 20,000 shields and innumerable swords were taken from the field by the Romans.

This battle marked the end of the Russian attempts to break the siege and drive the Romans off. They had lost too many men and were rapidly running out of provisions to continue the struggle. Despite his earlier refusal to contemplate asking for terms, Svyatoslav now so no other option before him. The emperor accepted the Rus' proposals for a peaceful withdrawal and the handing over of Dorostolon undamaged, with all the prisoners and booty the Rus' had taken, and agreed to permit the remnants of the Rus' army to cross the Danube without being attacked by the warships with the liquid fire projectors, which the Russians greatly feared. Indeed, John even agreed to resume friendly commercial contacts with the Rus', once Svyatoslav had reached home. In the event, the Russian prince was never to do so, dying in an ambush set at the mouth of the Dnieper by his erstwhile Pecheneg allies.

In a brilliant four-month campaign, carefully prepared and supported by a well-oiled logistical organization – one of the greatest strengths of eastern Roman military administration – the emperor John I had crushed and driven off one of the fiercest enemies the Romans had yet faced. Leaving a strong garrison in Dorostolon, he returned to Constantinople, where the great victory was celebrated with an imperial triumphal procession. The deposed Tsar Boris was asked to surrender his crown, and the eastern parts of Bulgaria were absorbed into the empire as a province. The Bulgarian campaign of 971 highlighted again the discipline, order and effectiveness of the imperial armies of the second half of the tenth century.

The Wars of Basil II

Basil II (976-1025) is generally held to have been one of the most effective and competent rulers of the eastern Roman empire. His early years were not easy but, despite beginning his reign with a civil war and military defeat in the Balkans, he continued and consolidated the conquests of his immediate predecessors, re-establishing the Byzantine empire as the paramount power in the region. After a long and gruelling war against a revived Bulgarian state, under the Tsar Samuel, he was finally victorious, entirely incorporating Bulgaria and its vassals into the empire, giving them their own provincial administration and establishing them as regular imperial provinces. The Danube once more became the imperial frontier in the north; the emirate of Aleppo and its more easterly neighbours became client states of the empire in the east. Here, the dynamic military power of the Egyptian Fatimid dynasty, whose interests likewise lay in exercising some control over the Syrian emirates and cities, now became the main enemy.

Basil became effective ruler only in 976, on the death from typhoid fever of John I. But he was still very young, and there were members of the aristocracy related to the previous emperors, Nikephoros Phokas and John Tzimiskes, who felt that they had better claims to imperial power. Both Nikephoros and John had, in effect, seized the throne, and had been able to legitimate their position only through marriage to the widow of emperor Romanos II – father of Basil and his brother Constantine – who had died in 963. It was a leading member of one of these ambitious noble clans, Bardas Skleros, who rebelled against Basil II shortly after his succession in 976; and it was another leader of an even more prestigious family, Bardas Phokas, whom the emperor called to his assistance in 978. The rebellion was defeated and Skleros escaped to the Caliphate where he was imprisoned. On his release in 987, however, and with Arab support, he returned and raised an army once more. Bardas Phokas was sent against him, but betrayed the emperor, first coming to an agreement with Skleros, then imprisoning him and declaring against Basil II himself. The emperor called upon the Russian prince Vladimir for help, and an agreement was reached which involved both Vladimir's acceptance of Christianity and his marriage to Basil's sister Anna. Vladimir also sent Basil a stout body of Norse-Russian troops (known in the Byzantine sources as Varangians). With their help, Basil was able to defeat Phokas, who died after a second battle in 989. And although Skleros continued in rebellion for a while, a reconciliation was soon arranged and peace restored.

Basil's early military ventures were largely unsuccessful (a factor which contributed to the desire in certain aristocratic quarters to replace him). In 986 he had marched against the reviving power of the Bulgarians, under their Tsar Samuel who, together with his brothers, had rebelled against Roman rule in Macedonia after the death of Tzimiskes, establishing a capital first at Prespa and later at Ohrid. Although taking up the older Bulgarian tradition, this was essentially a kingdom based in Macedonia, which now became the political centre of the new empire. From there he was able to extend his sway over the regions to the north and east, and by the mid-980s he controlled all the original Bulgarian state up to the Danube as well as the western Balkans, including much of Thessaly, Epiros and what is now Albania. He then began pushing directly into Byzantine Thrace, attacking Thessaloniki and other major centres in 985 and 986.

The young Basil had to take action before the empire's Balkan provinces fell away. An expedition led by the emperor marched north against the region of Serdica, but failed to take the town and, on his return, his forces were badly mauled in the Balkan passes, losing the imperial baggage in the process. The ensuing civil wars took up the emperor's attention for the next years, allowing the new Bulgarian power to extend and consolidate its hold. When next the emperor turned his attention to Tsar Samuel, he faced a very different problem indeed.

By 991, when Basil finally had the time to devote to the Balkan situation, Samuel's power was well established. Basil began by trying to forge diplomatic alliances with some of the other Balkan powers, such as the princes of Serbia, for example. In 991 Basil campaigned briefly and successfully in Macedonia, but eastern politics then took up his attention until 1001. In the meantime, in 997, Samuel had suffered a major defeat at the hands of one of Basil's generals, Nikephoros Ouranos, following a raid as far south as the Peloponnese. But it became clear that this would not affect his overall situation. Beginning in 1001, therefore, Basil began a series of regular, yearly campaigns that, with the strength of the well-disciplined Byzantine armies behind him, soon reduced Samuel's power to a fraction of its former extent. Basil's campaigns were well thought through. He first established a wedge of Byzantine-controlled territory stretching up from Thrace to the Balkan range and Pliska, thus cutting Samuel's core Macedonian lands off from the old Bulgarian heartlands. In a series of pincer movements he then progressively isolated the Tsar's forces, until by about 1007 the war had become a question of searching out and bringing Samuel's remaining forces to battle. The end for Samuel came in 1014 when, at the battle of Kleidion, a narrow pass in the Belasica mountains which Samuel had fortified against Byzantine attack, his remaining forces were caught in a pincer movement and annihilated. Samuel died shortly after the battle, possibly from a cerebral haemorrhage or heart attack, and within four years the remainder of his empire had collapsed in civil war and been absorbed into the empire. The whole Balkan region up to the Danube was, for the first time since the sixth century, again in Roman hands, and was to stay in Roman hands until the rebellions of the later twelfth century.

The effectiveness and inventiveness of Roman generalship during this period is exemplified by a number of battles fought during the reign of Basil II. One of the best known is the battle of the Spercheios river, fought in 997. Tsar Samuel had marched into Thrace, where he was able to ambush and capture Ashot, the son of the Byzantine *doux*, or commander, of the region of Thessaloniki, Gregory Taronites. In a vain attempt to rescue his son, Gregory too was drawn into a trap and surrounded, and died trying to cut his way out. Samuel then marched across northern Greece and down as far as the Gulf of Corinth, from where he entered the Peloponnese and proceeded to ravage and harry the land. Samuel's forces had managed to avoid the detachments placed to halt their advance into the Peloponnese and Greece, but on the march back towards his home territories he was forced to confront one of the empire's most able commanders, the general Nikephoros Ouranos, a close friend of the emperor Basil and author of an important military handbook. Nikephoros, who held the post of supreme commander of all the western armies, set out from Thessaloniki with his forces and crossed the mountains of Olympos to Larissa, where he left his baggage before proceeding. From Larissa he set out with a select and lightly equipped force to try and intercept Samuel's army. Moving by forced marches he crossed Thessaly and the plain of Farsala before arriving at the Apidanos river, which he crossed to reach the Spercheios, where his scouts had located the Bulgar encampment. Nikephoros pitched his camp on the bank opposite Samuel's army, but this did not dishearten the Bulgars: not only were there no nearby fords, but the river was in full spate due to particularly heavy rains.

Nikephoros was not prepared to give up, however. Scouts were despatched up and down the river for a considerable distance in both directions and eventually a fordable stretch was found, sufficient to permit the select force under Nikephoros's command to pass over. Marching along the bank of the river after nightfall, the troops were safely crossed over before dawn. Forming up on the opposite bank, they now marched back towards the Bulgar encampment and, just before dawn, fell on the imperfectly defended camp which Samuel had thought adequate. The Bulgar troops were caught completely unawares, and there was no organized resistance. The greater part of the Bulgar force perished or was captured. Samuel and his son Romanos, who had accompanied him, were both badly wounded and only escaped with their lives by hiding among the dead and injured until they could creep away. The Romans captured Samuel's baggage train and all his booty, and returned to Thessaloniki with a substantial body of captives.

A similarly stubborn refusal to give up when faced with apparently insurmountable physical obstacles was demonstrated by Basil II himself and his officers in the campaign of 1014. In the years preceding, the Roman strategy of attrition had worn down Bulgar resistance to such an extent that Samuel could no longer go on the offensive, but was limited to trying to prevent Byzantine incursions into his core territory and to preserve what lands and resources were still in his power. The Tsar's strategy was to attempt to prevent the damaging raids mounted by Basil each year into these Macedonian heartlands. Campaigning generally began in May, and the raids usually involved imperial units pushing up from Serres in the south, through the pass of Rupel and along the 'long plain' (Campulungu, or 'Kimbalonga' in its Greek form) formed by the Strymon valley itself. Following well-established

Bulgar practice, Samuel blocked many of the passes off with timber palisades and ditches, including the important pass at Kleidion (near the modern village of Kljuc), regularly employed by the imperial armies as they marched into Macedonia, despatching at the same time a diversionary attack against Thessaloniki by another route. The latter move was defeated by the local commander in the region, Theophylaktos Botaneiates, whose troops cut the Bulgar force to pieces. The attempt to block the pass also failed.

Confronted by the high palisade erected by the Bulgars, the eastern Roman forces at first tried to storm the obstacle, but after sustaining disproportionate losses in the attempt, found that they would have to march a long way westwards or eastwards in order to circumvent the obstacle, which would have meant calling off the campaign for that year. One of Basil's commanders, however, Niketas Xiphias, the commander of Philippoupolis, volunteered to lead a small force over the mountains in an attempt to find a way across and behind the enemy position. Basil's forces maintained their position before the pass, launching a series of small-scale assaults to keep the Bulgars occupied, while Xiphias spent some time scouting the area on either side of the pass. Eventually he located a narrow and difficult track to the west of the pass, which led across mount Belasica, and at dawn on 29 July Xiphias's small force fell on the rear lines of the Bulgar army with bloodcurdling yells. Order was never really established and, as panic gripped the Bulgar soldiers, the main imperial army under Basil, no longer faced by a determined and focused resistance from the palisade, were able to tear it down and begin the pursuit of their utterly disorganized foe. Many were killed, but the vast majority were surrounded and forced to surrender.

This was Samuel's last remaining army of any consequence, and its destruction effectively ended serious resistance. According to a slightly later source, some 15,000 prisoners were taken in all, and of these, Basil is supposed to have blinded all but one in every hundred, whom he left with one eye each to guide the rest back to Samuel. Whether the tale is true is hard to know, although there is probably some element of truth to it. At any rate, Samuel had a seizure or stroke of some kind when he saw what had happened to his soldiers, and died. Within the next four years Basil and his generals completed the subjugation of Bulgaria, and the Danube became once again the effective frontier of the Roman empire.

The successes of the period from about 960 to 1025 are impressive, but they were by no means uniform. The imperial armies had achieved a powerful reputation, so much so that by the 1030s the mere threat of an imperial army marching into northern Syria was enough to keep the local Muslim emirs in check. Yet while these successes were the result of a combination of good organization and logistics, intelligent tactics, well-armed, trained and disciplined soldiers, and good morale, the key still remained the competence and effectiveness of the commanders. Even under Basil II incompetent officers led their troops to disaster, so it can reasonably be maintained that the dependence on the charisma and intelligence of its leaders was one of the most significant inbuilt weaknesses of the imperial military system at the tactical level. Combined with short-sighted strategic planning and internal political conflict, this was to lead during the middle of the eleventh century to serious problems and to the erosion of the effectiveness of the field armies as well as the provincial defences.

6

Collapse and Recovery: The Eleventh and Twelfth Centuries

The successes of the generals who led the expansionist strategy of the second half of the tenth century had several unforeseen consequences. First, the thematic structures which had developed in the period from the later seventh to ninth centuries were substantially eroded. New command structures, strategic commands known as ducates and katepanates, much smaller territorially than the traditional themes, established a protective curtain between the inner regions of the empire and the frontier zones. But the traditional thematic militias were neglected. The logic behind the newly established strategic units was to address local threats or respond to the need to mobilize for larger expeditionary offensives, rather than major hostile incursions aimed at the heart of the empire. While the new structures did represent a defence in depth of sorts, the fragmentation of command around the periphery had obvious disadvantages when a major threat appeared. It was essentially up to the emperor, or one of the two commanders-in-chief, rather than a local commander, to assemble an appropriate force and march to deal with it. Much, therefore, depended on the competence of the leader in question. The empire still fielded an effective and feared campaign army, however, and as long as it remained well-led and successful, the empire's enemies were held at bay.

Strategy

By the 1040s it was felt that an effective system of alliances or buffer states and intelligent diplomacy had rendered inessential many of the expensive standing forces which had, following the successful expansion of the previous period, been established in the frontier provinces. Trade, economic and cultural influence as well as military threat kept the peace along the northern frontier on the Danube, for example, drastically reducing the costs of the forces which had been stationed in the region in the years following Basil II's reconquest of the area. Even military men, such as the soldier-emperor Isaac I Komnenos, saw that the costs of a large permanent standing force could not be borne in the long term. Emperors began actively to pursue a foreign policy which would permit them to call on vassals and the rulers of neighbouring powers for soldiers, and thus limit the demand on the empire's own resources.

During the middle years of the eleventh century the imperial defensive strategy broke down. This was largely a result of the fact that the balance between diplomacy and military strength was destroyed by civil war and provincial or military rebellion. The thematic militias had in any case long been neglected in favour of full-time, regionally recruited *tagmata* maintained on a permanent basis, and their demise cannot be blamed on the emperors of the eleventh century. But reductions in the overall military budget had induced a heavier dependence on non-Byzantine mercenaries than had been the case until the end of Basil II's reign. Foreign mercenary troops, especially of western knights – Franks, Germans and Normans – played an increasingly prominent role, usually under their own leaders. The defeat at Manzikert in 1071 was not in itself such a great disaster from a purely military perspective, but the ensuing civil war and internal disruption gave the invading Turks a free hand in central Asia Minor, and produced a very different political-strategic map of the region. Emperors from Alexios I onward spent the period from the 1080s until the 1180s attempting to recover the situation, ultimately without success. The wars of the period were fought increasingly using western tactics and panoply, but with elements of a still clearly Byzantine or East Roman tactical organization – contemporaries continue to remark on the order, cohesion and discipline with which the multi-ethnic and colourful Byzantine armies still fought.

Tactics and Tactical Organization

Mercenary units of professional soldiers, both indigenous Byzantines as well as, for example, the warrior-tribesmen of the steppe peoples or the mounted lancers of the Normans, continued to fight with order and discipline according to their own traditions and battlefield loyalties. But many units of the imperial armies were neglected during the middle years of the eleventh century. When the emperor Romanos IV set out on campaign to Syria in 1068, he had to spend some time and energy in recruiting new units and training them to fight effectively. A contemporary, Michael Attaleiates, paints a sad picture of the state of the thematic levy raised for the campaign of 1071, stating that such provincially recruited troops were entirely unfitted for warfare – they had been neither mustered nor paid or supplied with their traditional provisions for many years. The older men, who had some experience of fighting, were without mounts and equipment; the newer draftees had no experience at all and were quite without training, and the emperor had to mix them with the more experienced soldiers. In fact, however, Michael's own account of the campaigns of 1068-1071, including that of Manzikert, shows that the imperial armies still possessed an order, discipline and cohesion which is belied by many popular assumptions. We should also be wary of taking some of his comments too much at face value, since Attaleiates was keen to lay the blame for the decline of imperial military might on Romanos IV's incompetent bureaucratic predecessors by exaggerating the parlous condition of the army.

The indigenous forces were thus a mixture of regular mercenary units from the different parts of the empire, the older thematic soldiers, and foreign units. But the campaigns of Romanos IV against the Seljuk Turk raids in the late 1060s, which culminated at Manzikert, were by no means failures. On the contrary, the account of the eye-witness Attaleiates attests to a surprising degree of discipline and competence, with regularly entrenched and fortified camps, considerable tactical order, and well-organized lines of supply. According to another contemporary, Michael Psellos, the emperor Isaac I had revived the traditions of strict discipline and tactical order which central government neglect had threatened, and his forces were both effective and successful in battle. It was localized incompetence and failures in communications, combined with treachery and desertion, which brought about the downfall of Romanos IV's division at Manzikert.

But there is no doubt that, as a result of the politics and the policies of the middle of the eleventh century, the old army was disappearing. By 1073, shortly after the defeat at Manzikert, the government of Michael VII could raise only a few hundred troops to march against the rebel Frankish leader Roussel de Bailleul, relying mostly on Turkish allies. Although by the later part of the decade a reasonably effective, if small, central field army had been re-established, further civil wars meant that, in the early 1080's, Alexios I's army consisted almost entirely of mercenaries, largely non-Byzantine. As the empire became much more closely integrated into the tactical world of the lands around it, employing Seljuk, Pecheneg or Cuman horse archers, Norman, German and Frankish knights, Bulgarian and Anatolian light infantry, Georgians and Alans from the Caucasus, imperial guards recruited from outside the empire (Varangians, for example, from the 1070s chiefly made up of Anglo-Saxons who had left recently conquered Norman England), so its army became less 'Byzantine'.

At the end of the eleventh century, the Normans presented the imperial armies with a particular problem, in the form of the massed heavy cavalry charge. Although the Byzantines certainly knew about Norman heavy cavalry, they had only occasionally had to confront it themselves (they had used Norman mercenaries, for example, in Italy and Sicily in the 1030s and 1040s), and most of the warfare they had been involved in since the 1060s had been against light-armed, highly mobile enemies such as Turks and Pechenegs. The Byzantine heavy cavalry of the later tenth century had been armed with lances and maces, but the military manuals (and to a certain extent the historians' accounts of the battles in which they fought) suggest that they moved forward not at the charge, but at a slower pace, intended simply to roll over the less well-armed enemy cavalry or infantry, and helped by massed archery support. As we have seen from the account at the battles of Dorostolon, against committed and well-armed infantry, their impact was not always immediately successful. Although the evidence is unclear, during the course of the eleventh century the Normans in particular seem to have evolved an effective type of disciplined heavy cavalry charge using lances – the battle of Troina in 1041 is described as involving both Norman and Roman heavy cavalry charging in order and riding down the enemy lines. At Hastings, in 1066, it has been argued that the same tactics were employed, at least by some detachments of Duke William's cavalry; and the battle of Dyrrachion in 1081, discussed below, may well be evidence of a similar charge. Whether or not the chronology of the development is correct, and whether or not it also involved the use of especially bred and heavier warhorses at this stage (the evidence suggests almost certainly not) it seems that from the time of this battle on the Byzantines had to learn to cope with a particularly lethal form of disciplined assault.

Alexios I and John II tried to re-establish an indigenous army, but with very limited success. Under Manuel I, many indigenous units were re-equipped and trained in western style. The result was an army no different from any other multi-ethnic, polyglot mercenary army in its tactics and formations. But still, as the historian Niketas Choniates notes when reporting the harangue of the commander of the imperial troops fighting against the Hungarians in 1167, the formation, military equipment and training were the same for both sides. The difference lay in the superior order and tactical dispositions of the imperial troops, when these were properly exploited by an able commanding officer.

Manzikert 1071

In the period from the late 1040s until the late 1060s the Seljuk Turks under the Sultan Alp Arslan (1063-1073) had made considerable inroads into formerly Byzantine territory in eastern Anatolia. As ruler of Iran, Iraq and northern Syria – nominally for the Abbasid Caliph in Baghdad – Arslan had faced a problem with his unruly Turkmen nomads, whose desire for further booty and conquests could not be accommodated within the Islamic world. And so he had released them against the Christian powers to the north and west, where they were soon able to bring the kingdom of Armenia under his sway – the capital, Ani, was sacked in 1064 – and mount yearly raids deep into imperial lands. Plundering and destroying as they went, sacking several major cities, they had soon created a situation which the regular armies of the empire were only with extreme difficulty able to contain. In a series of campaigns between 1068 and 1070 the emperor Romanos IV (1068-1071) had led his armies in an attempt to bring the Turks to battle and destroy their power, but had been thwarted by their mobility, small numbers, and the large number of incursions which they mounted. The Turks were able literally to ride circles around the much slower moving imperial forces which, as we have noted already, were no longer as well-led or as effective as in the heyday of the Byzantine reconquests under Basil II.

In the winter of 1070-1071 Romanos prepared another major expedition, directed against the Seljuk garrisons which had been placed in the Byzantine border fortresses at Khliat and Manzikert in the east. His intention was certainly to re-establish the frontier defences as far as he could, although whether he also hoped to meet Alp Arslan himself in battle is a moot point. For in March or April 1071, when his preparations were well advanced, the emperor proposed a treaty with the Turkish Sultan, who was engaged upon the siege of Edessa, by which the latter would abandon his siege and the former would return the city of Hierapolis (Manbidj) to the Sultan's authority, taken by the emperor during his campaign in 1068. This would then enable the Sultan to resume his war with the Fatimid-controlled cities of Syria, in particular Aleppo, removing him from the scene in Asia Minor and leaving Romanos a free hand to re-assert Roman authority over the region, and perhaps set up a defensive chain that would hinder or prevent future Turkmen raids. Romanos's first offer of a truce was reinforced by a second embassy, which arrived at Aleppo in May, more or less demanding the exchange of the towns named in the first offer, and threatening war if no agreement was reached.

Romanos had already left Constantinople, and had begun mustering his troops in late February and March. By the time the Sultan received the second embassy, therefore, he must also have received news of the imperial advance towards his Armenian territories. Abandoning his negotiations with the governor of Aleppo, he seems precipitately to have headed back east, crossing the Euphrates with his own guards and a small retinue, to take command of the forces in Armenia and Mesopotamia and deal with the threat from Romanos.

The emperor's advance across Asia Minor was accompanied by several events that did not augur well for the success of the expedition. In the first place, he chose to leave the general Nikephoros Botaneiates behind, a competent officer whom, however, he suspected of potential disloyalty. Yet he chose to take with him Andronikos Doukas, eldest son of John Doukas, one of his rivals for the imperial throne, who certainly was disloyal to him. At the same time, Romanos began to distance himself from his troops and his officers, insisting eventually on establishing a separate baggage train and encampment for the imperial party, refusing to share in the hardships of the campaign but taking with him elaborate materials and equipment for his own accommodation. On the march from the Halys river to Sebasteia his guard of German mercenaries, the *Nemitzoi*, suffered some casualties at the hands of the local population, whose property and lands they had pillaged *en route*, and then complained to the emperor about their treatment. Romanos was forced to cow them into submission by threatening them with force from the other units encamped around them, and then dismissed them to a distant posting, away from the immediate area of the campaign; while at Sebasteia the emperor had to deal with possible opposition from the local Armenian population, who had been accused of making common cause with the Seljuk raiders during the previous year.

By late June the imperial forces had reached Erzurum (Theodosioupolis), where a decision had to be made as to which direction the army should take and how exactly the emperor wished to implement his strategy. There appears to have been some dissension. On the one hand, some of the generals suggested he move on, try to outflank the sultan and take the war into Seljuk territory, and bring him to battle. The emperor's last report of the Sultan was that he had departed in haste, indeed in a panic, from Aleppo, and it was assumed that he would need to go first to Iraq to raise his forces there before he could deal with the Roman attack. Others, including the generals Joseph Tarchaneiotes and Nikephoros Bryennios, argued rather that the emperor should wait, fortify the surrounding towns and strengthen their garrisons, lay waste the countryside to deprive the Turks of necessary supplies when they approached, and await events. The latter course of action seemed inappropriate, the more so since the army was clearly in danger of running out of supplies if it waited in one place for too long, and so the order was given to move on.

An estimate of the forces at the emperor's disposal at this point is difficult, but it is clear that he had by no means denuded the empire of troops for this campaign. A detachment of Varangians was certainly left in the imperial palace; a detachment of Frankish heavy cavalry under their leader Krispos had been left at Abydos; and since both the Normans and the Hungarians were a threat at different points in the Balkans, the garrisons in these regions will certainly not have been reduced. It may have been to these areas that the unruly German contingent was posted. The field troops in Syria, and in particular those under the *doux* or military governor of Antioch remained substantial, as later events demonstrate, even though some reinforcements to the emperor's field army had been sent from Syria. The contemporary sources also make it clear that, after the battle, considerable numbers of troops were still in their garrisons and posts throughout Anatolia.

Of the units which accompanied the emperor, some are mentioned in the sources by name. The Franks under Roussel de Bailleul, who may have numbered 500 or more; the five *tagmata* of the West, each of perhaps 1,000 men; a number of detachments of Oğuz (Turk) mercenaries, whose exact number is unknown; troops from Bulgaria; indigenous eastern thematic *tagmata* from Cappadocia, and probably also from Koloneia, Charsianon, Anatolikon (units from Pisidia and Lykaonia are mentioned in earlier campaigns for the 1050s), Chaldia (Trebizond) and Armeniakon, again perhaps in each case as many as 1,000 strong, but of dubious quality in many cases. Units from Cilicia and Bithynia are also mentioned in one of the sources. *Tagmata* from the field armies of Syria were also present, although it is not certain how many. In addition to these troops, there were also substantial numbers of Armenian infantry units. Where these were drawn from is unknown: possibly from the regions around Sebasteia and Theodosioupolis, as well as from the Syrian forces. In addition, there was a substantial body of Pecheneg mercenaries and allies and some units from allied or vassal states in the Balkans. Of the palace regiments, the soldiers of several other units, the *Hetaireai*, the *Scholai*, and the *Stratelatai* made up a reserve division, and there were detachments of Varangians also present. The total of the forces thus assembled can only be guessed at. The medieval Islamic sources reckon it at anything from 100,000 to 300,000, both preposterous in view of both the demography of the empire at the time and the logistics involved. But a grand total of perhaps 40,000 may be reasonable, and would certainly explain the emperor's apparent confidence and the fact that the Turkish Sultan was clearly worried by the size of the threat.

The emperor's plan seems to have been to take both Manzikert and Khliat, which lay somewhat to the south on the western shore of Lake Van. But he was completely misinformed of the movements of Alp Arslan and his troops. The latter, in fact, had not returned to Iraq at all; rather, he had marched directly towards the Armenian border by way of Amida and Mosul, then on to Khoi just to the north of Lake Urmia. There his vizier had proceeded to Azerbaijan to raise further troops, while he himself, having collected some 10,000 cavalry from his allies and vassals *en route*, had by now assembled a force of some 30,000 horsemen. Thus while Romanos thought that the Turkish leader was some way away, he was in fact just over 100 miles distant, with his scouts covering and reporting every move made by the Roman emperor. Already, therefore, Romanos was at a disadvantage, even if his forces were in a substantial majority.

From Erzurum/Theodosioupolis the emperor advanced eastwards. The troops were ordered to collect enough provisions for two months – a very considerable amount that necessarily entailed the use of large numbers of pack-animals and, possibly carts, slowing the army down somewhat. A substantial body of the Pecheneg allied force, closely followed by the Frankish troops under Roussel, were ordered ahead to the region around Khliat, which Romanos clearly perceived as the more difficult of his two first objectives, with instructions to collect fodder and provisions, prevent enemy damage to the harvest and, presumably, to secure it for the imperial advance. The emperor must have continued his march east along the same route, before turning south to cross the Araxes, and then east, either along the valley of the Murat Su, or a little further south (which is the route the forces under Roussel will have followed) at Mu (Taron), towards Manzikert itself.

Before reaching this first objective, he detached a further substantial force under Tarchaneiotes, with orders to assist Roussel in taking and garrisoning Khliat. According to Attaleiates, this included the elite of the army, most of the better and more battle-hardened units, including the Varangians and some of the Armenian infantry from the field forces under the *doux* of Theodosioupolis. He also notes that the troops remaining to Romanos were now fewer than those he had sent off to Khliat. We may surmise that, after the separation of these various detachments, it is likely that the forces remaining with the emperor at this point numbered only some 20,000 or so, and were therefore – contrary to Romanos's expectation and assumptions – barely superior in numbers, if at all, to the main Turkish host.

The detachment of the troops under Roussel and then Tarchaneiotes, based on the false assumption that the enemy would approach from the south or east of Khliat and was still some distance away, proved to be a major blunder. Unaware of the closeness of the Seljuk forces, which were by now approaching both Khliat and Manzikert from the east, the two Roman commanders were suddenly confronted by what seemed to be a substantial enemy force. What happened next has no explanation in the sources, for both forces appear simply to have about turned and moved with great haste away from the Seljuks, whom they seem neither to have reconnoitred, nor to have reported to the emperor, a mere 50km or less to the north. Both divisions simply marched off towards Melitene/Malatya on the Euphrates, and took no further part in the campaign.

There are two possible routes between Manzikert and Khliat, and it is likely that the troops under Tarchaneiotes took the slightly quicker, more easterly road, across the plain stretching south-eastwards from Manzikert, down towards the Süphan Daği. Since they were clearly able eventually to reach Melitene (Malatya), they must certainly have got as far as the junction with the westerly road down from Manzikert, just north of Khliat, where they perhaps also joined up with the troops under Roussel. It can, therefore, only have been at this point that the Seljuk troops appeared in strength, compelling the imperial forces to turn north along the westerly route back towards Manzikert, before turning westwards after a few kilometres, back through Taron, Harput and on to Malatya. It is likely that they may also have found this route back to the north, along which they would march to rejoin the emperor, cut by Seljuk forces, which would explain the decision to turn westwards, although a few fast riders might still have been able to get through to warn the emperor. Whether or not treachery played a role is unclear; more probably their understanding of the overall strategic situation encouraged their response, and the information required to assess this is simply not at our disposal.

Whatever the reason for this loss, the emperor was now deprived of some of his best and most reliable units. Unaware of the events to the south, he proceeded to Manzikert, which capitulated without a struggle, the garrison being released without punishment. Romanos set up his camp outside the fortress and on the banks of a small tributary of the Murat Su which flowed down from the Süphan Daği. The city was located on the northwestern edge of a roughly quadrangular rocky steppe region which stretches for some ten miles along a north-west/south-east axis, before rising gradually towards the foothills of the Süphan Daği, north-east of Khliat. This was an area thoroughly known to the Turks, but less familiar to both Romanos and his commanding officers, a fact which again proved to be a significant disadvantage to the Romans.

On the morning after the occupation of Manzikert, probably Wednesday 24 August, the emperor was informed that some of the detachments sent out to forage for supplies along the route south – towards Khliat, in fact – had been attacked and driven back by Turkish warriors. The commander of the left wing, Nikephoros Bryennios, was ordered to chase these raiders off; but in dealing with what turned out to be a much larger force than expected, soon found his units lured into ambushes and surrounded, so that he was compelled to withdraw to the camp. The emperor, still believing that this could not be the main Seljuk army, now sent out a much stronger force of cavalry under the Armenian commander Nikephoros Basilakes, the *doux* of Theodosioupolis. But Basilakes, ignoring the tenets of Byzantine tactics in respect of feigned retreats and the tactics of nomadic peoples, allowed his forces to engage in an uncontrolled pursuit of what he took to be retreating Seljuk troops. In fact, of course, the Turks had set an ambush, and not only were Basilakes's troops cut to pieces and driven back in flight, but he himself was captured.

Realizing that the Turks were present in greater strength than he had thought, but still entirely oblivious of Arslan's nearness, Romanos then ordered the whole left wing division to advance and drive the Turks off. But the latter had now retreated into the foothills surrounding the plain, and it was only when Bryennios reached the spot of the ambush on Basilakes that he learned, from a wounded survivor, what the true situation was. By this time – probably towards the middle of the afternoon – the Turks had arrived in real strength, and launched a determined attack on Bryennios's division, attempting to encircle it. The latter sensibly ordered a disciplined withdrawal, covering the movement of his own units by occasional charges, and at one point forcing the Turks into a real retreat. But the latter by now had the initiative, and it was with relief that Bryennios and his troops eventually reached the safety of the imperial camp. Bryennios himself was wounded – reportedly having two Turkish arrows fast in the armour on his back and a spear-thrust in the chest – although he was able to fight again the next day.

The emperor now realized that he was facing the main Turkish force, and that his information regarding Arslan's movements was clearly inadequate. The army was readied for a general assault but when drawn up for the advance the Turks had withdrawn completely into the hill country away to the south-east. In spite of scouts sent out to locate them, the whole enemy force had moved out of range, and the emperor was forced to withdraw to his camp.

That evening, however, the mobility and speed of the Turkish troops was demonstrated once more, for while a number of the Oğuz mercenaries were outside the camp doing business with local traders and merchants, Seljuk warriors appeared once again in the semi-darkness and swept in to harry those caught off guard outside the fortifications. Panic ensued as the Oğuz troops tried to hurry back inside the camp, while those inside the camp were equally confused by the fact that the Oğuz were hardly different in appearance from the Seljuk enemy, and the rumour spread that this was a full-scale assault upon the camp. But as suddenly as they had come the Turks disappeared, and although occasional raids took place during the night, no major attack was launched.

Next morning, 25 August, another Seljuk detachment attempted to seize control of the river bank opposite the Roman camp, but were driven off quickly by a concerted assault from the Byzantine infantry posted to defend the position. Shortly afterwards, however, a considerable body of the Oğuz warriors deserted to the Seljuks – their distant cousins – causing some anxiety that the remainder would follow. But they assured the emperor of their loyalty with an oath, and the worry subsided. Shortly afterwards there arrived in the imperial camp an embassy from Baghdad, from the court of the Caliph al-Muhalban, offering to negotiate. But Romanos would accept only conditions – including a Seljuk withdrawal – which it was clear the Turks could not, and so the embassy withdrew. It is also possible that he believed, or was persuaded, that the embassy was merely a ploy to delay the confrontation, allowing the Turkish Sultan to increase the forces at his disposal – the emperor having in the meanwhile sent messengers to recall the important body of troops he thought was still in the area of Khliat. In addition, and in spite of the situation of the army at the time, the Roman forces still had an impressive reputation, particularly in pitched battles where discipline and order were key elements; and it was generally felt that with the numbers of troops he had assembled and still available to him, the emperor had an excellent chance of inflicting a heavy defeat on the Turks, if he could bring them to battle.

It was, therefore, shortly after the departure of the Baghdad embassy, and on the morning of Friday 26 August, that the imperial army was drawn up outside the camp and prepared to advance on the Turkish host. The left wing was commanded by Nikephoros Bryennios and included his own western *tagmata* which, as *doux* of the west, he had commanded in Asia Minor for some time. The right wing, under Theodore Alyates, consisted of the Cappadocian and presumably most of the other Asia Minor units. The centre, under the emperor himself, included most of the guards units – the *scholai* included – and the Armenian heavy infantry. We may assume that the majority of the Roman heavy cavalry which remained with the main army (many had been sent off with Tarchaneiotes) were also in the centre, while the Pechenegs and Oğuz who remained with Romanos were disposed on the wings.

In spite of the arrogance and haughtiness which the emperor is reported by some sources to have displayed during the campaign, Romanos had the reputation of being a sensible and cautious general, and he knew the Turkish tactics well. The rearguard and reserve was, therefore, placed well behind the main force, able both to relieve the main line should it be forced to fall back, able also to close in and cut off any enemy units which attempted to encircle the main line and attack from behind. The rearguard included the *Hetaireai* and certain other elite units as well as regular *tagmata*, and possibly also a number of allied Turkish – Pecheneg or Oğuz – troops.

The terrain over which the battle was fought stretched over open, rocky ground from the city of Manzikert itself, with the entrenched and fortified imperial camp pitched a short distance to the south or south-east. From the city to the foothills to the south and south-east was a distance of between twelve and fourteen km of stony, rolling steppe land, the ground rising gradually before breaking up into an area of shallow gullies and stream-beds. At some distance from the Roman lines, but well in advance of this rougher land, Arslan had drawn up his own, less numerous force in a crescent formation, although he was himself not among the main body of troops, preferring to observe events from the higher ground to the rear. The Seljuk army was, in effect, divided up into a centre and two wings, but in traditional nomadic fashion these divisions in turn consisted of several smaller groupings which could, where needed, act independently.

Eastern Roman military practice demanded that, where an army of mobile horse-archers was to be attacked, the enemy should be brought to close action as swiftly as possible, to avoid undue casualties and attrition from long- and medium-range missile attack. The Roman force advanced, therefore, at a steady pace, in order with the rearguard keeping well back to protect the main line and flanks, while the Seljuks, equally disciplined, harried the Roman line with arrows while constantly but steadily moving back. While the centre withdrew, however, refusing any close engagement at all, the Turkish wings acted more aggressively, sweeping in to attack the Roman wings at close range before withdrawing again, thus forcing the Roman line to grow ever more ragged as the centre, pushing forward after the Seljuks opposite them, began to move well ahead, while the wings were held to a slower pace by the Turkish sallies.

By mid-afternoon the Byzantine centre division had reached and overrun the Seljuk camp – entirely emptied of its contents, of course – and were still pushing ahead, and when the afternoon drew to a close the emperor's own division had reached the rougher terrain ringing the edge of the plain across which his army had steadily advanced. Losses thus far seem to have been minimal, but on the flanks things were beginning to get out of hand. The constant shower of arrows was causing considerable annoyance to the Byzantine forces and, motivated by frustration rather than by tactical common sense or good discipline, many of the units attempted to charge their foes to bring them to battle. The Turks before them hesitated and then, in classic steppe style, feigned retreat, drawing the imperial forces into the rough ground where a series of ambuscades had been prepared.

It was now dusk. The emperor had been unable to come to grips with his enemy. He was no longer in close contact with the wings, which were only tenuously connected with his own division; and his army, which had left the main camp more-or-less undefended and extremely vulnerable to a swift mounted attack behind his lines, including his rearguard, was without supplies. To continue the advance into unknown and much rougher terrain, almost certainly prepared by the enemy, would have been disastrous. His army was still well-ordered and coherent, and an orderly withdrawal – which he had himself conducted in not dissimilar situations in the previous Anatolian campaigns – was now the only reasonable course of action.

It was at this point that disaster struck. Having given the order to withdraw, the centre began to pull back. But on the right wing the signal to withdraw was misunderstood by some soldiers and officers, who believed that the emperor had fallen. The rearguard was essential to the success of this withdrawal, of course, for it was the rearguard which would cover the units falling back and enable the manoeuvres to be carried out without undue haste and panic. But Andronikos Doukas was a sworn enemy of

Romanos IV, and it is clear from all contemporary accounts that he must have deliberately failed to follow the normal procedures. Rather than wait to cover the retreat of the main line, he reversed his own lines and simply marched back towards the camp, leaving Romanos's division exposed, and the wings entirely isolated. Although there is one near-contemporary account which tries to explain this action away, most accept that this was a deliberate act of treachery, designed to leave the emperor in the hands of the enemy and, Andronikos may have hoped, bring about his death – an event which would leave the path to the throne of a member of the Doukas clan uncontested. By the same token, these accounts all report the fact that Andronikos deliberately spread the rumour that the emperor had fallen in order to persuade the remaining divisions to abandon the field.

Seeing what was happening to the rearguard, and recognizing the confusion on the right wing, the Seljuks now launched an all-out attack. The right wing crumbled and dissolved in rout, fleeing back across the plain; the left wing, under Bryennios, seems to have withdrawn in order, until the Turkish units which had cut the right wing off from the centre swept into its rear and forced it, too, to break up in flight. Realizing the chaos the original misunderstanding had brought about, Romanos attempted to recall the panicking units and rally them to his own standard, but his signal was ignored and the central division too began to break up and withdraw, apparently in some order still, under the incessant barrage of Turkish arrows which now fell from all sides. The emperor and a small part of the centre were now entirely surrounded and, attempting a final stand, Romanos fought on, injured, until his horse was killed under him and, after a brief struggle on foot, he was knocked down. Only the next day, as the Turks went through the bodies collecting weapons and armour, was he recognized and taken before the Sultan.

Although the imperial army had dissolved at the end of the day's fighting, contemporary or near-contemporary claims that casualties were very high seem largely exaggerated, and the evidence suggests, on the contrary, that overall casualties were, in fact, quite light. The rearguard and reserve units under Andronikos Doukas escaped entirely unscathed and marched back to Constantinople – where Andronikos was immediately involved in the deposition of Romanos. Bryennios escaped similarly unscathed, and the left-wing units, in particular the *tagmata* of the west, were fighting effectively against Slavs and Pechenegs in the Balkans the following year. Of the units with the emperor in the centre and on the right wing, the Cappadocian *tagmata* seem to have been able to withdraw in some order, as did several of the elite units with the emperor himself, such as that of the *stratelatai*. Indeed, immediately after the battle, substantial numbers of units from these divisions had retreated on Dokeia (mod. Tokat, an important fortress on one of the main routes back to Constantinople, and to the south-east of Amaseia). There the emperor found them eight days later, after the Sultan had released him. Along with their commander Alyates, who had also escaped, the Cappadocian and other Asia Minor contingents vowed to support the emperor against the usurper who had been proclaimed in Constantinople upon the circulation of the false news of the emperor's death in battle.

It would seem, in consequence, that the actual losses incurred during the battle were quite limited, and affected largely the emperor's immediate retinue and bodyguard. A recent sensible analysis of the battle has estimated that, even if as many as 20% of the army were taken prisoner in the final hour before darkness fell, the overall losses in dead and wounded probably amounted to no more than 10% of those present at the beginning of the engagement. The most significant loss, apart from the capture of the emperor himself, seems to have been the imperial encampment and baggage train, which was abandoned as the various divisions and units withdrew towards Manzikert and beyond, and which was extremely rich – the sources emphasize the enormous quantity of booty that the Turks found there.

The reasons for these relatively light casualties are not hard to find. In the first place, the emperor's command was not finally cut off and surrounded until it was almost dark, so that the pursuit seems not to have been pressed beyond the imperial encampment itself. In addition, even as the other divisions withdrew, most of the Turkish troops were concentrated on the defeat of this body of troops around the emperor. This is significant from another point of view also, for, taken together with the Turkish tactics throughout the battle, it implies very strongly that the Seljuk forces were themselves nowhere near as numerous as many of the (later) medieval sources claim. Furthermore, Manzikert had been garrisoned and served as a refuge for many of the troops, and since the Turks did not attempt to retake it, it remained a safe haven until after the emperor's release.

In contrast to most popular judgements, therefore, the defeat at Manzikert was not a military disaster and did not entail the destruction of the eastern Roman army. On the contrary, the greater part of this army managed to make its way from the field with relatively few losses and in enough order to withdraw, by separate routes and at different rates, to comparative safety. The real disaster was of a political nature, for the capture of the emperor, which was soon broadcast throughout the political circles of the near and middle east, dramatically affected the general view of the Roman empire – a view certainly accepted until that point by the Turkish leader himself – that the Roman empire was a permanent, stable and unshakeable element of the political universe of the era. Romanos's capture showed that this was not the case, and encouraged a sea-change in attitudes to the power of the eastern Roman state.

By the same token, however, the ensuing civil war, which sapped the resources in troops and money on both sides, left Asia Minor undefended against the continuing incursions of Turkmen nomads and raiders, which Alp Arslan himself was relatively powerless to prevent. It also entailed the wearing down of the divisions which survived and the destruction of many units, so that the army of the eastern Roman empire suffered far more from this internecine strife than it had hitherto suffered at the hands of external enemies.

The Battle of Kalavryai 1078

The civil wars which marked the history of the empire from the early 1070s until the accession of Alexios I in 1081 thus witnessed a serious erosion of the empire's military strength. When Alexios seized power, he inherited the small but effective central army recruited during the reigns of the preceding emperors Michael VII (1071-8) and Nikephoros III (1078-81). This was made up of non-Byzantine mercenaries (Turks and

Franks, and the Varangians), some elite corps (the *Exkoubitoi*, the *Athanatoi*, the *Vestiaritai*), indigenous *tagmata* from Thrace and Macedonia, as well as from particular ethnic groups, such as Paulicians in the Balkans, Turks from the Vardar region, a force which numbered in total no more than about 20,000 men. He lost most of this army during his first years, following defeats at the hands of the Normans (at Dyrrachion in 1081) and the Pechenegs in 1089/90 – the army he assembled in 1089 consisted of the emperor's guards, a 500-strong units of Flemish knights, a levy of conscripted peasants, and a new unit of 2,000 men called the *archontopouloi*, consisting of the sons of former soldiers. After this army, too, had been defeated, by the winter of 1090 the emperor could muster a mere 500 soldiers. Thereafter, having recruited new units, he depended upon a combination of mercenary units, on the one hand, and units formed from the retainers or hired soldiers in the retinues of his extended family and the members of the aristocracy. Following his defeat of the Pechenegs at the battle of Lebounion in 1091, he was also able to recruit the surviving Pechenegs themselves, who henceforth formed a key element in the imperial armies. Alexios's resources were always stretched thinly, so that, apart from some provincial town militias and the retinues of local landlords and officials in the provinces, the central field army was the only effective force available to him.

In 1078 the general Nikephoros Bryennios rebelled against the emperor Michael VII Doukas, the latter having seized the throne after the defeat of Romanos IV at Manzikert. Michael's inability to deal effectively with the rebel soon led to his removal from power and the accession in March 1078 of Nikephoros III Botaneiates, an able and effective soldier who, however, suffered from a serious shortage of troops. To lead his fight against Bryennios Nikephoros III appointed an equally able strategist and tactician, Alexios Komnenos, and gave him the position of *domestikos* of the *scholai*, commander-in-chief of the field armies of the empire.

Bryennios had marched from his base at Dyrrachion (mod. Dürreš) on the Albanian coast across the southern Balkans along the *via Egnatia*, rallying much popular support *en route*, and gathering an army of some 12,000 men, the great majority battle-hardened veterans. By the time of Botaneiates's enthronement he had established himself at Adrianople, his home city. To oppose the rebel, Alexios had a small force of a few hundred Frankish heavy cavalry, 2,000 Turkish troops from allied emirs in Anatolia, the Chomatenoi, from Asia Minor, numbering perhaps 2,000, and the recently formed unit of the Immortals – *Athanatoi* (not connected with the earlier unit of the same name established by John Tzimiskes a century earlier), who may have numbered about 1,000. The total at his disposal was, therefore, a mere 5,500 or so, perhaps 6,500, greatly inferior to the enemy army, and a substantial portion of them new recruits or untried in battle. Turkish reinforcements were promised, but had not arrived when the emperor gave Alexios the order to advance to meet Bryennios and throw him back. In such a context, Alexios's only option was to attempt to draw the enemy into terrain prepared in advance and use ambush and feigned withdrawal to even the balance. As accounts of the battle show, Alexios's initial plan was a failure, and he was almost defeated. Yet by a brilliant tactical response, and by adopting the tactics he should probably have employed from the start, he was able to reverse the fortunes of the battle in a few moments, and end the day victorious. (See Map 9)

Alexios decided that he should move to block the main approach to Constantinople, leaving Bryennios no choice but to accept the challenge. Bryennios had pitched his camp not far away at Kedoukton (from Lat. *Aqueductus*), an open plain not far to the north-west. Marching into Thrace, Alexios encamped on the Halmyros river, a small stream to the west of mod. Erekli and not far from the fortress of Kalavryai or Galavria (mod. Gelivre) near Selymbria (mod. Silivri). He did not entrench or defend his camp, however, for according to the sources he wanted to be able to ambush and take Bryennios by surprise, since he was so greatly outnumbered. Here, his scouts were sent out to obtain information about Bryennios's movements, but some of them – they were Turks – were captured, and revealed Alexios's whereabouts and numbers to Bryennios. Having spied out the ground between the two camps very carefully, Alexios decided his best option was the draw Bryennios's forces down upon his own lines outside his undefended camp, preparing an ambush in the broken and undulating scrub country through which the enemy army would need to advance.

Bryennios had organized his force into the standard three divisions. On the right wing, his brother John was placed in command, with a force of about 5,000 consisting of Frankish mercenaries, units of cavalry from Thessaly, a unit of the *hetaireia* guard, and the *Maniakatoi*, a cavalry unit recruited from the Franks of southern Italy. On the left wing the commander Katakalon Tarchaneiotes commanded some 3,000 troops from Thrace and Macedonia; and in the centre Bryennios himself commanded some 3-4,000 or so men, consisting of Macedonian, Thracian and Thessalian units. On the extreme left, about a mile distant from the main battle line, a detachment of Pechenegs was posted, with orders to encircle and envelop the right wing of Alexios's army when the opportunity arose. Following traditional tactical precepts, each of Bryennios's divisions consisted of a forward line and, shortly behind it, a second line to act as reserve and reinforcement should the first line be forced to retire.

Alexios had divided his much smaller force into two divisions, the general Constantine Katakalon with the Chomatenoi and the allied Turkish troops on the right, Alexios himself with the Franks (in the centre) and the Immortals (to their left). A detachment of troops, probably from the Immortals, was sent ahead and off to the left flank to lay an ambush for the advancing enemy wing; while the Turks on the right were, according to one of the two major sources describing the battle, to guard against the possibility of an outflanking movement from the enemy Pechenegs.

The battle commenced as the forces under Bryennios advanced and came within range of Alexios's ambush. Here, the initial surprise of the attack succeeded for a few minutes in pushing the enemy line back in confusion. But bringing up his second line, John Bryennios quickly re-established order, and in a furious counter-charge, put the greatly outnumbered force of attackers to flight. The unfortunate consequence of this, however, was that the fleeing ambush detachment ran right into the waiting lines of Alexios's own left wing, and instantly caused a panic, so that his formation of poorly trained and inexperienced Immortals began to dissolve and run back from their positions. Although suffering some casualties, the majority seem to have reached safety some distance behind the field of conflict, where they were able to be rallied and their flight stopped. Alexios himself with a small retinue, thinking in the confusion of the fight that his division was still with him, continued to fight until he realized he was in danger of being completely cut off.

The pursuing enemy right wing now moved against the remaining force under Alexios, consisting of his Frankish troops, who put up a stout resistance. On Alexios's right, however, the contest was more even, until the enemy Pechenegs, who had successfully avoided the Turks detached to prevent an outflanking movement, had been able to sweep around and attack Katakalon's division in the flank and rear. The Chomatenoi, too, broke and fled, and it was probably the great numerical inferiority of the loyalist right wing which made this possible, for the Turkish allies were apparently fully engaged with holding their position against the troops under Tarchaneiotes. The Turks seem to have retired towards the rear of their position once the Chomatenoi had dissolved. Rather than following up their victory on the right, however, the Pecheneg troops of Bryennios's army now halted, still in good order according to the historian Bryennios, the grandson of the rebel commander himself, and turned aside to sack their own camp, which was full of the equipment and chattels of their own army! They then simply abandoned Bryennios's army and marched off homeward.

This certainly saved Alexios who, realizing that he was rapidly being isolated in the centre with the Franks and his own retinue, which was now beset on all sides, was advised to make good his escape. Apparently he had considered making a personal attack on Bryennios and trying to kill him, a development which might demoralize the enemy and swing the battle in his favour, but he was persuaded to give up this idea. The enemy troops around his division prevented his retiring directly, and he seems with only six men to have managed to ride through the mêlée and the enemy ranks in front of him and around the back of the enemy lines. Here he was met by the confusion caused by the Pechenegs who had started looting Bryennios's own camp and, seeing some grooms leading Bryennios's parade horse along with his imperial regalia, he and his followers managed to seize the animal and ride helter skelter for safety behind their own lines.

Alexios now rode towards a low hill behind his original position, on and around which a large number of his broken units had begun to reform, and here he announced that Bryennios was dead, showing them the parade horse and imperial swords as proof. He and his officers now began to reform the units for a renewed assault. They were encouraged by the fact that a detachment of Turkish allied troops had arrived, and while the Franks in Alexios's original left wing division had by now begun to surrender, the rear of Bryennios's army was in chaos, with the camp being looted by the Pechenegs, the rearmost units disrupted by fleeing camp attendants, and on the assumption that the battle was already won, no discernible order of battle had been maintained among the units making up the main battle line.

Alexios now decided to adopt a different strategy, utilizing his Turkish horse-archers to best effect, by dividing his force into three divisions. The central division, under his own command, was made up of the rallied Chomatenoi and Immortals but formed up not in a single dense body, but rather in several smaller groups, intermixed with similar small groups of Turkish mounted archers. The two wings were held back and concealed in the undulating ground, the plan being for Alexios's force to move forward, engage the enemy and entice them on in a disorderly rush, at which point they would be encircled by the units lying in wait.

Alexios's opening assault took Bryennios's troops by surprise, but after a while they re-established order and began to push him back. His men alternately resisted and then fell back, the Turkish mounted troops wheeling about and dashing through the gaps between his other units to keep the pursuers at a reasonable distance, all the while drawing the enemy force towards the location of the concealed troops. Bryennios's force, as Alexios had surmised, grew less and less disciplined as the pursuit wore on. Whether the whole of Bryennios's army was engaged in this action remains unclear. But when the running mêlée had passed the units waiting in ambush, the latter were given the signal to attack. Bursting out from their positions, they charged into the flanks and rear of Bryennios's units, which panicked and, losing all semblance of their former cohesion, turned to flight. The units behind them were likewise taken off guard and turned, and although Bryennios and his brother tried to rally the troops, they were cut off and surrounded with only a few men, and after a short while were forced to surrender. In this second phase of the encounter, Alexios had used, to outstanding effect, classic steppe tactics against a far superior force, not only in terms of numbers but also in terms of battle experience – Manzikert on a much smaller scale. Both armies had demonstrated, at different moments during the encounter, a degree of discipline which illustrates the strength and tenacity of eastern Roman military tradition and methods, but it was Alexios's clever exploitation of the chance offered him by the plundering of Bryennios's camp by his own Pecheneg allies which tipped the scales.

Dyrrachion 1081

Alexios was not always so lucky, and in the first years of his reign, beginning in 1081, he had to contend with major strategic problems as his empire reeled from the assaults of Pechenegs in the north, Normans in the west and Turks in Asia Minor. In late May 1081 the Norman duke Robert Guiscard, a member of the Hauteville clan which had carved out a substantial territory for itself in southern Italy, landed at Avlona on the Albanian coast with the intention of seizing for himself a territory in the western Balkans. He had already taken Bari, the last Byzantine stronghold in Italy, in 1071, and had firm designs on the Byzantine territories in the Balkans. This was his first, and long-planned, move. His landing was unopposed and by the middle of June his force had marched north to encircle and lay siege to the regional capital and Byzantine fortress of Dyrrachion (mod. Dürreš).

The city was extremely well-defended, situated on a long and narrow peninsula which ran parallel with the coast but separated from it by a brackish and marshy lagoon. The powerful defences, which dated from the sixth century, had been well-maintained, and the city was in a position to withstand a long siege. Guiscard had a fleet with him, and his initial plan was to try to take the city by storm from both land and sea – a desperate undertaking given the strength of the defences and the garrison. In the event, the emperor's allies, Venice, sent a strong fleet which arrived before this plan could be realized, and completely routed the Normans at sea, while the garrison then sallied out, taking the Normans by surprise and inflicting substantial casualties on them. While Venetian and Roman vessels now maintained a blockade of Robert's forces by sea, the invaders also had to put up with the difficult conditions in their encampment, where fever broke out over the following weeks and rendered a large number of both ordinary soldiers and knights out of action.

In spite of these set-backs, Robert would not give up, and continued to press the siege with all the means at his disposal. The emperor Alexios I, only very recently enthroned, now decided that he must march west and drive the aggressors off, since they presented a substantial threat to the empire's Balkan provinces, which since the virtual complete loss of control over the Anatolian region, was now crucial to its survival. As the emperor marched to meet him, meanwhile, Guiscard had constructed a number of siege engines, with which he proceeded to bombard the garrison in an effort to wear it down, while at the same time his scouts informed as the emperor approached. At Thessaloniki Alexios received reports of a sally by the garrison which had been less than successful, resulting in some casualties, including the commander George Palaiologos, who received an arrow in the temple (although he survived). He also received a report as he marched on that Guiscard had now constructed a large siege-tower, which threatened the walls.

The size of the two armies is, as usual, difficult to assess. Anna Komnena gives a figure of 30,000 for the Norman host, consisting of a core of some 1,300 heavily armed cavalry supported by lighter cavalry and a large draft of infantry and footsoldiers, some of dubious quality. The figure is, again, probably exaggerated, but it was nevertheless a very substantial force, and the emperor almost certainly had a smaller army with which to engage the Normans. To pit against this Alexios had with him the Thracian and Macedonian *tagmata*, perhaps 5,000 strong; the *exkoubita*, a guards unit which may have numbered 1,000; the *vestiaritai*, similarly an elite unit of probably the same number; a body of Frankish knights under Constantine Humbertopoulos; the corps of Manichaeans, consisting of two units totalling 2,800 men together; the various *tagmata* of Thessalian cavalry, whose numbers are unknown; some 2,000 Turkish allied troops from Asia Minor, along with levies from Thrace and the other Balkan provinces; a corps of Armenian infantry, probably several thousand strong; the Varangians, perhaps 1,400 strong; and an unknown number of light infantry archers and slingers. His total force numbered perhaps 18-20,000, although it may have been slightly larger.

The emperor had sought the advice of his senior officers, including George Palaiologos, who had visited him in his camp, about whether or not to attack. The garrison had successfully destroyed the first siege-tower built by the Normans, who now embarked upon the construction of a second. Arguing that time was on the emperor's side, the more senior officers – including Palaiologos himself – urged caution, but there were those who counselled an immediate attack, advice which Alexios himself favoured. But while he hoped to catch the Normans unawares and still in position around the defences of Dyrrachion, Robert had scouts posted who informed him of the imperial army's approach. Alexios advanced to a range of low hills opposite the Norman camp on the neck of the peninsula, preparatory to an attack on the Norman encampment the next day. His camp was entrenched along the higher ground, with the sea and the lagoon on the left and some distance ahead, and with a sudden steep escarpment to the right, which defined the area in which the two sides could manoeuvre. The emperor's plan was to attack the Norman camp simultaneously from the city and from the salt-marshes, while the main force would march around to the neck of the peninsula, closing it off and attacking the Normans from the rear. But Guiscard was too intelligent a tactician to allow himself, with superior numbers, to be boxed in, and during the night of 17th-18th October he moved his army out and along the peninsula, to draw it up in battle order on the mainland facing Alexios, its rear to the lagoon.

Although he had already sent off a body of troops through the marshes against Robert's camp, Alexios now revised his plan and reformed his lines in three divisions opposite the Normans. Guiscard himself commanded the centre, with his son Bohemond commanding the Norman left and the count of Giovinazzo the right, on the seaward flank. On the Roman side Alexios commanded the centre, with the Varangians in the front line, while Gregory Pakourianios and Nikephoros Melissenos commanded the left and right wings respectively. Detachments from the garrison in Dyrrachion and light troops from Alexios's force who had been detailed to attack the Norman camp found it abandoned, and at about the same time Alexios ordered a general advance. His Varangians had been ordered to precede the main line by a few yards, and behind them a strong force of infantry archers was ordered to move through their ranks, loosing off a volley before retiring behind the Varangian line. This manoeuvre was to be repeated as long as possible during the advance until the two armies should come into contact, and may have been Alexios's response to the danger posed by the Norman heavy cavalry force.

As the armies drew close to one another, Robert sent out a detachment of cavalry in the centre to charge forward and then retire hastily, in an effort to draw the Varangians out of their position; but they were met by the archers' volleys and retired without success. Then the units on the Norman right under count Ami suddenly charged forward against the point where the Roman centre and left wing divisions met, directing their attack against the left flank of the Varangian line. But while the Varangians stood and stoutly resisted the attack, the Roman left wing under Pakourianos, and including some of Alexios's best troops, surged forward and broke the Norman formation, which disintegrated. The majority of these troops seem to have been conscripts and less experienced cavalry, and fled back in panic towards the coast, where many perished in the sea before the remainder were rallied by Robert's wife, who appeared in full panoply and cantered up and down the shore-line in an effort to reform them.

In the meantime the Norman left wing and centre engaged in skirmishing with the Roman forces opposite, and with the Norman right broken, their centre, along with most of Guiscard's heavy cavalry, looked in danger of being outflanked. At this point the Romans appeared to be winning the fight, but the Varangians had been unable to resist joining in the pursuit of the fleeing Norman troops, and had become separated from Alexios's main line. Tired by the chase and by the weight of their equipment, they were in no position to resist a determined assault. Guiscard now sent against them a strong force of Norman spearmen which took them unexpectedly in the flank, and within a short time the Varangian formation had been broken up with heavy casualties. Some of the remaining Varangian soldiers fled for refuge to a small chapel which stood nearby, where the Normans shut them in and set fire to the building. The whole detachment perished.

Deprived of his left wing, which was still pursuing the broken Norman right wing and had lost all order, and with his centre now exposed, Alexios found himself subject to the charges of Guiscard's heavy cavalry, which had been held in reserve. Divided into a number of smaller detachments, these now crashed at several points into Alexios's line. The infantry archers and skirmishers who had been placed behind the Varangians, if they were still in position (the account makes no mention of them at this stage) could have offered little, if any, resistance to such an attack. No mention is made of the fate of the Roman right, but along with the main battle line of the Roman centre, these two divisions, without their heavy Varangian infantry in the van, soon disintegrated. The emperor and his retinue and guards resisted as long as they could, but were soon compelled to fall back and flee, the emperor escaping only after a long pursuit and numerous attempts had been made to take or kill him by the Norman forces, which were now able to encircle the remaining Byzantine troops at leisure. The imperial camp, with its rich booty, was left defenceless and was taken by the victorious Normans.

Alexios was undoubtedly a good tactician, but he was badly let down by the indisciplined rush to pursue the beaten enemy wings, a cardinal sin in the Byzantine tactical manuals. He had also failed to take adequate account of the effectiveness of the Norman heavy cavalry charge, which punched through his lines with little resistance. In later battles, he tried to avoid having to confront such charges directly, and would also order the archers to shoot at the Normans' horses, which were generally unarmoured. The defeat was especially serious for an empire already so desperately short of manpower and resources, and Alexios had to start almost from scratch to rebuild his army thereafter. It is remarkable that, within a few years, he had succeeded so far as to be able to throw the Normans out of the Balkans and defeat the Pechenegs and the Seljuks – although in the case of the last enemy the arrival of the first crusade was undoubtedly an important factor in the recovery of Byzantine fortunes in Anatolia.

Losses at the battle were very heavy on the Byzantine side – some 5,000, perhaps as many as 25% of the whole army, including most of the Varangian corps. Norman losses for the whole army are not known, although there must have been substantial casualties among the troops on the two wings that broke and fled back towards the sea or the lagoon. Among Robert's Norman heavy cavalry, however, a contemporary Norman report puts losses at a remarkable thirty!

The Komnenian Recovery

Careful planning, intelligent and skilful internal policies and sensible strategy enabled Alexios I to stabilize the situation between his accession and 1105. Tactics appropriate to the different enemies the empire faced, especially against Pechenegs and Turks, were refined. The Pechenegs were completely defeated and, as part of the treaty drawn up afterwards, were established within the empire, and in return had to serve in the imperial army. By wearing them down and avoiding pitched battles like Dyrrachion, the Normans were eventually thrown out of Epirus and Albania; and the difficult situation with regard to the Turks in north-western Asia Minor was stabilized. In achieving these results, there is no doubt that Alexios's clever use of the armies of the first Crusade, which passed through Byzantine territory in 1097-1098, played an important role. He also introduced some important fiscal and military administrative reforms to re-establish a coherent central administration and palatine establishment. Under Alexios's son John II (1118-1143) substantial regions of western Anatolia were reconquered. Under John's successor Manuel I (1143-1180) imperial power in the Balkans was re-affirmed and strengthened, and Roman armies began gradually to extend Byzantine control into central Anatolia, in an attempt to re-assert Roman rule there. But while the empire faced the Hungarians on the Danube with some success, its ultimate failure in Asia Minor spelled the end of the East Roman empire in its established territorial form. In 1176, in a strategically premature and tactically misjudged attempt to eliminate organized Turkish opposition in central Asia Minor, the imperial field army, with the emperor present, was ambushed and defeated at the battle of Myriokephalon. This expensive enterprise was thus wasted, and as a result of changes in the international situation and rebellion in the Balkans, the empire was never again in a position to go onto the offensive in Asia Minor on this scale again. The 'Turkification' and Islamization of central Asia Minor was already under way; the empire could henceforth do little to prevent its completion. The eastern Roman empire, which had once straddled Europe and Asia, became an increasingly European state.

The Battle of Semlin/Sirmium 1167

Eastern Roman relations with the kingdom of Hungary were particularly strained during the 1150s and 1160s, for the growing power of Hungary had become an important player in the international political scene, in particular in relation to Byzantine policy towards the German empire, the pre-eminent power in central and eastern Europe and Italy. Hungarian interest in the north-western Balkans, especially in Rascia/Serbia and the Dalmatian coast, was perceived by the government at Constantinople as a destabilizing element in the region and a threat to imperial interests. Manuel tried to address the issue by applying both military and diplomatic pressure, sending frequent expeditions to intimidate dissident rulers in the region into following the imperial line and interfering in the dynastic politics of the Hungarian court. In 1164 Manuel led an expedition across the Danube to re-establish Byzantine control over the region of Sirmium (taking its name from the fortress of the same name, modern Sremska Mitrovica, on the left bank of the Sava), but although he was successful, the hostilities continued into 1165 and, in 1166 with a three-pronged attack. No decisive victory was won by either side, however, until in 1167 the general Andronikos Kontostephanos was placed in command of a combined field army. By skilful strategic manoeuvring he managed to bring the Hungarian field armies, which had joined forces, to a pitched battle near the fortress of Semlin in the district of Sirmium. The result was a stunning Byzantine victory which demonstrated once again that Byzantine tactical order and discipline could carry the day even when the enemy were not outnumbered and employed the same technology. (See Map 9)

Kontostephanos drew up his forces in three divisions, as usual, at some distance from the river Sava, to his rear. The main battle line was shielded by a screen of horse archers – Turks and Cumans – and some western mercenary knights, who had made up the vanguard of the army. The centre, which had constituted the rearguard on the march, was commanded by Kontostephanos himself, and consisted of the imperial guards units, including the Varangians and *Hetaireiai*, units of Italian mercenaries from Lombardy (probably lancers), and a unit of 500 Serbian allied infantry. On the left wing, which had been the second division on the march, were the regular Roman and allied units arrayed in four taxiarchies or 'brigades', and on the right – the third division on the march – were placed the elite Roman units and German mercenaries, together with some Turkish units. Behind each wing division, and following standard Roman practice, were placed units to cover the Roman flanks or to outflank the enemy and take him in the rear should the opportunity arise; and behind the centre was drawn up the reserve, three taxiarchies of infantry and archers, with a number of heavily armoured Turks, probably infantry also.

The Hungarian commander drew his army up in three divisions in a single broad battle line. Although the Byzantine sources say that he mixed infantry and cavalry together without distinction, this most probably reflects a battle order with infantry drawn up in the centre and behind the cavalry, upon which the Hungarians clearly relied for the effectiveness of their attack.

The battle commenced with the Roman light-armed troops skirmishing forward to harry the opposing lines with arrows and to persuade them to mount a charge, before which they were to retire. This was successful, and the whole Hungarian line surged forward. The Roman left wing, with the exception of two brigades, was immediately pushed back and broke in feigned rout towards the river, where it quickly reformed. In the centre and on the Roman right the charge was held. The Roman right then counter-charged, and at the same time the regrouped Roman left-wing units also charged, smashing into the Hungarians who were pinned by the two taxiarchies which had not withdrawn. Kontostephanos now counter-attacked in the centre and ordered forward the infantry reserve along the whole front, driving the Hungarian forces back. The enemy divisions then began to break up in disorder and the whole Hungarian army turned to flight.

Kontostephanos won the battle because of intelligent tactical dispositions, in particular the weakening of the Hungarian line by the feigned withdrawal on the Roman left. Although the sources do not make this manoeuvre explicit, the fact that the units which were driven back reappear in perfect order a short while after their 'rout', together with the fact that two of the four brigades which made up the Roman left wing division held their position, with the effect of pinning the Hungarian right, makes this very probable. The counter-charge of the Roman line, followed by the sudden impact on the Hungarian line of the heavy infantry reserve, then took the Hungarian divisions off balance, since they seem to have had no reserve upon which to fall back or to call for support. Byzantine or eastern Roman sources always emphasize Roman order against non-Roman disorder, and this is certainly something of a literary motif in Byzantine accounts of battles (especially when Roman officers do not maintain it, and thus lose a battle). Nevertheless, the fact that it is a literary motif does not mean that it was not usually true, for, as we have seen, Byzantine commanders who used order and discipline effectively were usually victorious. Of course, order and discipline alone were not enough – sensible and intelligent leadership was just as vital.

The Battle of Myriokephalon 1176

The battle of Sirmium illustrates the fact that in the 1160s, even with a very different type of army from that which had won the great victories of the later tenth and early eleventh centuries, and different yet again from the thematic forces which had defended the empire from the seventh century, eastern Roman armies, when well-led and disciplined, were capable of winning striking victories, and remained a key instrument of imperial foreign policy. By the 1170s in Asia Minor the emperor Manuel had succeeded in establishing a real equilibrium with the Seljuk Sultanate of Konya (Ikonion) and had been gradually pressing forward around the frontier regions, with the ultimate intention of recovering the central Anatolian plateau, lost in the aftermath of Manzikert a century earlier. Imperial forces had been able to reoccupy Cilicia in the south, and the principality of Antioch recognized Byzantine overlordship. The main problem facing the emperor in the east was the fact that his western policies were constantly threatened by the activities, diplomatic or otherwise, of the German emperors, who saw the eastern Roman state as the main challenge to their power in the central Mediterranean, and went so far as to tacitly support the Seljuk Sultan Kilidj Aslan against the eastern Roman emperor. Manuel had therefore to dispose his resources carefully to avoid appearing to neglect his Balkan territories, yet at the same time to assemble sufficient manpower to mount an effective challenge to the Seljuks. An important aspect of his policy in the east was maintaining good relations with the Crusader states in Syria and Palestine, and at the same time remaining on good terms with the emirs of Aleppo who served as a valuable counter-weight to the Seljuk power to their north. When the ruler of Aleppo, Nur ad-Din, died in 1174, the balance of power in the region shifted a little away from Byzantium, as Nur ad-Din's successor, Saladin, was more interested in affairs in Egypt and to the south.

Manuel decided, in consequence, that a strategy to eradicate the Seljuk power would pay the best results in the short-term, and began preparations for a major expedition aimed at Ikonion, the Seljuk capital itself. It is debatable whether, had his strategy paid off and he had been able to defeat the Seljuks and take the city, the policy could have worked in the long term, in view of the firm hold the Turks had by now established in the region. Nevertheless, having re-fortified a number of fortresses which directly challenged Seljuk power, war broke out and Manuel's army, accompanied by a large siege and baggage train – stretching, according to the emperor himself in a letter he later wrote to Henry II of England, along ten miles of the route – set out in the summer of 1176 to confront the Seljuk leader in what, it was hoped, would be a decisive encounter.

Kilidj Aslan was, understandably, in some consternation about the imperial attack, which posed a serious threat to his realm. He sent to Manuel offering to negotiate but the emperor, convinced of the superiority of his forces, refused and marched on. The Seljuk Sultan had only one option, to defend his territory as best he could. Accurately assessing the routes the imperial army could follow, he decided that his only chance lay in ambushes and delaying actions. The obvious location for a defensive action was one of the passes across the mountains onto the central Anatolian plateau, on the eastern edge of which Konya was located. Manuel's approach was from the west, but his route took him somewhat to the north first, before he could proceed along the road from Pisidian Antioch south-eastwards along the eastern shore of Lake Pousgouse (mod. Beyşehir Gölü), and then eastwards. Following this road, his army would have to march through the important pass of Tzybritze along the road to Ikonion, if they were to besiege the city. This was the direct route, which the emperor had traversed once before during an expedition beyond Roman territory in 1146. The pass is about 15 miles in length and follows a winding course, curving down in a south-easterly direction before bending around to the north-east once more. Wooded in places and offering plenty of cover to any force wishing to set an ambush, it is entered by a narrow defile several miles in length, before this opens out into a narrow plain some 9 miles long, with sloping ground on one side, steeper cliffs on the other. Near the beginning of the plain (and about 6 miles from the head of the pass), and some 2 miles from the road to the north, stood the ruins of an abandoned fortress (still visible today as mod. Asar Kalesi), the medieval Myriokephalon ('thousand peaks', after the numerous mountains behind it). The ground throughout its length is broken and rugged, adding to the difficulties of any military force trying to keep in formation, a point noted by the contemporary historians. At the head of the pass the cliffs close in again and the road passes through another defile before emerging onto the hilly plateau about 25 miles from Konya.

The Turks had already destroyed as much of the available seasonal forage as they could along the route followed by the imperial forces. They had also poisoned or otherwise rendered unusable the main watering places. The result was that the Roman forces were already suffering from a shortage of water and forage, and dysentery had afflicted many of the troops in the army. The Sultan's forces occupied the pass and, on approaching it, Manuel had to decide whether or not to attack. In spite of advice to the contrary, which warned him of the danger of ambuscades, he opted to make a frontal attack, although there was at least one nearby alternative, which although difficult, would have brought the army out onto the plain near the town of Philomelion (Turkish Ak ehir), and which was followed by the forces of the third crusade in 1190. The reasons for his decision are not stated; but it may have been due to the fact that Manuel was anxious about the army's need for water and forage and had no option apart from turning back – a humiliation which, at this stage, he was unwilling to contemplate. It is also possible that, being familiar with the contours of the pass from the 1146 expedition, he expected the Turks to let his army pass through and harass him on the far side.

The size of the Seljuk force is unknown. The numbers of the imperial army are likewise difficult to assess, but the siege- and baggage train is reported to have included 3,000 carts, and an army stretching over more than ten miles, marching five abreast, would number something in the order of 25,000 men. The accuracy of this estimate depends on terrain, width of the marching column, numbers of horses and so forth, so it is only the very crudest guide. The army was divided, following standard practice, into several divisions, each of which seems to have consisted of a balanced force of cavalry, archers and infantry, except the van, which was made up chiefly of infantry. A contemporary account based on the reports of those present on the campaign describes the imperial column as made up of the van division (as noted, chiefly infantry, largely of the palace regiments), followed by the main division (made up of the eastern and western *tagmata*), the right wing under Baldwin of Jerusalem followed by the pack and baggage train, and then the siege train, and then the Roman left wing. This was then followed by the emperor's own division and picked troops, followed in turn by the rearguard under the trusted senior commander, Andronikos Kontostephanos – a classic Roman marching order.

Manuel is reported to have taken no account of the rough terrain through which his army now had to pass. The heavily laden pack-animals did not have their loads redistributed and lightened; the carts carrying the siege-engines were not redeployed to make their passage more quickly; no advance parties were sent through to try to locate and dislodge the Turkish ambushes. Following the emperor's decision, the Roman vanguard pushed on and marched through the defile into the pass. The predominantly infantry force seems to have taken the Turks by surprise, for it was able to push through with only token opposition – possibly the Turks were still getting into position at this point, since the sources are not clear about when Kilidj Aslan sent in his troops.

The march through probably took between five and six hours, and given the length of the imperial column, which had almost certainly extended as the troops defiled through the narrower sections, the van will have reached the head of the pass by the time the rear divisions were entering. Close behind the van division, the main division marched hastily through; but it was at this point that the Turks in the heights above and around the pass seem to have launched their attack, falling on the Roman right wing and the baggage train in particular, which had followed more slowly and had become strung out over a longer distance. One source speaks specifically of the failure of the right-wing troops to maintain any sort of battle-order or use their archers to fend off the Seljuk attacks. The right wing suffered heavy casualties and its troops broke formation and began to run both forwards and to the rear. Baldwin himself fell in the action. Many of the soldiers tried to take refuge on a small hill, but large numbers were also injured when they fell into the dry ravine between the road and the raised ground. The Turks had set several ambushes along the length of the pass, according to a contemporary source in seven different 'trench-like' valleys through which the route passed, and no sooner had some soldiers made their way out of one ambush than they fell into the next. Meanwhile, the van division, which had escaped the main attack, was through the pass, where it established its own fortified encampment on a hill, soon to be followed by the main division. Choniates notes specifically that the Turks left these divisions alone once they had pushed through the pass and encamped.

The divisions behind the baggage also began to panic and dissolve as the effects of the Turkish attack became evident and as they came upon the carnage of the draught and baggage animals and their handlers, mercilessly shot down by the Turkish archery and now partly blocking their path. Turkish arrows now rained down upon the rearmost Roman units, whose path was blocked by the destruction of the siege and baggage train, and for a while it is reported that the emperor himself resigned all hope and simply sat passively awaiting his fate. The situation was not improved by a sudden dust-storm which blew up, making it impossible for a while for the troops on either side to make out their foe. The emperor was then galvanized by some of his soldiers and officers and, exerting himself to re-establish some discipline, was able to reform the various detachments into a defensive formation, managing to get the rest of the force through the pass where it joined the van and centre divisions. The rearguard seems to have followed through without suffering from the Seljuk attacks, and arrived at the fortified encampment as dark fell.

Analysis of events after the battle, and in particular of all the information pertaining to the numbers and strength of eastern Roman armies in the next year or two, strongly suggest that overall casualties appear, in spite of Choniates's dramatic account, not to have been heavy, except among the troops of the right wing, which seems to have been almost annihilated. But the whole baggage and siege train was destroyed, its personnel and animals killed or captured. That evening the army took up a defensive position on and around the hill occupied by the van division, where it spent the night repelling the sorties and attacks of the Turkish mounted archers. Without the equipment Manuel had brought with him the expedition could not hope to achieve its aim of taking Konya and, given his difficult situation and following discussions with his officers, the emperor now accepted Kilidj Aslan's offer to negotiate, and was able to withdraw without further loss.

The defeat, while not costly in manpower, was expensive in terms of opportunities lost through poor tactics. For even though the correct procedure was followed up to the point at which the army arrived before the pass, military handbooks advised that such locations should either be avoided or, where absolutely unavoidable, carefully scouted out in advance. It was a standard tenet of eastern Roman military practice that, where an army has to pass through a narrow defile or pass, or where the soldiers might be able to march only two abreast or even in single file, cavalry should dismount and their horses, with the baggage, should be placed in the centre. A detachment of troops should also be left behind to hold it until the army returns. While the emperor seems to have followed these precepts in part, his failure to consider other options, or to scout the pass and take adequate account of the ways in which the Turks had disposed their defences, was substantially responsible for the defeat and the loss of the siege train.

As with Manzikert, with which Manuel himself compared the defeat, Myriokephalon has usually been grossly exaggerated, at least in terms of casualties and the after-effects on the army. For it was certainly not a catastrophe. The loss of the siege train was indeed a disaster for the expedition and for Manuel's strategy, however, and threw the emperor into a fit of depression for a while, encouraging a gloomy reaction to the failure. But its longer-term effects were more damaging to the empire, for Manuel was never again in a position to assemble such a costly expeditionary force. Yet even after the battle, the Turks were unable to press what little advantage they had been able to derive from it. The empire's armies were still intact and in place, and a year later, were able to inflict a dramatic defeat on an invading Seljuk force while maintaining the empire's position in the Balkans. Only after Manuel's death in 1180 and the collapse of his carefully constructed system of diplomatic checks and balances did the real collapse in imperial power begin once more.

Conclusion

The battles lost and won by eastern Roman armies between the sixth and twelfth centuries reflect very closely the internal as well as the external history of the empire. Its social and economic, as well as its political and administrative structures are mirrored in the ways in which the army was organized. The weaknesses and strengths in training and tactical or strategic organization, the social origins, training and skills (or lack of them) of the officers who led the armies, the logistical arrangements for maintaining and supplying soldiers, the military technology employed in equipping the troops and making war, all these aspects are part and parcel of eastern Roman culture. We should not forget, either, the ideological element, for the need to justify and explain warfare and violence in a self-consciously Christian society was strongly felt, and much was, in consequence, written about the subject which can help us understand how people in that world thought about it.

Given its strategic location, beset on all sides throughout its existence with enemies or potential enemies, the empire's survival as a major political entity throughout the period I have covered is a remarkable tale of endurance and of organizational and ideological flexibility. One obvious reason for this success is the fact that eastern Roman military administration, represented in particular by a centralized fiscal system and close control of necessary resources in manpower and materials, gave the Byzantine government an advantage which none of its foes enjoyed. This system was, until the twelfth century, greatly in advance of those of its neighbours. With central government maintaining an effective grip on this resource-extracting organization, it was able to direct resources according to the requirements of defence or offense to the best effect. Of course, politics and internecine strife interfered with this, so that the effective and appropriate employment of men and matériel did not always happen. Those in authority had to recognize where the priorities lay and, as the empire's political history so clearly shows, this was not always the case.

The armies of the eastern Roman empire were frequently defeated, sometimes disastrously so. They were often appallingly badly led. Yet until the later part of the twelfth century, they usually possessed a clear strategic and tactical organizational advantage over most of their enemies. And it was this, together with the state's effective management and control of resources, which enabled them to recover so quickly and so often. But practical logistical arrangements were not the only reason for this resilience. It was also a result of a long and respected tradition of military writing maintained by soldiers, reflected in the awareness among the upper levels of Byzantine society of the past achievements of imperial armies. Most significantly, both the historical narratives and the military manuals could explain those achievements as the results of Roman order, discipline and tactical cohesion, good logistical arrangements and – last, but by no means least – a clear understanding and recognition of the fundamental role played by divine support!

There were times, as the examples I have used frequently show, when discipline and tactical order were neglected. Yet the eastern Roman tradition of military writing and an acute sense of the past kept the precepts set out in the tactical handbooks in mind. It was on the basis of this framework, and with the victories associated with the application of this advice, that competent generals were able to strengthen and enforce the discipline, training and tactical skills which provided the empire for so long with such an effective tool of foreign policy and which shielded it for so long against so many foes.

Beginning during the eleventh century, the Roman technical and organizational advantages noted above were fairly rapidly eroded away. Western European states, which had gradually over the previous centuries been evolving different but equally effective social structures, could now put large numbers of well-disciplined and well-equipped soldiers into the field. New developments in tactics occurred in the west, not in Byzantium. Without its earlier advantages, the strategically disadvantageous position occupied by the eastern Roman state began to tell. In combination with dynamic economic and technological changes, the eastern Roman empire, still bound by its late ancient fiscal and political assumptions, proved itself unable to compete.

The battles I have described represent only a tiny fraction of those fought by Byzantine armies between the sixth and twelfth centuries. I have selected them partly because they are those for which most evidence survives (although a few more could be added to this list) and partly because they exemplify the developments the armies of the empire underwent across the period, which I have described in the accompanying discussion. If I have been able to shed a little more light, and perhaps a little less romance, on the armies of the eastern Roman state, then this book will have served its purpose.

Sources and Discussion

General Bibliography and Further Reading

G.T. Dennis, 'The Byzantines in Battle', in N. Oikonomides (ed.), *To empolemo Byzantio (Byzantium at war)* (Athens, 1997) 165-7S
K. Dixon, P. Southern, *The Late Roman Army* (London, 1996)
J.F. Haldon, *Byzantium: a History* (Stroud, 2000)
J.F. Haldon, *Warfare, State and Society in Byzantium c. 550-1204* (London, 1999)
AD Lee, *Information and Frontiers. Roman Foreign Relations in Late Antiquity* (Cambridge 1993)
T.S. Miller, J.S. Nesbitt (eds), *Peace and War in Byzantium* (Washington DC 1995)
D. Nicolle, *Medieval Warfare Source Book, 1: Warfare in Western Christendom.* London 1995)
D. Nicolle, *Medieval Warfare Source Book, 2: Christian Europe and its Neighbours* (London 1996)
The Oxford Dictionary of Byzantium. ed. A. Kazhdan *et al*, 3 vols (New York-Oxford 1991)
M. Whittow, *The Making of Orthodox Byzantium, 600-1025.* London 1996)

1 The Geography of Byzantine Warfare

C. Cahen, *Pre-Ottoman Turkey: A General Survey of the Material and Spiritual Culture c. 1071-1330* (London 1968)
M. Cary, *The Geographic Background of Greek and Roman History* (Oxford 1949)

F.W. Carter, ed., *An Historical Geography of the Balkans* (London-NY-San Francisco 1977)
J.F. Haldon, *Warfare, State and Society in the Byzantine World 565-1204* (London 1999) 46-66
R.S. Lopez, 'The Evolution of Land Transport in the Middle Ages', *Past and Present* 9 (1957-58) 17-29
N.J.G. Pounds, *An Historical Geography of Europe, 450 BC-AD 1330* (Cambridge 1973)
W.M. Ramsay, *The Historical Geography of Asia Minor*, Royal Geographical Society, Supplementary Papers IV (London 1890/Amsterdam 1962)
J.M. Wagstaff, *The Evolution of the Middle Eastern Landscapes* (Canterbury 1984)
M. Whittow, 'The Strategic Geography of the Near East', in *idem*, *The Making of Orthodox Byzantium, 600-1025* (London 1996) 15-37

Detailed surveys of climate, geography and communications of the central Byzantine lands can be found in the Admiralty geographical handbooks:

Greece, I: *Physical Geography, History, Administration and Peoples*, Naval Intelligence Division, Geographical Handbook Series, B.R. 516 (London 1944)
Greece, II: *Economic geography, ports and communications*, Naval Intelligence Division, Geographical Handbook Series, B.R. 516A (London 1944)
Greece, III: *Regional Geography*, Naval Intelligence Division, Geographical Handbook Series, B.R. 516B (London 1945)
Turkey, I, Naval Intelligence Division, Geographical Handbook Series, B.R. 507 (London 1942)
Turkey, II, Naval Intelligence Division, Geographical Handbook Series, B.R. 507A (London 1943)
Volumes for Albania, Yugoslavia and Bulgaria are also accessible.

The routes are discussed in detail by Ramsay, *Historical geography*. Since this pioneering study several other useful publications have appeared which deal with the Byzantine road-system in Anatolia: see J.G.C. Anderson, 'The road system of eastern Asia Minor with the evidence of Byzantine campaigns', *Journal of Hellenic Studies* 17 (1897) 22-30; and E. Honigmann, *Die Ostgrenze des byzantinischen Reiches von 363 bis 1071* (Brussels 1935). More recently the series *Tabula Imperii Byzantini* (Austrian Academy, Byzantine Institute, Vienna) has produced a series of detailed historical-topographical texts analysing and describing all the provinces of the Byzantine empire, and accompanied by detailed maps.

For a brief general assessment of the Byzantine strategy in Asia Minor in the eighth and early ninth centuries, see J.A. Arvites, 'The Defence of Byzantine Anatolia During the Reign of Irene (780-802)', in S. Mitchell (ed), *Armies and frontiers in Roman and Byantine Anatolia* (British Archaeological Reports, International Series 156, Oxford 1983) 219-36.

For information and discussion of Byzantine logistical arrangements, which were fundamental to the empire's military organisation, see J.F. Haldon, *General issues in the study of medieval logistics: sources, problems and methodologies* (Leiden); and J.F. Haldon, 'Roads and communications in Byzantine Asia Minor: wagons, horses, supplies', in J. Pryor, ed., *The logistics of the Crusades* (Sydney).

2 Justinian's Wars

The accounts of battles in the *Wars* of Procopius, who was an eye-witness to many of the engagements fought by the general Belisarius, are often detailed enough in respect of topography and troop movements or dispositions to produce a fairly detailed account of the course of a particular battle. But there are sometimes contradictions and gaps in his narratives, so that I have occasionally supplied a detail on the basis of probability, drawn from details offered in accounts of other battles by the same author. In comparison with Procopius, however, Agathias is less clear in his account of battles, and far less knowledgeable about warfare and military matters. But by exploiting the evidence from other writers of the same period, and particularly Procopius (a little earlier), it has been possible to produce a fairly coherent account of the battles in question, and one which cannot be too far from the way the encounters actually developed.

Dara

Sources: *Procopius, History of the Wars*, ed. and trans. H.B. Dewing (Cambridge, Mass.-London, 1914-1928) I, xiii; *Theophanis Chronographia*, ed. C. de Boor, 2 vols. (Leipzig, 1883, 1885) 180-181; English translation in: *The Chronicle of Theophanes Confessor*, ed. and trans. C. Mango, R. Scott (Oxford, 1997) 274-275; *The Chronicle of John Malalas. A translation,* by E. Jeffreys, M. Jeffreys, R. Scott *et al*. (Byzantina Australiensia IV, Melbourne 1986) 18.50.

Discussion: J.B. Bury, *History of the Later Roman Empire from the Death of Theodosius I to the Death of Justinian*, 2 vols. (London 1923/New York 1958) II, 82-85; E. Stein, *Histoire du Bas-Empire II: de la disparition de l'empire d'Occident à la mort de justinien (476-565)* (Paris-Bruxelles-Amsterdam 1949) (repr. Amsterdam 1968) 288; A.H.M. Jones, *The Later Roman Empire: a Social, Economic and Administrative Survey*, 3 vols. and Maps (Oxford 1964) 271. Note that the graphic representation of the battle presented here is schematic. In reality, the ditch dug by the Roman forces was at a considerable distance from the city wall: for an excellent discussion, see C. Lillington-Martin, 'Archaeological and ancient literary evidence for a battle near Dara gap, Turkey, AD 530: topography, texts and trenches', in A.S. Lewin and P. Pellegrini, eds., *The late Roman army in the Near East from Diocletian to the Arab conquest.* BAR International series 1717. Oxford 2007), 299-311.

Tadinae

Sources: Procopius, *Wars*, VIII, xxix-xxxii.21.

Discussion: H. Delbrück, *History of the Art of War*, 4 vols., trans. Walter J. Renfroe, Jr. (Lincoln-London 1990) II, *The Barbarian Invasions*, 351-61; Bury, *History of the Later Roman Empire* II, 261-267; A. Pertusi, 'Ordinamenti militari, guerre in Occidente e teoria di guerra dei Bizantini (secc. VI-X)', in *Ordinamenti militari in Occidente nell'alto medioevo* (Settimane di studio del Centro Italiano di studi sull'Alto Medioevo, XV, 2. Spoleto 1968) 631-700, at 644-647.

Casilinus

Sources: *Agathiae Myrinaei Historiarum libri V*, ed. R. Keydell (Berlin, 1967) ii, 1-14; English translation in: *Agathias, History*, trans. J.D.C.Frendo (Berlin-New York, 1975).

Discussion: Stein, *Bas-Empire*, II, 605-608; Bury, *History of the Later Roman Empire* II, 278-280; Jones, *Later Roman Empire*, 291; Delbrück, *The Barbarian Invasions*, 369-374; Pertusi, 'Ordinamenti militare', 650-652.

General Bibliography

J.C. Barrett, A.P. Fitzpatrick, L. Macinnes (eds), *Barbarians and Romans in North-West Europe* (British Archaeological reports, International

Series 471. Oxford 1989)
J. Crow, 'Dara, a Late Roman Fortress in Mesopotamia', *Yayla* 4 (1981) 12-20
J. Crow, B. Croke, 'Procopius and Dara', *Journal of Roman Studies* 73 (1983) 143-159
K.R. Dixon, P. Southern, *The Late Roman Army* (London 1996)
M. Dodgeon & S.N.C. Lieu, *The Roman Eastern Frontier and the Persian Wars, AD 226-363* (London 1991)
H. Elton, *Warfare in Roman Europe, AD 350-425* (Oxford 1996)
P.M. Freeman & D.L. Kennedy (eds), *The Defence of the Roman and Byantine East* (British Archaeological reports, International Series 297. Oxford 1986)
J.F. Haldon, *Warfare, State and Society in the Byzantine World 565-1204* (London 1999)
B. Isaac, *The Limits of Empire. The Roman Army in the East* (Oxford 1990)
AD Lee, *Information and Frontiers. Roman Foreign Relations in Late Antiquity* (Cambridge 1993)
The Oxford Dictionary of Byzantium, ed. A. Kazhdan et al., 3 vols., (New York-Oxford 1991)
R.S.O. Tomlin, 'The Army of the Late Empire', in J. Wacher, ed., *The Roman world* I (London 1987/1990) 107-33
R.S.O. Tomlin, 'The Late Roman Empire AD 200-450', in P. Connolly, ed., *Greece and Rome at War* (London 1981/1989) 249-61
M. Whitby, 'Procopius' Description of Dara', in *The Defence of the Roman and Byzantine East* (Oxford 1986) 737-783
C.R. Whittaker, *Frontiers of the Roman Empire. A Social and Economic Study* (Baltimore-London 1994)

3 After Justinian

Solachon

Sources: The account of the battle in Theophylact Simocatta is lacking in some details, and I have used my imagination a little in supplying them, consonant with what I believe is plausible in the context, from other accounts by the same author of battles on the same front at this period. See *Theophylacti Simocattae Historia*, ed. C. de Boor (Leipzig, 1887; revised and emended edn. P. Wirth, Stuttgart, 1972), ii, 1-5; English translation in: *Theophylact Simocatta, History*, trans. M. and M. Whitby (Oxford, 1986).

Discussion: The best account of the wars on the eastern front during this period is in L. M. Whitby, *The Emperor Maurice and His Historian: Theophylact Simocatta on Persian and Balkan Warfare* (Oxford 1988)280-282, with notes and the older literature. See also J.B. Bury, *History of the Later Roman Empire from Arcadius to Irene (395 AD to 800 AD)*, II, 95-107; and M.J. Higgins, *The Persian War of the Emperor Maurice (582-602)* (Washington DC, 1939). For the sixth-century context and operational procedures, see F. R. Trombley, 'The operational methods of the late Roman army in the Persian war of 572-591', in A.S. Lewin and P. Pellegrini, eds., *The late Roman army in the Near East from Diocletian to the Arab conquest.* BAR International series 1717. Oxford 2007), 321-356, with extensive further literature.

Jabiya/Yarmuk

Sources: The sources for the battle are numerous and complex. None is contemporary with the events, although several were written shortly afterwards and drew on purportedly eye-witness accounts. All contain elements of legend, and are influenced by the ideological perspective of their respective authors. Thus while the Byzantine accounts attempt to explain the defeat away as a result of Muslim treachery and cunning, or of jealousies within the Byzantine command, eastern Christian accounts see in the imperial defeat a divine punishment for the heresy of the emperor Heraclius or the Romans in general; while the numerous Islamic accounts are anxious both to establish the credentials of the particular characters with which the author identifies for dynastic or regional political reasons, as well as to stress the divine support received by the Muslims against the Christians. Disentangling all this material is virtually impossible, with the result that several different versions of the battle could be produced – probably the best attempt to analyse all the relevant sources, and to take into account the various Islamic traditions, is in L. Caetani, *Annali dell'Islam*, 10 vols. (Milan, 1905-1926/repr. Hildesheim, 1972), see vol. 3, 499-613, esp. 508-530 for the topography and location of the conflict. I have tried in the above to produce as consensual a view as possible, based on both sensible strategic and tactical considerations as well as on the various discussions in the secondary literature.

Discussion: For the most useful recent modern account, with a full bibliography of secondary works, a discussion of the background to the battle as well as of the different source traditions, see W.E. Kaegi, Jr., *Byzantium and the Early Islamic Conquests* (Cambridge, 1992), 112-146. See also J.W. Jandora, 'The Battle of the Yarmuk: A Reconstruction', *Journal of Asian History* 19 (1985) 8-21. But a strong case has now been made to re-date this battle from 636 to 638, and to explain the imperial defeat as in part the results of an outbreak of plague which decimated the Byzantine army and severely affected its morale at that time. See D. Woods, 'Jews, rats, and the battle of Yarmuk', in A.S. Lewin and P. Pellegrini, eds., *The late Roman army in the Near East from Diocletian to the Arab conquest*. BAR International series 1717. Oxford 2007), 367-376.

General Bibliography

E.W. Brooks, 'The Arabs in Asia Minor (641-750) from Arabic sources', *Journal of Hellenic Studies* 18 (1898) 182-208

K.R. Dixon, P. Southern, *The Late Roman Army* (London 1996)

F.M. Donner, *The Early Arabic Conquests* (Princeton 1981)

J.F. Haldon, 'Administrative Continuities and Structural Transformations in East Roman Military Organisation c. 580-640', in J.F. Haldon, *State, Army and Society in Byzantium*, no. V (Aldershot 1995)

J.F. Haldon, 'Seventh-Century Continuities: the *Ajnâd* and the 'Thematic Myth'', in Averil Cameron (ed.), *States, Resources and Armies: Papers of the Third Workshop on Late Antiquity and Early Islam* (Princeton, 1995) 379-423.

J.F. Haldon, *Byzantium in the Seventh Century: The Transformation of a Culture* (Cambridge 1990/1997)

J.F. Haldon, *Warfare, State and Society in the Byzantine World 565-1204* (London 1999)

J.D. Howard-Johnston, 'The Two Great Powers in Late Antiquity: A Comparison', in Cameron (ed.), *States, Resources and Armies*, 157-226

P.M. Freeman & D.L. Kennedy (eds), *The Defence of the Roman and Byantine East* (British Archaeological Reports, International Series, 297. Oxford 1986)

B. Isaac, *The Limits of Empire. The Roman Army in the East* (Oxford 1990)

C.R. Whittaker, *Frontiers of the Roman Empire. A Social and Economic Study* (Baltimore-London 1994)

4 Bulgars and Arabs

The sources for this period rarely offer any details of what happened during a battle. Most were in any case written after the events they describe, and drew on a range of older sources. I have tried to piece together enough essential information for each battle from such sources, but I have necessarily had to fill in many gaps and resolve contradictions, and so my interpretation represents only one possible version of the events in question. I have based my account on the sources for the whole period and on what is known about the organization, fighting capabilities and social context of the armies of the time.

Pliska

Sources: Theophanes, *Chronographia*, 490-491; trans. Mango/Scott, 672f.; I. Dujcev, 'La chronique byzantine de l'an 811', *Travaux et Mémoires* 1 (1965) 205-54; text 210-16.

Discussion: Bury, *Eastern Roman empire*, pp. 344-5.

Versinikia

Sources: Theophanes, *Chronographia*, 500; trans. Mango/Scott, 684; *Scriptor incertus de Leone Armenio*, in: *Leonis Grammatici Chronographia*, ed. I. Bekker (Bonn 1842) 335-362, at 337-338 (new ed. with commentary and translation by Fr. Iadevaia, *Scriptor incertus. Testo critico, traduzione e note* [Messina 1987]); *Theophanes continuatus*, 13-15 (in: *Theophanes continuatus, Ioannes Caminiata, Symeon Magister, Georgius Monachus continuatus*, ed. I. Bekker [Bonn 1825] 1-481).

Discussion: Bury, *Eastern Roman Empire*, 350-1, with sources; and for an important modern re-assessment of the sources and the course of the battle, D. Turner, 'The Origins and Accession of Leo V (813-820)', *Jahrbuch der Österreichischen Byzantinistik* 40 (1990) 171-203, esp. 187-193.

Anzen

Sources: The sources for the battle of Anzen are confused, partly because several elements of the story recur in accounts of other battles, both before and after this date. In this account, I have drawn on the basic narratives for the battle of 838, supplementing them with topographical and other information from accounts of battles which took place in the same area.

Byzantine sources: *Leonis Grammatici Chronographia*, ed. I. Bekker (Bonn 1842) 222, 224; *Symeonis Magistri ac Logothetae Annales a Leone*

Armenio ad Nicephoram Phocam, in: *Theophanes continuatus*, 603-760 at 636-7, 638; *Iosephi Genesii Regum libri quattuor*, edd. I. Lesmüller-Werner, I. Thurn (Berlin-New York 1978) 48-49; *Theophanes continuatus*, 127-129. References to other battles but which actually refer to the battle of 838 can also be found in the same sources at different locations: *Genesius*, 43-44 and *Theophanes continuatus*, 113-114 and 116-118, for a battle supposedly earlier than Anzen, but actually describing aspects of that fought in 838; and *Genesius*, 65-66 and *Theophanes continuatus* 177 for a battle of Anzen in 858, but again describing that of 838.

Arabic and other eastern sources from a variety of important chronicles and histories are conveniently collected, with French translations, in A. A. Vasiliev, *Byzance et les Arabes I: La dynastie d'Amorium (820-867)*, éd. fr. H. Grégoire & M. Canard (Brussels 1950/1968) 331-2, 333-4 (Mas'udi); 299-301, 309 (Tabari); 275 (Ya'qubi). Other references to the battle can be found in: *La Chronique de Michel le Syrien, Patriarche Jacobite d'Antioche*, ed. et trad. J.B.Chabot, 4 vols. (Paris 1899, 1091, 1905, 1924), see vol. 3, 95, and in several other later chronicles which drew on earlier material.

Discussion: Bury, *Eastern Roman Empire*, 264-5; and W. Treadgold, *The Byzantine Revival 780-842* (Stanford 1988) 300-1 and notes.

Marj al-Usquf ('Bishop's Meadow') and Lalakaon 863

Sources: *Theophanes continuatus*, 179-83; *Genesius*, 94-7; Ioannes Skylitzes, *Synopsis Historiarum*, ed. J. Thurn (Berlin-New York 1973), 139. The relevant Arabic sources are in Vasiliev, *Byzance et les arabes*, I, 277 (Ya'qubi); 325 (Tabari).

Discussion: G. Huxley, 'Michael III and the battle of Bishop's meadow (AD 863)', *Greek, Roman and Byzantine Studies* 16 (1975) 443-450, including all the previous secondary literature and analysis of the sources.

Bathys Ryax 878

Sources: *Theophanes continuatus*, 272-274; *Genesius*, 86-88.

Discussion: W.E. Kaegi, Jr., *Byzantine military unrest 471-843: an interpretation* (Amsterdam 1981) 281-282.

Acheloos 917

Sources: Skylitzes, *Synopsis historiarum*, 203.81-96.

Discussion: S. Runciman, *A history of the first Bulgarian empire* (London, 1930) 160-161.

General Bibliography

H. Ahrweiler, 'L'Asie mineure et les invasions arabes', *Revue Historique* 227 (1962) 1-32

J.F. Haldon, *Warfare, State and Society in the Byzantine World 565-1204* (London 1999)

J.F. Haldon, *State, Army and Society in Byzantium. Approaches to Military, Social and Administrative History* (Aldershot 1995)

J.F. Haldon, *Byzantine Praetorians* (Bonn-Berlin 1984)

J.M. Hussey, ed. *The Cambridge Medieval History*, IV: *The Byzantine Empire*, 2 parts, revised ed. (Cambridge 1966)

R.-J. Lilie, *Die byzantinische Reaktion auf die Ausbreitung der Araber* (Miscellanea Byzantina Monacensia, 22. Munich 1976)

D. Obolensky, *The Byzantine Commonwealth. Eastern Europe 500-1453* (London 1971)

P. Stephenson, *Byzantium's Balkan frontier. A Political Study of the Northern Balkans, 900-1204* (Cambridge, 2000)

A.A. Vasiliev, *Byzance et les Arabes* I: *La dynastie d'Amorium (820-867)*; II: *Les relations politiques de Byzance et des Arabes à l'époque de la dynastie macédonienne (Les empereurs Basile I, Léon le Sage et Constantin VII Porphyrogénète) (867-959)*, éd. fr. H. Grégoire & M. Canard (Brussels 1950/1968)

M. Whittow, *The Making of Orthodox Byzantium, 600-1025* (London 1996)

5 Warfare in the Age of Reconquest

The historical sources for this period, especially the *History* of Leo the Deacon, who seems to have been an eye-witness to some of the battles fought by John Tzimiskes, are generally fuller in the detail they offer on battles and related activities. The accounts given in this chapter, in consequence, involve very few elaborations by me, and as usual, those I have included are grounded in the evidence for the period. The best general discussions of the warfare of the period are to be found in G. Dagron, H. Mihaescu, in: *Le traité sur la Guérilla (De velitatione) de l'empereur Nicéphore Phocas (963-969)* (Paris 1986) and E. McGeer, *Sowing the Dragon's Teeth. Byzantine Warfare in the Tenth Century* (Washington D.C. 1995).

The Raid of 956

Sources: Mutanabbi, trans. M. Canard, in Vasiliev, *Byzance et les arabes*.

Discussion: J. Howard-Johnston, 'Byzantine Anzitene', in S. Mitchell, *Armies and Frontiers in Roman and Byantine Anatolia* (British Archaeological Reports, International series 156. Oxford 1983) 239-90, on whose analysis my account is based.

Raids of 950, 958, 960

Sources and discussion: M. Canard, *Histoire de la dynastie des Hamdanides* (Paris 1953) 763-768; 795; 801-803; *Leonis diaconi Caloensis Historiae libri decem*, ed. C.B. Hase (Bonn 1828) §2, 5 (for the raid of 960).

Feigned retreat 970

Sources: Leo diac., *Historia*, vi, 109-111.

Discussion: McGeer, *Sowing the dragon's teeth*.

Dorostolon 971

Sources: Leo diac., *Historia*, viii, 9-10; ix, 1-8; Ioannes Skylitzes, *Synopsis Historiarum*, ed. J. Thurn (Berlin-New York 1973) 294-309.

Discussion: S. McGrath, 'The battles of Dorostolon (971). Rhetoric and reality', in T.S. Miller, & J.S. Nesbitt (eds), *Peace and war in Byzantium* (Washington DC 1995) 152-64, also with full details of the older literature.

Battle of the Spercheios River 997

Sources: Skylitzes, 341-342.

Battle of Kleidion 1014

Sources: Skylitzes, 348-349.

General Bibliography

H. Ahrweiler, 'L'Asie mineure et les invasions arabes', *Revue Historique* 227 (1962) 1-32

Campaign Organisation and Tactics: ed. and trans. G.T. Dennis, in: *Three Byzantine Military Treatises*. Text, transl. and notes (Washington D.C. 1985) 241-335 (text 246-326)

Constantine Porphyrogenitus, Three Treatises on Imperial Military Expeditions, ed., English trans. and commentary J.F.Haldon (Vienna 1990)

G.T. Dennis, 'The Byzantines in Battle', in Oikonomidès (ed.), *Byzantium at War*, pp. 165-78
J.F. Haldon, H. Kennedy, 'The Arab-Byzantine Frontier in the Eighth and Ninth Centuries: Military Organisation and Society in the Borderlands', *ZRVI* 19 (1980) 79-116
J.F. Haldon, *Warfare, State and Society in the Byzantine World 565-1204* (London 1999)
E. McGeer, *Sowing the Dragon's Teeth. Byzantine Warfare in the Tenth Century* (Washington D.C. 1995)
T.S. Miller, & J.S. Nesbitt (eds), *Peace and War in Byzantium* (Washington DC 1995)
S. Mitchell, *Armies and Frontiers in Roman and Byantine Anatolia* (British Archaeological Reports, International series 156. Oxford 1983)
N. Oikonomidès, (ed.), *To empolemo Byzantio (Byzantium at war)* (Athens 1997)
Skirmishing: ed. and trans. G.T. Dennis, in: *Three Byzantine Military Treatises*, 137-239 (text 144-238)
(also ed. with French transl. and extensive, detailed commentary, in G. Dagron, H. Mihaescu, in: *Le traité sur la Guérilla (De velitatione) de l'empereur Nicéphore Phocas (963-969)* (Paris 1986)
P. Stephenson, *Byzantium's Balkan frontier. A Political Study of the Northern Balkans, 900-1204* (Cambridge, 2000)
A. Toynbee, *Constantine Porphyrogenitus and his World* (London 1973)
M. Whittow, *The Making of Orthodox Byzantium, 600-1025* (London 1996)

For analysis of the 'guerrilla' strategy described in detail in the treatise, see G. Dagron, H. Mihaescu, *Le traité sur la Guérilla (De velitatione) de l'empereur Nicéphore Phocas (963-969)* (Paris 1986) 195- 237.

6 Collapse and Recovery

Manzikert 1071

Sources: All the details I have included in my account can be found in the historical record, although the sources for the battle are numerous and often contradictory. They can be divided very roughly into three major groups, the Byzantine, the eastern Christian (Armenian, Syriac, Arabic) and the Islamic (Arabic) (there are in addition one or two western sources, the only important one being the *Gesta Roberti Wiscardi*, which is nearly contemporary). But by far the most important and useful are the accounts of the eye-witness Michael Attaliates, who was present in the emperor's entourage; and those of the grandson of the general Nikephoros Bryennios, commander of the left wing at Manzikert, also called Nikephoros Bryennios. All the other sources are later, in some cases very much later, and the Islamic sources in particular are often replete with legend and myth about Alp Arslan himself and the events before and during the battle: *Michaelis Attaliotae Historia*, ed. I. Bekker (Bonn 1853) 147-167; *Nicéphore Bryennios, Histoire*, ed. P. Gautier (Brussels 1975) 111-119; Islamic and non-Byzantine sources are presented and discussed by C. Cahen, 'La campagne de Mantzikert d'après les sources musulmanes', *Byzantion* 9 (1934) 613-642.

Discussion: For an excellent discussion of the military implications of the battle, with an up-to-date bibliography of sources and secondary literature, see J.-C. Cheynet, 'Mantzikert: un désastre militaire?', *Byzantion* 50 (1980) 410-38. Also very important are C. Cahen, 'La campagne de Mantzikert d'après les sources musulmanes', *Byzantion* 9 (1934) 613-642; and three discussions by Sp. Vryonis, jr.: in his *The decline of medieval Hellenism in Asia Minor and the process of Islamization from the eleventh through the fifteenth century* (Berkeley-Los Angeles-London 1971) 96-103 with notes; 'The Greek and Arabic sources for the battle of Mantzikert, 1071 AD', in Sp. Vryonis, jr., ed., *Byzantine Studies. Essays on the Slavic World and the Eleventh Century* (New York 1992) 125-140; and his 'A Personal History of the History of the Battle of Mantzikert', in N. Oikonomidès (ed.), *To empolemo Byzantio (Byzantium at war)* (Athens 1997) 225-244. A. Friendly, *The Dreadful Day: The Battle of Manzikert, 1071* (London 1981) offers a clear account of the battle, but his understanding of its outcome and results largely ignores the evidence (properly assessed by Cheynet, for example), so that he adopts the traditional view that it was indeed a military disaster. For sensible comments on the numbers involved, see Delbrück, *Medieval warfare*, 198.

Kalavryai 1078

Sources: Anna Komnene, *Alexiad*: text and French translation in: *Anne Comnène, Aléxiade*, ed. B. Leib, 3 vols. (Paris 1937, 1943, 1945); index, P. Gautier (Paris 1976); English translation: *The Alexiad of the Princess Anna Commune*, trans. E.R.A.Sewter (Harmondsworth 1969), i, 4-6 (Sewter translation, 38-45)
Nicéphore Bryennios, Histoire, ed. P. Gautier (Brussels 1975)

Discussion: N. Tobias, 'The tactics and strategy of Alexius Comnenus at Calvrytae, 1078', *Byzantine Studies* 6 (1979) 193-211.

Dyrrachion 1081

Sources: Anna Comnena, *Alexiad*, iv, 1-8 (Sewter translation, 135-153); Gesta Roberti Wiscardi, ed. M. Mathieu, *La geste de Robert Guiscard* (Palermo 1961) 225f.

Discussion: R. Willoughby, 'The Shock of the New', in *History Today*, 49/8 (Aug 1999) 37-42. Willoughby argues that the battle provides the first evidence, after Hastings, of the Frankish/Norman heavy cavalry charge with couched lance, although this is dubious. Already in 1041 Byzantine and Norman heavy cavalry had ridden down Saracen cavalry and infantry, described in a near-contemporary hagiograhical text in language not dissimilar to that used by Anna Comnena. See Haldon, *Warfare, State and Society*, 223 and note. Specially bred heavier war-horses are first evident in the sources from the twelfth century, and Byzantine horses were certainly no smaller or lighter than those used by the Normans at this period. See the excellent discussion and analysis in A. Hyland, *The Medieval Warhorse. From Byzantium to the Crusades* (Stroud 1994).

Battle of Semlin/Sirmium 1167

Sources: *Nicetae Choniatae Historia*, ed. J.A. Van Dieten, 2 vols. (Berlin-New York 1975); English translation: H.J. Magoulias, *O City of Byzantium. The Historia of Nicetas Choniates* (Wayne State, 1984) 152-7; John Kinnamos, *Epitomê*, ed. A. Meineke (Bonn 1836); English translation in C.M. Brand, *The Deeds of John and Manuel Comnenus* (New York 1976) 271-3.

Discussion: P. Magdalino, *The Empire of Manuel I Komnenos, 1143-1180* (Cambridge 1993) 78-81 (general background and context); and Stephenson, *Byzantium's Balkan frontier*, 239ff.

Myriokephalon 1176

Sources: Choniates, *Historia*, 176ff,; Kinnamos, *Epitome*, 56.

Discussion: R.-J. Lilie, 'Die Schlacht von Myriokephalon (1176): Auswirkungen auf das byzantinische Reich im ausgehenden 12. Jahrhunert', *Revue des Études Byzantines* 35 (1977) 257-275.

There is some disagreement over the location. The traditional view places the pass in question along the Çay valley, in the north-western reaches of the Sultan Dağ mountains, but this does not accord with all the details given in certain medieval sources. More recently, an alternative location identifies the pass as the modern Bağirsakdere Boğazi, a description of which matches closely the medieval accounts, running eastwards from modern Yunuslar and Kızılören, and about a day's march west of Konya. See M.F. Hendy, *Studies in the Byzantine monetary economy, c.300-1450* (Cambridge 1985) 146-154 for the revised view. The traditional identification is presented in several works. See the literature cited in Hendy; and also N. Mersich, 'Tzibritze. Zum Austragungsort der Schlacht von Myriokephalon (1176)', *Byzantios. Festschrift H. Hunger* (Vienna 1984) 241-246. For the various locations associated with the site, see K. Belke, N. Mersich, *Tabula Imperii Byzantini* 7: *Phrygien und Pisidien* (Denkschr. d. Österr. Akad. d Wiss., phil.-hist. Kl. 211. Vienna 1990) 193 (Asar Kalesi), 307 (Kizilören), 355 (Yunuslar).

General Bibliography

M. Angold, *The Byzantine empire 1025-1204. A Political History* (London 1984)

J. France, *The Crusades* (London 2000)

S. Franklin, J. Shepard (eds), *Byzantine Diplomacy* (Aldershot 1992)

J.F. Haldon, *Warfare, State and Society in the Byzantine World 565-1204* (London 1999)

P. Magdalino, *The Empire of Manuel I Komnenos, 1143-1180.* Cambridge 1993)

N. Oikonomidès (ed.), *To empolemo Byzantio (Byzantium at war)* (Athens 1997)

J. Shepard, 'The Uses of the Franks in Eleventh-Century Byzantium', *Anglo-Norman Studies* 15 (1993) 275-305

R.C. Smail, *Crusading Warfare, 1097-1193*, ed. C. Marshall (Cambridge 1995)

P. Stephenson, *Byzantium's Balkan Frontier. A Political Study of the Northern Balkans, 900-1204* (Cambridge, 2000)

Sp. Vryonis, jr., *The Decline of Medieval Hellenism in Asia Minor and the Process of Islamization from the Eleventh through the Fifteenth Century* (Berkeley-Los Angeles-London 1971)

List of Illustrations

Maps

Glossary

Annona Military rations issued from taxation collected in kind; Gk. *synone*

Apotheke A state depository for various goods and materials; in the seventh to ninth centuries the warehouse, and the district to which it pertained, under the control of a *kommerkiarios*

Archontes Holders of imperial titles or offices; provincial landholding elite dominating towns

Bandon Originally a banner or pennant; later the unit designated by the flag. Numbered variously from 50-400 depending on period and context. By the tenth century *bandon* referred also to a district from which soldiers were recruited; also called in this sense a *topoteresia*.

Chomatenoi Soldiers recruited from the district of Choma in Asia Minor

Comitatenses Soldiers/units of the field armies under their *magistri militum*, fourth to seventh centuries (cf. *limitanei*)

Cursus publicus the public postal, transport and relay system (see *Dromos*)

Diocese Lat. *dioecesa*, Gk. *Dioikesis*, an administrative unit consisting of several provinces; from the 4th century the episcopal administrative unit of the Church

Dioiketes Fiscal administrator responsible for the land-tax, usually in a single diocese, from the seventh century

Dromos Greek term for *cursus publicus*

Drouggarios (Lat. *drungarius)* Commander of a group of units – *banda* – within a *thema*

Ducatus The command held by a *dux*. In its later Byzantine form, *doukaton* referred to the command and the region under the authority of the *doux*.

Dux In later Roman period, commander of a military unit; commander of a unit of *limitanei*, or garrison troops; in the middle and later Byzantine period the title *doux* was re-introduced as a high military rank

Dynatos literally, a 'powerful person', so described because of his position in the military or administrative establishment of the state

Excubitores Small palace bodyguard recruited from Isaurian mountain people by the emperor Leo I. During the seventh century they became a show troop, but the unit was revived as a larger active elite regiment under Constantine V in the 760s, as the *exkoubita*. It disappears during the later 11th century

Foederati 'Federates', from the later 4th century barbarian troops recruited on the basis of a treaty by which they and their families were allowed to move onto imperial territory and share the land and its income with the indigenous population and landlords. During the sixth century the term came to mean units of non-Roman mercenaries (although Romans could also join) brigaded together; and during the 7th century the whole corps was posted to Asia Minor, probably Lycaonia, where they formed a subdivision or *tourma* of the *Anatolikon* theme. The term disappears after the early 12th century.

Genikon (sekreton) The general treasury and main fiscal department of government after the seventh century

Kastron 'Fortress', but after the 7th century also used to mean 'town' or 'city'

Kastrophylax 'Castle guardian', governor of a fortress

Katepano Military officer in command of independent unit and/or district (8th-12th centuries); imperial provincial/regional governor (after the 13th century)

Kleisoura Small frontier command; district along/behind the frontier (esp. later 8th-10th centuries)

Komes (Lat. *comes*) The later equivalent of tribune (Gr. *tribounos*), the commander of a *bandon*

Kommerkiarioi Fiscal officials responsible for state-supervised commerce and the taxes thereon. During the 7th and 8th centuries had a much expanded role in the fiscal system and the supplying of the armies; from the middle of the 8th century reverted to chiefly commercial functions.

Limitanei Provincial garrison troops in the later Roman period

Magister militum Divisional military commander, replaced by the *stratêgos* after *c.*660

Magister Officiorum 'Master of offices', leading civil minister and close associate of the emperors in the later Roman period

Paulicians An eastern Asia Minor sect of the 7th – 9th centuries. During the mid-9th-century they took over much of eastern Anatolia and fought the empire with the support of the Caliphate. They were crushed by Basil I. Many were transported at different times to Thrace during the seventh-tenth centuries, where they introduced their beliefs to the Balkans.

Praetorian Prefecture The largest administrative unit of the empire from the time of Constantine I, under a praetorian prefect (originally a commander of the praetorian guard). Each prefecture was divided into dioceses, then provinces, and had its own fiscal administrative and judicial structure

Prokathemenos Town/fortress governor of the Comnene period

Pronoia Attribution of fiscal revenues, usually to a soldier in return for military service. Appears first on a limited basis in the 12th century; eventually included lifelong and heritable grants

Protonotarios Chief fiscal administrator of a theme from *c*.820 – mid-11th century

Rus' One of the names for the Scandinavian settlers of the lands which later became known as Russia. The name Rus' is probably Swedish, rather than Slavic, in origin, although the issue is still debated. The generic Byzantine term for these people was Varangians, although the classicizing term *Tauroscythians* was also used.

Scholae In the period from Constantine I until the later 5th century a crack cavalry unit; by the later 5th century a show force. The units were reformed and became once more elite regiments under Constantine V, forming until the 11th century the core of the imperial field armies

Strateia (1) State military service, generally used of any state service whether military or not

(2) Service in the army

(3) the obligation to support a soldier/a property whose tenant/owner was subject to such an obligation

Strategos A general; in Byzantine times usually the governor of a military district or *thema*, and commander of its soldiers

Stratiotes A soldier; by derivation (from the 10th century) a holder of 'military' land, subject to the obligation to support a soldier

Stratiotikon logothesion Fiscal department which dealt with recruitment, muster-rolls and military pay from the 7th century

Tagmata (1) Elite field units recruited by Constantine V. They formed the core of imperial field armies until the eleventh century
(2) any full-time mercenary unit – used especially of foreign mercenary troops in the 10th -12th centuries

Thema A 'theme', from the middle of the 7th century the district across which soldiers were quartered, and from which they were recruited; an administrative unit; the army based in such a region. The first *themata* were the field armies under their *magistri militum* (see above), withdrawn into Asia Minor and garrisoned across the empire's territory. The Greek form of their names were derived from their earlier Latin designations (thus the Anatolikon theme was formerly the army of the *magister militum per Orientem*; the Armeniakon theme formerly the army of the *magister militum per Armeniam*; the Thrakesion theme formerly the army of the *magister militum per Thracias*, and so on)

Tourma A division within a thematic army; an administrative territorial unit within a theme

Tourmarches The commander of a *tourma*

Tzakones (or *Lakones)* From the southern Peloponnese, they served as light-armed troops

Varangians Mercenary unit first recruited during the reign of Basil II, consisting of Russian and Scandinavian adventurers and mercenaries

Index

Acknowledgements

The usual thanks are to be expressed towards friends, family and colleagues for their patience, help and advice during the writing of this volume. I am especially indebted to my friend David Turner, who kindly put his house in Greece at my disposal for the final stages of writing, to Henry Buglass for his excellent maps and line drawings and to Graham Norrie for the photographic work. Thanks also to Jasper and Charlie for eating the first version of Chapter 2 and compelling me to start again with a better one!

THE HISTORY PRESS

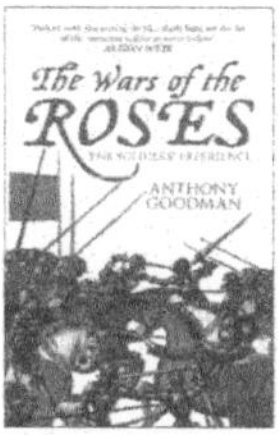

The Wars of the Roses

The Soldiers' Experience

ANTHONY GOODMAN

'Fascinating... a meticulous work' ***TLS***

'Sheds light on the lot of the common soldier as never before' ***Alison Weir***

'Fascinating reading' ***BBC History Magazine***

£12.99

0 7524 3731 3

Byazntium: A History

JOHN HALDON

'A triumph of synthesis'

Speculum: A Journal of Medieval Studies

£12.99 0 7524 3472 1

The Great Dying

The Black Death in Dublin

MARIA KELLY

'An infectious chronicle... pacy popular history' ***The Irish Sunday Times***

£14.99

0 7524 2338 X

A History of the Black Death in Ireland

MARIA KELLY

'A fine example of how history can be made interesting to the layman as well as the scholar' ***The Irish Times***

'A remarkably vivid and perceptive account. Written with verve, it makes a compelling read' ***Maurice Keen***

£12.99 0 7524 3185 4

The Crusades

MALCOLM BILLINGS

'Demonstrates that one can write in the light of the most recent research without losing excitement and colour' ***Jonathan Riley-Smith***

£12.99

0 7524 2974 4

The Welsh Kings

Warriors, Warlords & Princes

KARI MAUND

£12.99

0 7524 2973 6

The Return of the Vikings

The Battle of Maldon 991

DONALD SCRAGG

'An accessible, well illustrated study... a lively historical introduction' ***BBC History Magazine***

£17.99

0 7524 2833 0

The Byzantine Wars

JOHN HALDON

A ***BBC History Magazine*** Book of the Year 2001

£12.99

0 7524 4565 6

If you are interested in purchasing other books published by The History Press, or in case you have difficulty finding any of these books in your local bookshop, you can also place orders directly through our website: www.thehistorypress.co.uk

THE HISTORY PRESS

William II Rufus, the Red King

EMMA MASON

'A thoroughly new reappraisal of a much maligned king. The dramatic story of his life is told with great pace and insight'
John Gillingham

£25

0 7524 3528 0

William Wallace The True Story of Braveheart

CHRIS BROWN

'A formidable new biography... sieves through masses of medieval records to distinguish the man from the myth' ***Magnus Magnusson***

£17.99

0 7524 3432 2

Elizabeth Wydeville: The Slandered Queen

ARLENE OKERLUND

'A penetrating, thorough and wholly convincing vindication of this unlucky queen'
Sarah Gristwood

'A gripping tale of lust, loss and tragedy'
Alison Weir

A ***BBC History Magazine*** Book of the Year 2005

£9.99 978 07524 3807 8

The Battle of Hastings 1066

M.K. LAWSON

'Blows away many fundamental assumptions about the battle of Hastings… an exciting and indispensable read' ***David Bates***

A ***BBC History Magazine*** Book of the Year 2003

£12.99 978 07524 4177 1

The Welsh Wars of Independence

DAVID MOORE

'Beautifully written, subtle and remarkably perceptive' ***John Davies***

£12.99

978 07524 4128 3

Medieval England

From Hastings to Bosworth

EDMUND KING

'The best illustrated history of medieval England' ***John Gillingham***

£12.99

0 7524 2827 5

A Companion to Medieval England

NIGEL SAUL

'Wonderful... everything you could wish to know about life in medieval England'
Heritage Today

£19.99

0 7524 2969 8

The Prince In The Tower

MICHAEL HICKS

'The first time in ages that a publisher has sent me a book I actually want to read' ***David Starkey***

£9.99

978 07524 4386 7

If you are interested in purchasing other books published by The History Press, or in case you have difficulty finding any of these books in your local bookshop, you can also place orders directly through our website:
www.thehistorypress.co.uk

THE HISTORY PRESS

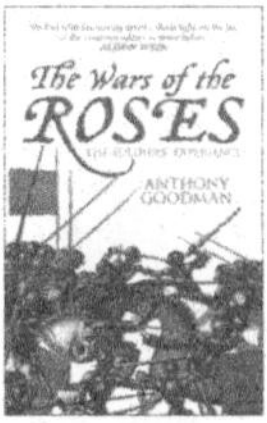

The Wars of the Roses
The Soldiers' Experience
ANTHONY GOODMAN
'A fascinating book' ***TLS***
£12.99
0 7524 3731 3

The Vikings
MAGNUS MAGUNSSON
'Serious, engaging history'
BBC History Magazine
£9.99
0 7524 2699 0

William the Conqueror
DAVID BATES
'As expertly woven as the Bayeux Tapestry'
BBC History Magazine
£12.99
0 7524 2960 4

Agincourt: A New History
ANNE CURRY
'A tour de force' ***Alison Weir***
'*The* book on the battle' ***Richard Holmes***
A ***BBC History Magazine*** book of the year 2005
£12.99
0 7524 2828 4

Hereward The Last Englishman
PETER REX
'An enthralling work of historical detection'
Robert Lacey
£17.99
0 7524 3318 0

The English Resistance
The Underground War Against the Normans
PETER REX
'An invaluable rehabilitation of an ignored resistance movement' ***The Sunday Times***
£12.99
0 7524 3733 X

Richard III
MICHAEL HICKS
'A most important book by the greatest living expert on Richard' ***Desmond Seward***
£9.99
0 7524 2589 7

The Peasants' Revolt
England's Failed Revolution of 1381
ALASTAIR DUNN
'A stunningly good book... totally absorbing'
Melvyn Bragg
£9.99
0 7524 2965 5

If you are interested in purchasing other books published by The History Press, or in case you have difficulty finding any of these books in your local bookshop, you can also place orders directly through our website:
www.thehistorypress.co.uk